Karl J. Schmidt is Assistant Professor of History at Missouri Southern State College, USA, where he teaches Asian history. He has also taught at Florida State University and Tallahassee Community College. Educated at the University of South Florida and Florida State University, USA, Dr. Schmidt, who is both a cartographer and a historian, has travelled extensively and conducted research in South Asia.

ATLAS AND SURVEY OF
SOUTH ASIAN
HISTORY

India, Pakistan, Bangladesh, Sri Lanka, Nepal, Bhutan

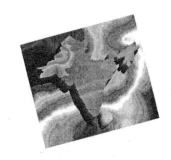

Karl J. Schmidt

**VISION
BOOKS**

N. DELHI ● BOMBAY
H Y D E R A B A D

ISBN 81-7094-337-X

© M.E. Sharpe, Inc., USA

This edition published in 1999 by
Vision Books Pvt. Ltd.
(Incorporating Orient Paperbacks)
24 Feroze Gandhi Road, Lajpat Nagar III,
New Delhi-110024 (India)
Phone: (+91-11) 6836470/80
Fax: (+91-11) 6836490
E-mail: visionbk@del2.vsnl.net.in

in arrangement with
M.E. Sharpe, Inc. USA

Printed at
Rashtra Rachna Printers
C-88, Ganesh Nagar, Pandav Nagar Complex,
Delhi-110092 (India).

[Authorised edition for sale in India and Indian Sub-continent only.]

To Nadine

and

Emily

Contents

FOREWORD

History is the study of time and place. If our postmodern culture ignores both, our schools and colleges are especially neglectful of geographical knowledge. Teachers of world history are particularly aware of that neglect.

In the right hands, maps, like pictures, are worth thousands of words. Karl J. Schmidt has the right hands. He is both a cartographer and a historian of South Asia. His artfully drawn maps and lucid commentaries tell a history of South Asia that reads like moving pictures.

Schmidt's *An Atlas and Survey of South Asian History* fills an important gap. The last South Asian atlas intended for students, published in 1959 with maps ending in 1939, has long been out of print. But Schmidt has done far more than update an old approach with maps for the last fifty-five years. He has rethought South Asian history and drawn maps that tell the stories of recent scholarship. Schmidt forsakes the India Office vision ("India under Lord Minto," "India under Dalhousie") for a cartographic history of indigenous South Asia, including, for example, a series on the growth of the Delhi Sultanate and a rich array of non-political maps on South Asian economic, social, and cultural history.

These are maps for the contemporary classroom and general reader. Clear and easy to read, they are beautifully complemented by Schmidt's graceful and informative prose. Whether this collection is used as an "illustrated" text to be read from beginning to end or as a reference tool, it is a long overdue resource for teachers and students of South Asian and world history.

Kevin Reilly

INTRODUCTION

Geographers define South Asia as that part of Asia encompassing India, Pakistan, Bangladesh, Nepal, Sri Lanka, and Bhutan. Historically, the interconnections among these countries have been vital, and I have accepted this geographical definition in creating this atlas. Myanmar (Burma) has not been treated in depth because, both geographically and historically, Burma belongs to Southeast Asia, not South Asia. I have included text and maps on Burma only when its history has had an interconnection with South Asia, for example, when, in the nineteenth century, it was absorbed as part of the British Indian Empire, and later, when it was invaded by the Japanese during the Second World War.

My main reason for undertaking this project was to provide a small, affordable atlas of the history of South Asia for use by students at the undergraduate and graduate level as well as for teachers and South Asian specialists in need of a useful reference book. The last small atlas on South Asian history produced for student use was C. C. Davies's *An Historical Atlas of the Indian Peninsula*, second edition (1959). In addition to being long out of print everywhere except India, the Davies atlas is also out of date. The focus of the atlas was strictly political, and since 1959 much new scholarship has been undertaken, especially in the areas of economic and social history. The only other historical atlas on South Asia is Joseph E. Schwartzberg, ed., *A Historical Atlas of South Asia* (1993). Schwartzberg's effort is admirable, but the atlas is too massive and expensive (the cost is US$250) to be of real use to students, who must, I think, have easy access to an atlas—one they can purchase on their own.

This work is an attempt to fill the void between the Davies and Schwartzberg atlases. In writing the map texts, I have made use of much fresh scholarship in the field. I have not attempted to incorporate much information from journal articles, which are often too specific to be of use in a general work of this kind, and have preferred instead to draw upon the many books and monographs written on South Asia's history in the last twenty years. I found the growing list of volumes in *The New Cambridge History of India* to be especially valuable, as they incorporate and synthesize much recent scholarship. I do want to make clear, however, that this atlas is not a work of original scholarship. As a South Asianist historian, I am acutely aware of the need for specialization in one's research in a field as massive as this one. I have, therefore, in undertaking this atlas, attempted to synthesize the research of many individual scholars; the works I found most useful are credited in the bibliography. Both students and specialists may find the glossary and index to be especially valuable aids in using the atlas. Terms in the text in **boldface** are listed in the glossary. The index contains well over 700 individual entries and refers the user to both text and map references. In the body of the work itself, maps that do not cover the whole of South Asia have a small inset box indicating which part of South Asia the maps cover; dashed lines at the bottom of some indicate that the extent of the map exceeds the extent of the standardized inset map area.

While most maps represent a synthesis of many works, I do want to acknowledge that Map 3 is indebted to G. A. Zograph's map in *Languages of South Asia* (1982); Map 45 is indebted to Irfan Habib's economic map of the Mughal Empire in *An Atlas of the Mughal Empire* (1982); finally, Map 66 is indebted to maps in K. M. de Silva's *A History of Sri Lanka* (1981).

Geography, Climate, and Languages

1   Geography of South Asia

Geography can have a significant effect on the overall development of human cultures. The availability of water for agriculture, the productivity of soils, and the topography of the land can force humans to adapt themselves to the geographical conditions of a given area or region. While the effects of geography on South Asian societies cannot be definitively measured, the course of the region's history is due, in part, to its distinctive geography and location (see Map 1.1).

Geologically, South Asia (the Indian "subcontinent") forms the northeastern segment of the Australian tectonic plate, a portion of the earth's crust which has continued to move northward, albeit extremely slowly, to collide with the much larger Eurasian plate. Subsequent stresses produced by the impact of the two plates created the Himalayas, a young mountain range by geological standards.

South Asia comprises three well-defined physiographic provinces or physical regions within its approximately 4.32 million square kilometers (1.72 million square miles): (1) the northern mountain ranges, (2) the Indo-Gangetic or North Indian Plain, and (3) the Indian Plateau, which includes the Central Indian Plateau, the Deccan Plateau, and the Tamil or Southern Plateau, including Sri Lanka (see Map 1.2).

The northern mountain ranges can be divided into three groups. The Hindu Kush, Karakoram, and Greater Himalayan ranges have an average elevation of 6,700 meters (20,000 feet) and contain the well-known Mount Everest (8,847 meters/29,028 feet) and Mount Kanchenjunga (8,507 meters/28,208 feet). The Sulaiman, Mahabharat, and Patkai ranges comprise mountains which range from 1,500 meters (5,000 feet) to 3,650 meters (12,000 feet). The last of the ranges is the Outer Himalayan, which consists of low foothills or piedmont. Travel in the northern mountain ranges is difficult; mountain passes are few and are closed for most of the year due to copious snowfall.

The Indo-Gangetic Plain is the product of the alluvial deposits of three major rivers: the Indus, the Ganga (Ganges), and the Brahmaputra. Each of these rivers has its headwaters in the Himalayas, and each is, therefore, fed initially by melting snow and ice. As these rivers flow out into the Indo-Gangetic plain, they are joined by numerous tributaries. The Indus has as its major tributaries the five Panjabi rivers of Jhelum, Chenab, Ravi, Beas, and Sutlej. The availability of water from these five tributaries makes the upper Indus valley one of the most productive agricultural regions in all of Asia. The Ganga counts among its main tributaries the Yamuna, Sarda, Gandak, and Kosi rivers. They all add significantly to the Ganga's flow as it moves eastward to drain into the Bay of Bengal. The Ganga River valley's deep alluvial soils, excellent river flow, and long growing season combine to make it India's most productive farming area and, as a result, also its most populous (historians estimate that since the introduction of sedentary agriculture to the region, the Ganga River valley has been India's most populous region). The Brahmaputra has three major tributaries: the Tista, Manas, and Lahit rivers. The valley through which the Brahmaputra flows is substantially narrower than that of the Ganga, is less densely populated, and is subject to recurrent flooding.

The northernmost part of the Indian Plateau is known as the Central Indian Plateau. This plateau extends from the edge of the Indo-Gangetic plain in the north to the edge of the Vindhya mountains in the south, beyond which lies the large Deccan Plateau, situated between the Western Ghats (hills) on the Arabian Sea and the Eastern Ghats on the Bay of Bengal. Several rivers—the largest of which are the Godavari and the Krishna—empty into the bay from the Deccan Plateau due to the decrease in elevation from west to east. In terms of soils, those of Deccan are mainly heavy and black, products of basaltic lava flows 65 to 70 million years old. Overall, these soils are fertile, but their productivity varies according to rainfall amounts.

Finally, the Southern Plateau marks the southernmost region of South Asia. The plateau consists of low hills and interspersed valleys. Along the southern edge of both the Western and Eastern Ghats in the Southern Plateau lie littoral zones known respectively as the Malabar and Coromandel coasts. Due to overall climate and effect of the monsoon (see Maps 2.1-2.4), these two littorals are very fertile and productive and, after the Indo-Gangetic Plain, contain the largest regional concentration of population in South Asia.

The relationship between South Asia's physical and political geography can be seen by comparing Maps 1.2 and 1.3. Physical features such as mountain ranges, rivers, and deserts have traditionally defined regional core areas within the subcontinent. They often marked the frontiers and boundaries between most South Asian political entities until the late modern period.

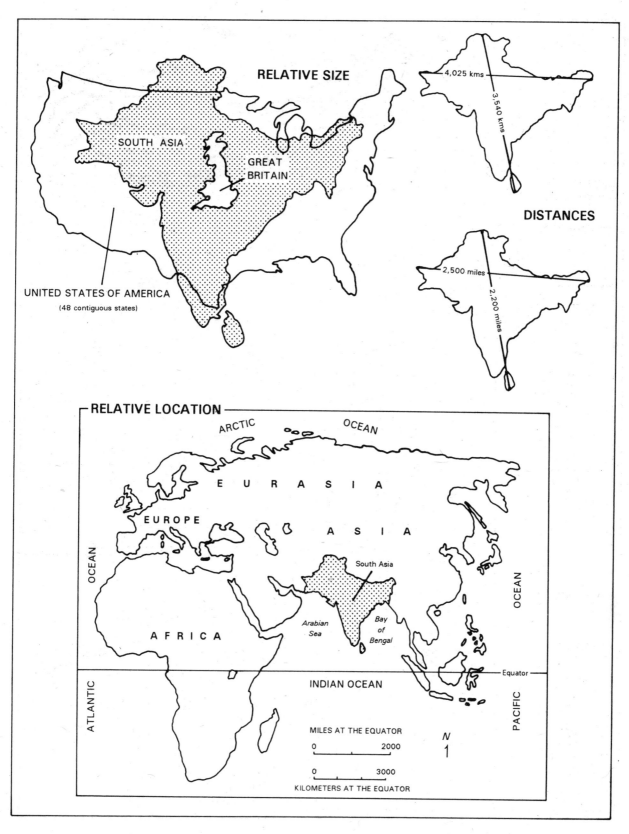

Map 1.1 Size and Location of South Asia

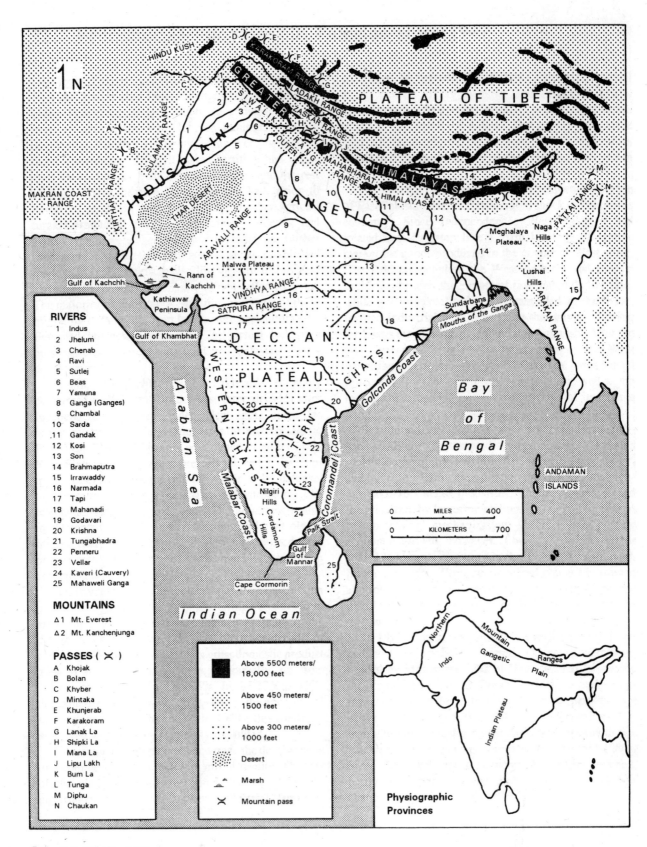

Map 1.2 Physical Features

RIVERS
1 Indus
2 Jhelum
3 Chenab
4 Ravi
5 Sutlej
6 Beas
7 Yamuna
8 Ganga (Ganges)
9 Chambal
10 Sarda
11 Gandak
12 Kosi
13 Son
14 Brahmaputra
15 Irrawaddy
16 Narmada
17 Tapi
18 Mahanadi
19 Godavari
20 Krishna
21 Tungabhadra
22 Penneru
23 Vellar
24 Kaveri (Cauvery)
25 Mahaweli Ganga

MOUNTAINS
△1 Mt. Everest
△2 Mt. Kanchenjunga

PASSES (✕)
A Khojak
B Bolan
C Khyber
D Mintaka
E Khunjerab
F Karakoram
G Lanak La
H Shipki La
I Mana La
J Lipu Lakh
K Bum La
L Tunga
M Diphu
N Chaukan

Above 5500 meters/ 18,000 feet
Above 450 meters/ 1500 feet
Above 300 meters/ 1000 feet
Desert
Marsh
✕ Mountain pass

Physiographic Provinces

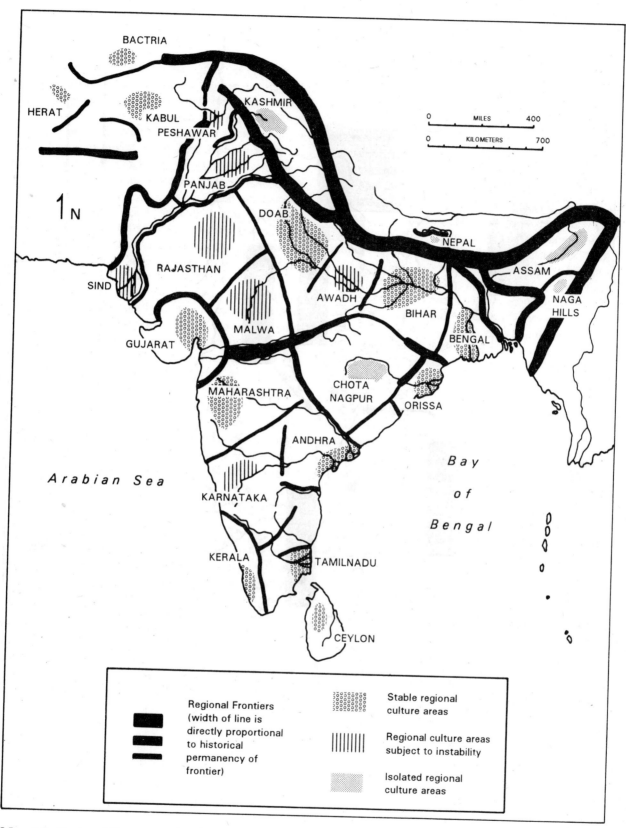

BACTRIA

HERAT

KABUL
PESHAWAR

KASHMIR

PANJAB

1 N

DOAB

NEPAL

ASSAM

RAJASTHAN

SIND

AWADH

BIHAR

NAGA
HILLS

GUJARAT

MALWA

BENGAL

MAHARASHTRA

CHOTA
NAGPUR

ORISSA

Arabian Sea

ANDHRA

Bay

of

KARNATAKA

Bengal

KERALA

TAMILNADU

CEYLON

| 0 | MILES | 400 |
| 0 | KILOMETERS | 700 |

Regional Frontiers
(width of line is
directly proportional
to historical
permanency of
frontier)

Stable regional
culture areas

Regional culture areas
subject to instability

Isolated regional
culture areas

Map 1.3 Regional Frontiers and Culture Areas

5

2   South Asian Climates

Because of the vastness of South Asia, it is difficult to generalize about climatic conditions, as many variations within the subcontinent exist (see Map 2.3). Despite the difficulty, it is possible to broadly classify South Asian climates in terms of seasons. Unlike in North America or Europe, seasonality in South Asia is determined less by temperature and more by variations in precipitation.

Because of its proximity to the equator and other geographical factors, South Asia has only three seasons per year: the cool or winter monsoonal season, the hot season, and the wet or summer monsoonal season. Although each season is accompanied by definite temperature regimes, the three-season scheme is based primarily on variations in precipitation and affects mainly the northern two-thirds of South Asia.

The cool or winter monsoonal season lasts from approximately late October or early November to early March and is characterized by cool to warm days (21°-27°C/70°-80°F) and cool, crisp nights with overnight temperatures often dropping to or below freezing (0°C/32°F). High pressure over the Asian landmass creates an outflow of cold, dry, continental air toward the lower pressure systems prevalent over the oceans. This outward flow of air constitutes the winter monsoon. Although this airflow does pass directly over the subcontinent, its effect is tempered somewhat by the Himalayas. During this season, early morning fogs are common. Precipitation is infrequent and comes mainly in the form of rain, although in the higher elevations, such as the Himalayas, snowfall is prevalent.

By March, the weather begins to change again. The hot season arrives and lasts until early July. Precipitation all but disappears, and, as a result, temperatures begin to rise dramatically. Daytime temperatures in the 38°-43°C (100°-110°F) range in the Central Gangetic plains are not uncommon, while nighttime temperatures average in the 16°-18.5°C (60°-65°F) range. Temperatures in the Thar desert and the Indus plain can average even higher. Working under these conditions can be quite oppressive, especially out of doors.

Finally, by early June in the far south, and early July elsewhere, the wet or summer monsoonal season arrives, bringing with it much-needed rainfall. The action of the winter monsoon reverses and now moist, warm air is drawn from over the Indian Ocean toward the lower pressure areas which dominate over the sub-continent. Contrary to popular belief, the summer monsoonal season does not result in a four-month-long unremittant deluge. The movement of the monsoon northward into the South Asian landmass from the southwest is gradual, extending over a period of four to six weeks before it reaches all areas. Rainfall is plentiful in most areas, even copious in some, but usually occurs only once per day, much like the convective thunderstorms common over much of North America during the summer. Although the rainfall is a welcome relief from the dry conditions which preceded it, average temperatures do not decline sharply; therefore, dry, hot days are replaced by wet, hot days of high humidity. In July, daytime average temperatures of 27°-32°C (80°-90°F) are common over most of the northern two-thirds of the subcontinent, with temperatures exceeding 32°C (90°F) in the desert areas of the Indo-Pakistani border. Nighttime temperatures are not appreciably lower. The summer monsoon begins to recede from the northern-most areas of South Asia beginning in late August or early September under pressure from cooler continental airmasses; thereupon, the seasonal cycle begins anew.

The cycle of seasons affects the various areas of South Asia in different ways and no generalization about climate and weather in South Asia can accurately replace a scientific analysis of climate based on net solar radiation, air temperature, precipitation, and the movement of air masses. Map 2.1 illustrates the various climates of South Asia ranging from the cold, arid climate of northern Kashmir and Ladakh, to the very wet, humid climate of southern Sri Lanka and north-eastern India. Map 2.2 indicates the average annual precipitation values present throughout the subcontinent.

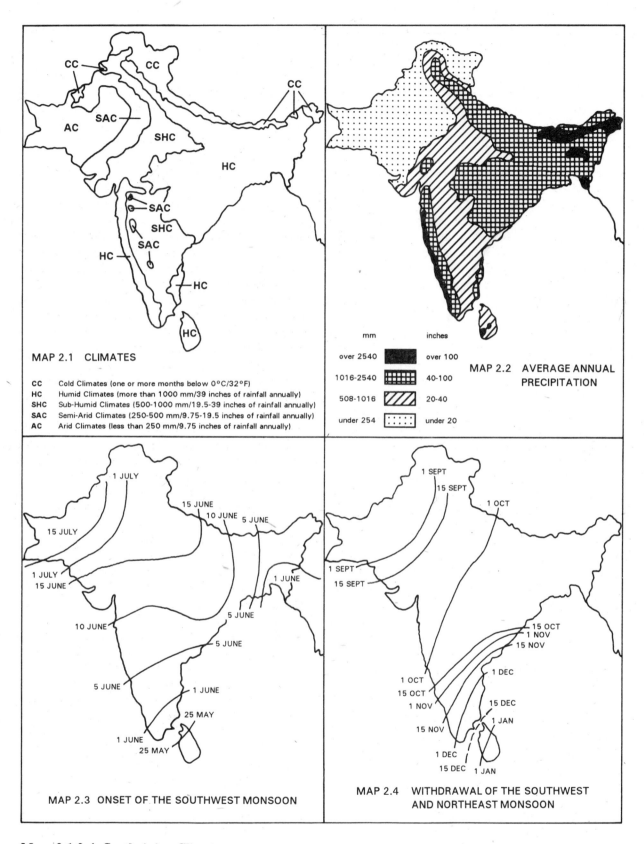

MAP 2.1   CLIMATES

CC   Cold Climates (one or more months below 0°C/32°F)
HC   Humid Climates (more than 1000 mm/39 inches of rainfall annually)
SHC   Sub-Humid Climates (500-1000 mm/19.5-39 inches of rainfall annually)
SAC   Semi-Arid Climates (250-500 mm/9.75-19.5 inches of rainfall annually)
AC   Arid Climates (less than 250 mm/9.75 inches of rainfall annually)

mm		inches
over 2540		over 100
1016-2540		40-100
508-1016		20-40
under 254		under 20

MAP 2.2   AVERAGE ANNUAL PRECIPITATION

MAP 2.3 ONSET OF THE SOUTHWEST MONSOON

MAP 2.4   WITHDRAWAL OF THE SOUTHWEST AND NORTHEAST MONSOON

Maps 2.1-2.4 South Asian Climates

3 Languages of South Asia

The over 1,100 million people of the six countries of South Asia speak over fifty distinct languages, eighteen of which are classified by linguists as major national languages. South Asian languages can be divided into three broad groupings: Indo-Aryan, Dravidian, and Munda.

The Indo-Aryan language group, the Indian branch of the multitudinous Indo-European language family, constitutes the largest of the three groups. Linguistic historians believe that gradual Aryan migration into South Asia resulted in the diffusion of several related Aryan dialects throughout the northern part of the subcontinent. Collectively, these dialects are known as Old Indo-Aryan. The oldest example of Old Indo-Aryan is the Vedic language used in the *Rig Veda* (c. 1500 BCE). Later developments in Old Indo-Aryan include Epic Sanskrit (c. 1000-400 BCE) and Classical Sanskrit (c. 400 BCE-600 CE). Even as Sanskrit evolved over the centuries, it remained primarily a literary language used by orthodox **Brahmans**. The main vernacular languages, comprising Middle Indo-Aryan, but contemporaneous with the two forms of Sanskrit, were Pali (used in Buddhist canonical writings) and Prakrits (in common usage by the advent of Ashoka's reign, 268 BCE). By c. 500 CE, another form of Middle Indo-Aryan language, Apabhramsha, had entered popular usage over a wide area of northern India and formed a final transition to the various languages of New Indo-Aryan (post-1000 CE)—the language group comprising those in use today. The main languages of New Indo-Aryan are (ranked according to number of current speakers): Western and Eastern Hindi (321 million), Bengali (180 million), Urdu (96 million), Western and Eastern Panjabi (89 million), Bihari (70 million), Marathi (67 million), Rajasthani (44 million), Gujarati (39 million), Oriya (31 million), Assamese (23 million), Sindhi (17 million), and Sinhalese (13 million).

The second major South Asian linguistic group comprises the Dravidian languages. Dravidian languages, as spoken by indigenous populations, are confined to South Asia and seem to have no links to any outside language families. Linguistic historians have been unable to determine whether ancient Dravidian speakers were indigenous to South Asia or, like the Aryans, came from outside the subcontinent, but apparently at a much earlier date. Pockets of Dravidian languages in what are now Pakistan and parts of northern India seem to indicate that at one time Dravidian speakers inhabited a much larger area of the subcontinent than they currently do, but were displaced early on by Indo-Aryan-speakers. Dravidian is now confined, with a few minor exceptions, to southern India. Unlike the voluminous research that exists on Indo-Aryan languages, very little historical research has been undertaken on the Dravidian languages. This lacuna is as much due to the difficulty of conducting the research as it is to the shortage of scholars in the field. The main Dravidian languages are (ranked according to number of current speakers): Telugu (71 million), Tamil (67 million), Kannada (43 million), and Malayalam (35 million). Minor languages include: Belari, Brahui, Gadaba, Gondi, Kodagu, Kolami, Konda, Koraga, Kota, Kui, Kurukh, Kuvi, Malto, Manda, Naiki, Parji, Pengo, Toda, and Tulu. Speakers of these minor languages range from a few million each to less than one thousand. The majority of the minor languages are spoken by 200,000 or less.

The last major language group in South Asia, comprising the twelve Munda languages, is also the smallest. Linguistic historians believe that the Munda languages definitely predate the arrival of Indo-Aryan in South Asia, and may, they postulate, also predate Dravidian. Munda-speakers probably inhabited a much wider area than they do today, but over the centuries have yielded to expanding Indo-Aryan and Dravidian speakers. Geographically, the Munda languages are now almost entirely confined to remote hill and forest areas of Bihar, Orissa, and Madhya Pradesh. The three most widely-spoken Munda languages are Santali, Mundari, and Kherwari. Minor languages comprise Bonda (or Remo), Didey (or Gta), Gutob (or Gadaba), Juang, Kharia, Korku, Mowasi, Parengi (or Gorum), Sawar (or Sora). Many of the minor languages are rapidly losing ground and may disappear entirely as they are subsumed by the subcontinent's predominant languages.

In addition to the three language groups discussed above, several other languages are commonly spoken in South Asia. These include Tibeto-Burman languages like Nepali (14 million) and Tibetan (5 million); Iranian languages like Pushtu (21 million) and Baluchi (4 million); and Dardic languages like Kashmiri (4 million). French and Portuguese are also spoken in small pockets in India and, due to South Asia's colonial heritage, English is widely spoken throughout the six countries of the subcontinent.

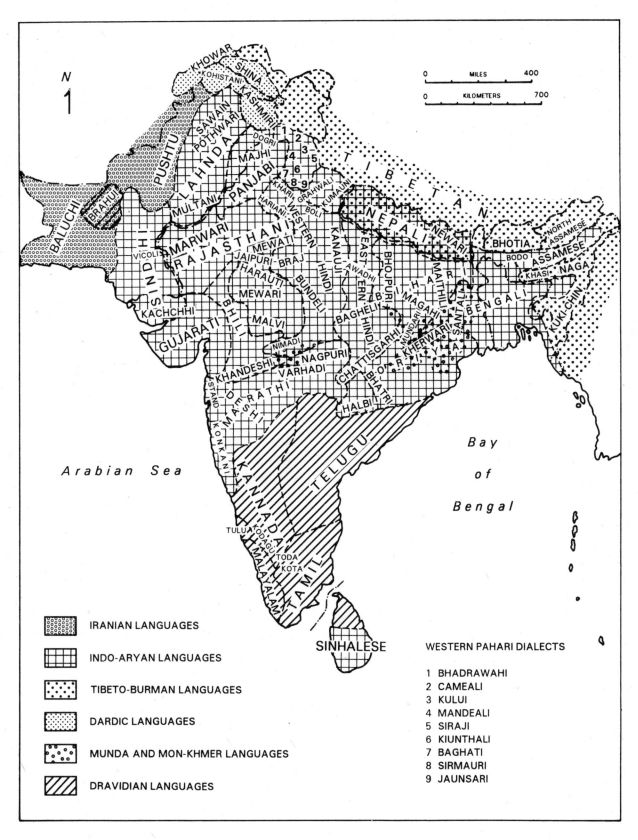

Map 3 Languages of South Asia

Legend:

- IRANIAN LANGUAGES
- INDO-ARYAN LANGUAGES
- TIBETO-BURMAN LANGUAGES
- DARDIC LANGUAGES
- MUNDA AND MON-KHMER LANGUAGES
- DRAVIDIAN LANGUAGES

WESTERN PAHARI DIALECTS

1 BHADRAWAHI
2 CAMEALI
3 KULUI
4 MANDEALI
5 SIRAJI
6 KIUNTHALI
7 BAGHATI
8 SIRMAURI
9 JAUNSARI

Political and Military History

4   Harappan Culture (Indus Valley Civilization)

In 1921, Daya Ram Sahni of the Archaeological Survey of India began work on a site on the Ravi river in what is now Pakistan. The site, known as Harappa, contained evidence of a culture over 1,000 years older than any other yet discovered in South Asia and one which dated back to c. 2350 BCE, making it one of the four oldest centers of civilization in the world. Sahni had discovered what subsequently became known as the Harappan or Indus Valley Civilization.

Based on their size and the diversity of archaeological evidence, three main cities formed the center of the Harappan Civilization: Harappa, Mohenjodaro, and a recently discovered site, Ganweriwala. All three cities are remarkably similar in size, design, and structure. Harappa is the smallest of the three and covers an area of approximately 65 hectares (160.5 acres). Ganweriwala and Mohenjodaro are nearly the same size at 81.5 hectares (201.3 acres) and 83 hectares (205 acres), respectively. The cities were all planned in much the same way: each was dominated by a "citadel," built atop a mound of brick, overlooking the main city; each of the cities appears to have been surrounded by a large and massive brick wall, perhaps designed to serve the dual purpose of protecting the cities from attack and from intermittent river flooding. Main streets were laid out in a grid pattern, remarkable in their regularity and precision. Buildings appear to have been stratified based on primary use. Residential structures were built away from and below the citadel, while official structures (used for grain storage, or religious or governmental purposes) were built either closer or next to the citadel and often on the same level as the citadel. Careful and uniform building construction as well as such seemingly "modern" urban innovations as cesspools, sewers, drains, and baths indicate that the Harappans enjoyed a relatively high standard of living.

The Harappan economy seems to have been based on twin pillars of agriculture and trade (Allchin and Allchin 1982). The alluvial soils of the Indus valley provided rich, fertile, easily worked ground to grow a variety of crops including grains such as wheat, barley, and rice; legumes; dates; oil seeds such as mustard and sessamum; and cotton. In addition to crops, Harappans made use of several domesticated animals such as sheep and goats for food, supplemented by wild game such as deer, boar, tortoise, and various fowl.

Archaeologists have suggested (Possehl 1982; Ratnagar 1982) that the geographical positioning of several Harappan cities was based, in part, upon the need to take advantage of nearby natural resources or to serve as centers for the overland, river, or sea trade. Harappa was an important nexus of several riverine and overland trade routes and was situated close to the mineral resources of the Sulaiman mountain range. Mohenjodaro not only was located in the fertile Indus floodplain but was also well positioned to take full advantage of the resources of Rajasthan and Baluchistan. Like Mohenjodaro, Ganweriwala also had access to the resources of Rajasthan, especially the rich copper mines of Ganeshwar. Beyond the larger core cities of the Harappan Civilization, archaeologists have discovered many smaller settlements, some apparently built to fulfill specialized economic needs. Lothal, for example, was a small, compact community which lay along the Harappan frontier at the edge of the Kathiawar peninsula. It was well-situated to draw upon the resources of Deccan and Rajasthan, as well as the seaborne trade with the coastal states of the Arabian peninsula and the Gulf. Evidence of the sea trade is suggested by the existence at Lothal of what appears to be a dock for sea-going vessels.

Despite its well-developed cities and economic infrastructure, the Harappan Civilization began to decline shortly after 1900 BCE and vanished completely c. 1700-1600 BCE. Several theories for this decline have been postulated by archaeologists, among them: that successive waves of Aryan invaders attacked and destroyed Harappan cities and farms; that a decrease in rainfall led to aridification of the Harappan periphery and to a subsequent inward population migration which the center could not effectively absorb; that a great flood engulfed Mohenjodaro and dislocated a large segment of the Harappan population who then fell victim to pestilence and disease; or that a series of earthquakes over an extended period of time disrupted the food production capability of the Harappans, from which they never recovered. Although for many years the first theory held sway among many archaeologists, many now speculate that changes in the environment, either human- or nature-induced, disrupted the delicate balance of the Harappan Civilization and brought about its eventual demise (Agrawal and Sood 1982).

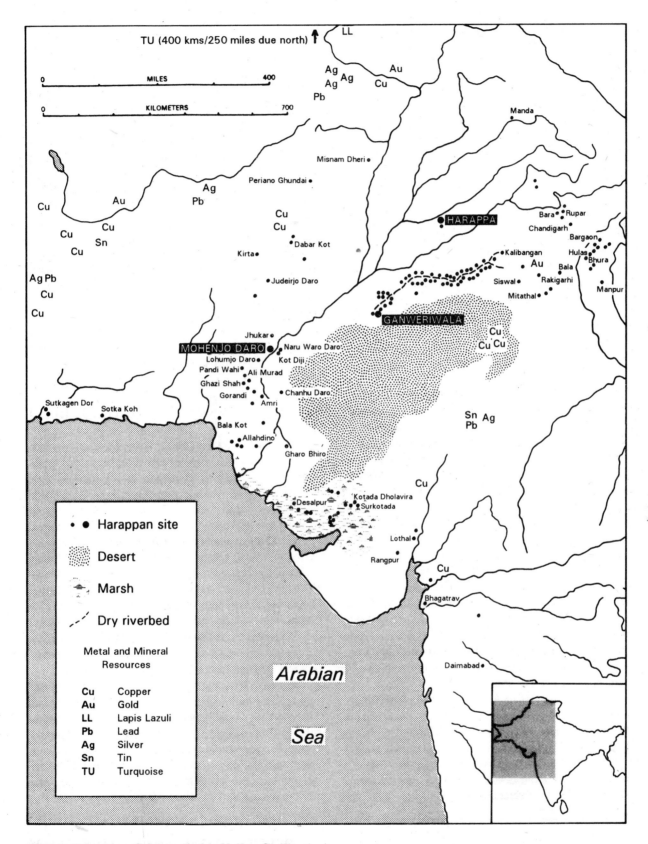

Map 4 Harappan Culture (Indus Valley Civilization)

13

5   Indo-Aryan South Asia, c. 1000 BCE

The first millennium BCE in South Asia has traditionally been referred to as the Early Vedic Age because the primary historical source for this period is the *Rig Veda*. Unfortunately, much of the historical and geographical information contained in the *Rig Veda* is not verifiable in the ordinary sense; therefore, presenting an accurate map of South Asia c. 1000 BCE entails some difficulty and is by necessity limited to the northern part of the subcontinent.

Another significant historical problem in dealing with this time period is that no agreement (and indeed, some controversy) exists among historians as to the original home of the Aryans, the creators of the *Rig Veda*. Several theories have been postulated by historians over the last century regarding the original habitat of the Aryans. The advocates of these competing theories can be divided into two broad groups: "externalists" and "internalists."

Externalists argue that c. 2000 BCE the Aryans either migrated to, or invaded, South Asia from outside. They believe that the Aryans came from either the steppes of Central Asia, from Southwest Asia, from southeastern Europe, or even from as far away as the Arctic. According to externalists, early Aryan migration into South Asia took place gradually, c. 2000-1200 BCE, as the Aryans moved from the mountain passes of Afghanistan eastward into Panjab and the area around modern Delhi. Linguistic evidence strongly suggests that the Aryans did indeed come from outside of South Asia and that their point of origin was somewhere in Central Asia.

In contrast to the externalists, internalists theorize that the original home of the Aryans was located in South Asia itself. They argue that none of the *Vedas* contain any mention of migration or of foreign lands and that this fact casts doubt on the external origins theories. Internalists believe that the Aryans came from Kashmir and from there, moved out onto the plains of Panjab and northern India.

All of the theories of Aryan origins are exceedingly problematical due to an almost exclusive reliance on the *Rig Veda* as an evidentiary source. Unless significant additional historical or archaeological evidence is uncovered, the debate over this issue is likely to continue (for a more detailed summary of the various theories, see A. Bhattacharjee 1988; and de Gila-Kochanowski 1990).

Leaving aside the problem of Aryan origins, it is clear that the Aryans had, by c. 1000 BCE, become well-established in northern India. As the Allchins point out (1982), the interaction of indigenous Harappan culture and Aryan culture over several centuries probably produced a synthesis of the two cultures; the result can be called Indo-Aryan. It is still unclear, however, precisely what the nature of that synthesis was, but a careful analysis of the *Rig Veda* does illustrate Indo-Aryan culture, including economic and political systems, as well as the level of their technology.

Although there is no systematic discussion of the Indo-Aryan economy in the *Rig Veda*, scattered references do indicate that during this early period, the Indo-Aryan economy was a mixture of pastoralism (based on the breeding and trade of cattle, sheep, and horses), and agriculture (based on the cultivation of barley and wheat). The change from a nomadic pastoral economy to one in which agriculture played a large and growing role, led to an ever-increasing specialization of labor, which, in turn, was reflected in the stratification of Indo-Aryan society and the development of the **jati**, or **caste system**.

Early Indo-Aryan political structures seem to have been based on some type of patriarchal **lineage** system, with several lineages taken together forming a clan. Competition and friction among the various Indo-Aryan clans for influence and authority seems to have created an impetus to further migration within South Asia and to the establishment of additional settlements throughout northern India (Thapar 1984). These Indo-Aryan settlements centered initially on Panjab, but gradually encompassed an area extending from the western tributaries of the Indus on the west to the Yamuna and Ganga rivers on the east. According to Thapar (1984), the Indo-Aryan clan-based lineage system formed a precursor to the later development of state-based political systems in northern India by c. 500 BCE.

Although iron age technology had made inroads among the Indo-Aryans by 1000 BCE (Allchin and Allchin 1982; N. R. Banerjee 1965), most Indo-Aryans still used tools made from stone, copper, and bronze. Heavy reliance on older and less efficient technologies made the clearing of dense forests slow and difficult, and served, until iron came into widespread use after 800 BCE, as a check on Indo-Aryan expansion into the Gangetic valley.

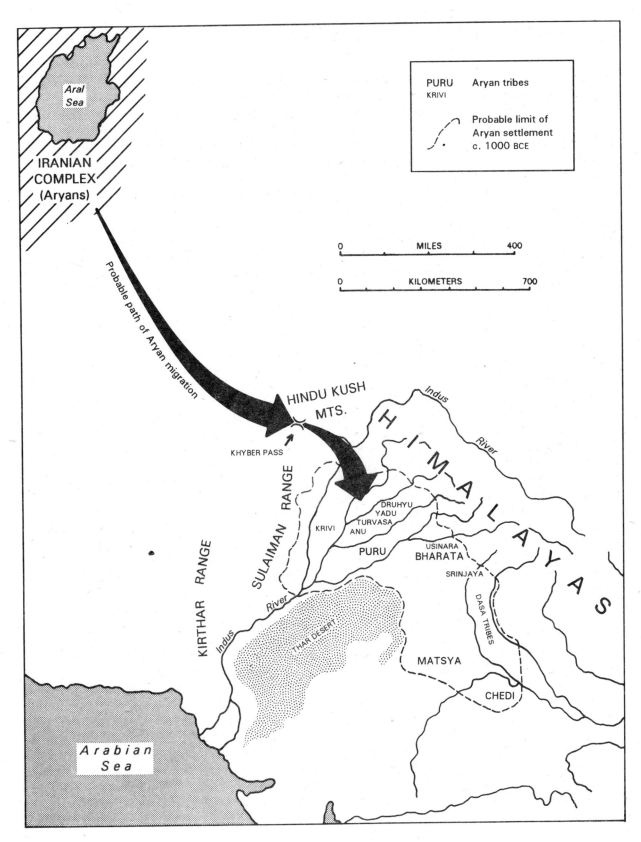

Map 5 Indo-Aryan South Asia, c. 1000 BCE

6　Republics and Kingdoms in Northern India, c. 700-450 BCE

Republics and kingdoms in northern India developed as a response to changing political circumstances after 1000 BCE. As the Indo-Aryans gave up their nomadic traditions and became increasingly settled in various areas, their peoples laid permanent claim to those particular territories. Maintaining territorial claims required leaders to foster a sense of separate identity among their respective peoples which led, in turn, to the development of the state. State formation also required the development of more complex forms of political organization than the earlier, lineage-based society of the Indo-Aryans could provide. As a result, by c. 500 BCE, the Aryans shifted from earlier, simpler forms of government to the development of republics and monarchies (Thapar 1984).

Initially, the constraints of their technology prevented the Indo-Aryans from settling in the Ganga River valley. They found it easier to clear for settlement the hill areas which bordered the valley rather than the more densely forested river valley below. Subsequent Indo-Aryan groups, equipped with efficient iron technology, were able to clear the dense forests for agriculture and settle the Ganga River valley itself. Differences in the temporal sequence of settlement were also reflected in governmental systems. When the hill areas were settled, their governments reflected the prevailing preference for the republican form of government. Likewise, when the Ganga lowlands were later settled, the governments established reflected the type in current vogue: monarchy. As the Indo-Aryans spread eastward beyond their core area of Panjab, and in response to changing political needs, they discarded the elements of their lineage-based governments which most resembled "direct democracy" and chose instead a more efficient type of government featuring an assembly in which the interests of the different lineages were indirectly represented. When Indo-Aryan states became larger over time, and therefore more difficult to administer, and as leaders became increasingly interested in the continued growth of their own power, their governments became gradually more centralized and autocratic.

The sixteen major states (*mahajanapadas*) during this period, as mentioned in the ancient Buddhist text, *Anguttara Nikaya*, were (from roughly west to east): Kamboja, Gandhara, Kuru, Surasena, Matsya, Avanti, Asmaka, Panchala, Chedi, Vatsa, Kosala, Kashi, Malla, Vrijji, Magadha, and Anga. Located primarily in the Gangetic plains, most of these states were monarchies, with large, splendid capital cities, flourishing economies, and well-developed administrative systems. The development of these states was directly linked to the rise of large, fortified urban centers which acted as focal points for the efficient spatial concentration of trade, as well as religious, political, and military activities. Of the six largest cities in the Central Gangetic plains, five were capitals of major states.

With large armies supported by increased revenues derived from agriculture and trade, and driven by the desire to increase the size of their respective territories, king fought king in a series of bloody, internecine wars until most of the states, including most of the republics, had been destroyed. The victors absorbed the vanquished until by c. 500 BCE only four of the sixteen states survived: Magadha, Kosala, Kashi (all of which were kingdoms), and the Vrijji republic.

In the competition between states, and more specifically, between kingdoms and republics, the republics seem to have lost more frequently. This was probably due more to the inherent inefficiency of republicanism than to any actual superiority of the monarchical system. For example, republican governments require more time than monarchies to arrive at decisions, and have difficulties preventing personal ambition and political partisanship. In addition, the Indian republics tended to be small in areal extent, tended to occupy poor land with limited natural resources, and were hampered by poor communications due to unfavorable terrain. This situation contrasted markedly with the majority of the kingdoms, which were large in extent, occupied areas with good agrarian, timber, and iron resources, and had, for the most part, excellent communications and transportation facilities through the Ganga and its tributaries (Sharma 1968).

Of the four states which survived the many wars of the late sixth century BCE, Magadha witnessed the most dramatic rise to power. Over the next eighty years, two of its kings, Bimbisara (c. 540-493 BCE) and Ajatashatru (c. 493-461 BCE), drove Magadha to preeminence among the states in the Gangetic plain. Magadha retained its importance in the politics of the area and later formed the core of the Mauryan Empire.

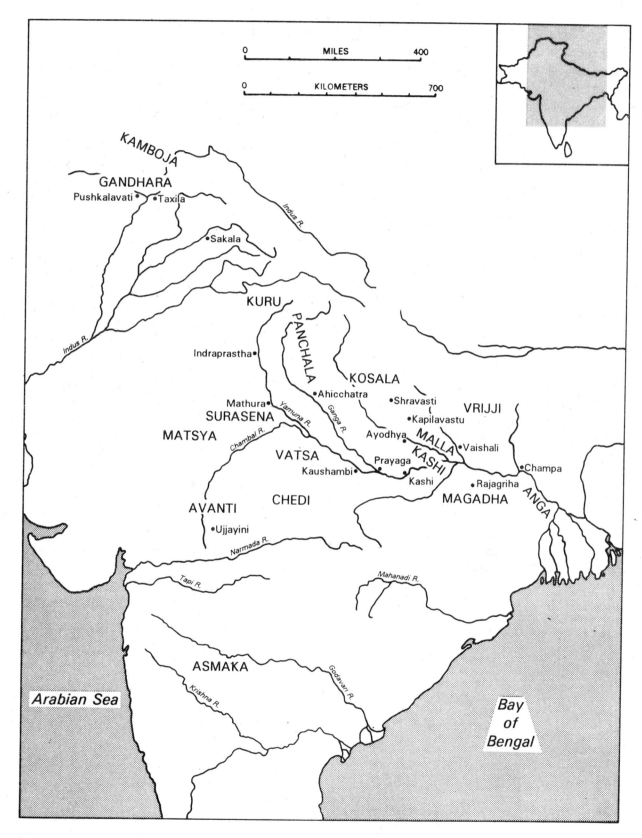

Map 6 Republics and Kingdoms in Northern India, c. 700-450 BCE

17

7   The Greeks in South Asia, 550-50 BCE

Greek activities in South Asia began soon after the Persian king and founder of the Achaemenid Empire (550-330 BCE), Cyrus the Great (r. 558-529 BCE), extended Persian hegemony from the Hindu Kush mountains in Afghanistan to the Ionian-Greek settlements in Asia Minor. Cyrus and his successors imported thousands of Ionian-Greek artisans and mercenaries from the western marches to add both technical skill and martial manpower to the maintenance of the empire. Many of these same Ionian mercenaries, after helping to establish Achaemenid dominion over what is now Afghanistan, settled in that area. In addition, the Persians regularly exiled politically rebellious Greeks in the western empire to the Persian "Siberia" of Bactria, Gandhara, and the Indus valley. Once there, the exiles formed their own settlements and colonies with the encouragement of the Persian government. Descendants of some of these ex-mercenaries and exiles would later serve in Alexander's army during his invasion of India.

In 336 BCE, at the age of twenty, Alexander III became king of Macedon. Over the next two years, he crushed several rebellions against his rule and thus established his dominion over Greece. In 334 BCE, Alexander embarked on a campaign of military conquests in Persia so extensive and so brilliantly executed that he would later become known as Alexander "the Great." After five years of warfare in Persia, Alexander destroyed Achaemenid power forever. His usurpation of that great empire all but complete, Alexander undertook a final major campaign in the summer of 327 BCE in order to establish himself as ruler over all remaining Achaemenid territory. His objective: India.

Alexander crossed the Hindu Kush mountains with a force of some 70,000 infantry and 10,000 cavalry—the largest force he had yet commanded. A marvel of logistical competence, this force would grow to some 125,000 soldiers after reinforcements arrived from the west. Alexander encountered little Indian resistance until he reached the upper Indus valley region (Panjab) in 326 BCE. There, at a crossing of the river Jhelum (Hydaspes), Alexander fought and defeated the Indian ruler, Paurava (Porus), and took control of Panjab. Soon after, Alexander compelled his army eastward toward the "Eastern Ocean" (presumably the Ganga River). When they reached the banks of the Beas (Hy-phasis), however, Alexander's army, exhausted by battle and the long marches through torrential monsoonal rains, mutinied and forced him, ultimately, to return to Persia. He died soon thereafter in Babylon in 323 BCE.

Seleucus Nikator (d. 280 BCE), one of Alexander's generals, became heir to the empire upon Alexander's death. As Seleucus I, he founded the Seleucid Dynasty (364-12 BCE) and ruled over much of western Asia from his capital at Antioch in Syria. In 305 BCE, Seleucus concluded a treaty with the Indian emperor, Chandragupta Maurya (r. 321?-297 BCE), which fixed the crest of the Hindu Kush mountains as the boundary between the Seleucid and Mauryan Empires. The two emperors also exchanged ambassadors.

As Mauryan power waned, so too did that of the Seleucids. Under Seleucus's grandson, Antiochus II (c. 261-247 BCE), Bactria, one of the Indo-Greek vassal states, declared its independence from Seleucid control around 250 BCE. Advancing Greco-Bactrian armies, probing the weakening Mauryan frontier, recaptured the city of Purushapura (Peshawar) from the Mauryans in 190 BCE and all of Panjab by 180 BCE. By the middle of the second century BCE, the invading armies of the Bactrian king, Menander (r. 160-130 BCE), with his capital at Sakala, had conquered Indraprastha (Delhi) and Mathura, and had even attacked (but did not occupy) the old Mauryan capital of Pataliputra (Patna) itself. Greek territory in South Asia reached its apex under Menander.

Following Menander's death, his immediate successors vied for control of Greek kingdoms in South Asia until descendants of another Greek monarch, Eucratides (who had been murdered by one of his own sons c. 155 BCE), invaded Gandhara and touched off fifty years of bloody warfare among the Greeks in South Asia. In approximately 80 BCE, hordes of **Shaka (Scythian)** horsemen invaded the upper Indus valley from Baluchistan and cut off Greek kingdoms in Panjab from others in the trans-Hindu Kush area. Greek kingdoms in Panjab perished rapidly with the Shaka onslaught. The last of the Indo-Greek states in India, the core state of Bactria, ruled by Hermaeus, was extinguished and its people killed or dispersed, when it was attacked by both the Shakas and the **Parthians** c. 50 BCE.

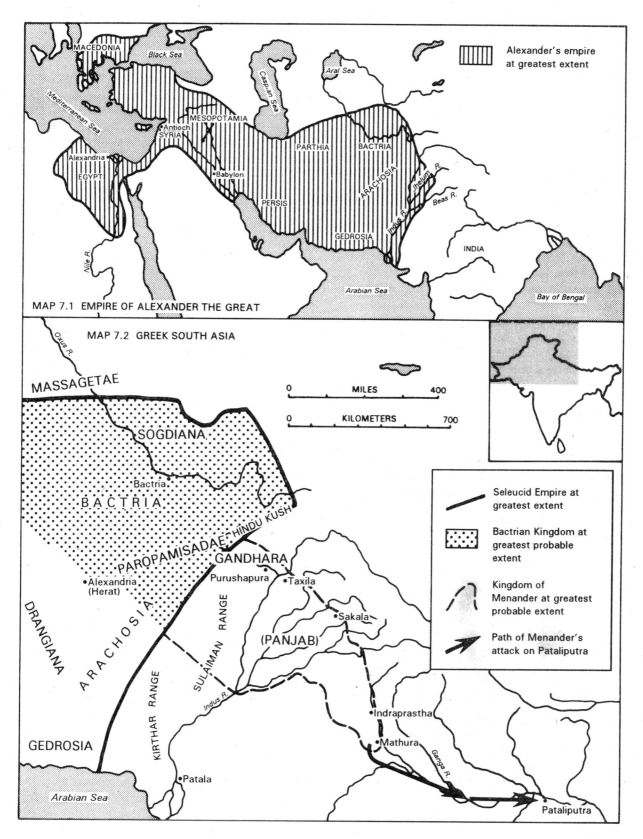

Maps 7.1–7.2   The Greeks in South Asia, 550–50 BCE

19

8   Growth of the Mauryan Empire, 321-232 BCE

The Mauryan Empire, the first to encompass nearly all of India, owed its creation to the rise of Magadha, its core state, as well as to a number of strong, intelligent, and able rulers. From c. 550 BCE, the powerful leadership of kings Bimbisara and Ajatashatru paved the way for Magadha's political and economic dominance over the Gangetic plain. Magadha's initial geographical position, as well as subsequent imperial conquests, endowed it with plentiful natural resources: forests for timber, elephants for the army, and iron ore which could be traded or used for making weapons. Access to the Ganga river trade enabled Magadhan kings to derive revenue from both internal and, after the conquest of the state of Anga (for location, see Map 6), foreign trade. With these resources, Bimbisara and Ajatashatru created a very powerful state; even after their deaths, three usurpations of the throne, and three changes of dynastic rule over more than a century, Magadha was still the strongest state in India when Alexander and his armies arrived in 326 BCE.

The last usurper of the Magadhan throne, and founder of a new dynasty and empire, was Chandragupta Maurya (r. 321?-297 BCE). The details of Chandragupta's rise to power are obscure, but tradition has it that Chandragupta was befriended at an early age by a Brahman named Kautilya who tutored him in the art of statecraft and the uses of war. Chandragupta utilized his new knowledge to raise an army, and to attack the Magadhan frontier, which had been weakened earlier by a series of Greek offensives. After many successful campaigns, Chandragupta conquered Magadha, and reputedly killed the last Nanda ruler of Magadha himself before usurping the throne at Pataliputra c. 321 BCE.

Following the precepts laid down by his mentor, Kautilya, the Mauryan emperor set about consolidating his hold over his newly acquired empire. He implemented an efficient administrative system; built up his army; and established an extensive spy network to gather intelligence both externally and internally. In 303 BCE, Chandragupta defeated the Greek Seleucus Nikator, after the latter attempted to regain lost Greek territories in northwestern India. The two rulers signed a peace treaty in which Seleucus ceded all territories east of the Hindu Kush mountains to Chandragupta. The details of Chandragupta's empire-building activities after the treaty with Seleucus are vague, but by the end of his reign, Chandragupta seems to have incorporated most of northern India into the Mauryan Empire.

Very little is known about the reign of Bindusara (r. 297-272 BCE), Chandragupta's son, but during his lifetime he undertook several military campaigns in southern India, conquering and incorporating into the Mauryan Empire almost all of the subcontinent, except the Southern Plateau and Kalinga.

The conquest of Kalinga was left to Bindusara's son and the most famous of the Mauryan emperors, Ashoka (r. 268-232 BCE). In 261 BCE, Ashoka conquered Kalinga, but only after a very bloody campaign, during which 100,000 Kalingans were killed and 150,000 were forced from their homes. This campaign not only devastated Kalinga, but reportedly forever changed Ashoka's life. Although Ashoka is remembered as the greatest monarch of ancient India, this reputation is not based on his military prowess, or even the fact that the Mauryan Empire reached its apex under his long reign. His high reputation is based on the fact that after the Kalinga campaign, Ashoka renounced warfare, later converted to Buddhism, and spent the rest of his life as a benevolent ruler over most of South Asia, pursuing a policy known as **Dhamma**, the doctrines of which were inscribed on a multitude of rocks and pillars throughout his dominions.

The Mauryan Empire lasted another fifty-two years after Ashoka's death, but was in decline during that entire period. The decline seems to have been the result of several factors. First, the empire was divided in half at Ashoka's death, with twin capitals at Taxila and Pataliputra. This division weakened the empire by forcing the western part to devote much energy to developing a new imperial organization, directed from Taxila, thereby diverting vital resources from the defense of the northwestern frontier against the Greeks. Second, Ashoka's successors were weak rulers and probably did not inspire the same level of confidence and loyalty from either the bureaucracy or the people. In such an atmosphere, it seems likely that Ashoka's successors abandoned Dhamma in favor of more conventional, i.e., less compassionate, imperial policies to shore up their diminishing power. This retrogression probably produced a backlash, weakening the empire further. Finally, it seems likely that problems common to large empires—disparities in urban-rural income; cultural dissimilarities; contrasts in regional levels of economic development—all increased the tendency toward disunity and aided in the empire's final collapse c. 180 BCE (Thapar, 1973; 1987).

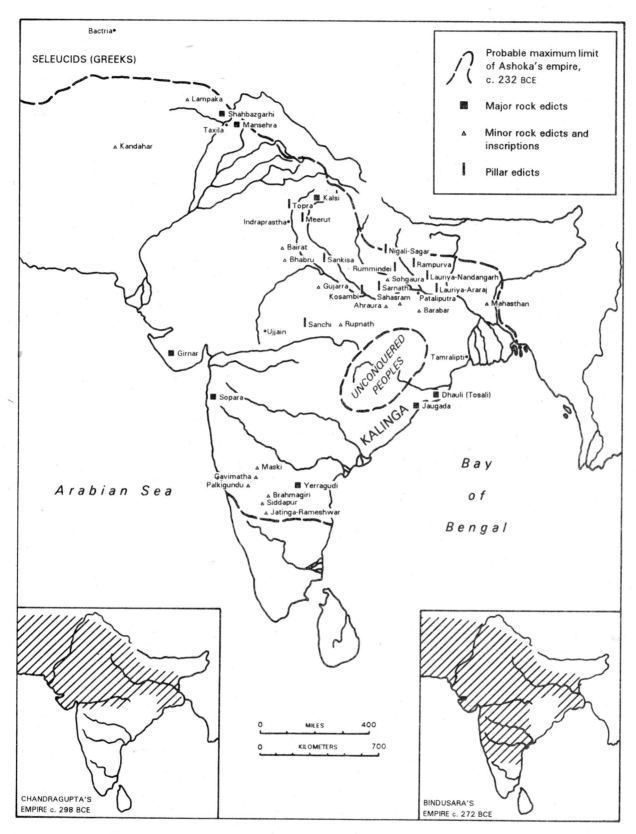

Map 8 Growth of the Mauryan Empire, 321-232 BCE

Bactria•

SELEUCIDS (GREEKS)

△ Lampaka

■ Shahbazgarhi

Taxila ■ Mansehra

△ Kandahar

■ Kalsi

❘ Topra

Indraprastha• ❘ Meerut

△ Bairat

△ Bhabru ■ Sankisa

Rummindei

△ Gujarra ■ Sohgaura ❘ Nigali-Sagar

Kosambi ■ Sarnath ❘ Rampurva

Sahasram ❘ Lauriya-Nandangarh

Ahraura △ Pataliputra ❘ Lauriya-Araraj

△ Mahasthan

❘ Sanchi △ Rupnath △ Barabar

•Ujjain

■ Girnar

UNCONQUERED PEOPLES

Tamralipti•

■ Sopara

■ Dhauli (Tosali)

KALINGA Jaugada

△ Maski

Arabian Sea

Gavimatha △

Palkigundu △ ■ Yerragudi

△ Brahmagiri

△ Siddapur

△ Jatinga-Rameshwar

Bay

of

Bengal

Probable maximum limit
of Ashoka's empire,
c. 232 BCE

■ Major rock edicts

△ Minor rock edicts and
inscriptions

❘ Pillar edicts

| 0 | MILES | 400 |
| 0 | KILOMETERS | 700 |

CHANDRAGUPTA'S
EMPIRE c. 298 BCE

BINDUSARA'S
EMPIRE c. 272 BCE

9   South Asia, c. 185 BCE-320 CE

In c. 185 BCE, the last Mauryan emperor, Brihadratha, was assassinated by his commander-in-chief, a Ujjaini Brahman named Pushyamitra. Usurping the Mauryan throne, Pushyamitra (r. c. 180-151 BCE) established the Shunga dynasty (180-72 BCE), which ruled from Pataliputra over the remains of the defunct Mauryan empire. The Shungas sought to preserve their hold over the kingdom by employing a philosophy of militarism and by reviving **Brahmanical Hinduism**. While Pushyamitra maintained a large army primarily for conquest, he also protected the kingdom from attacks by Bactrian armies. During Pushyamitra's lifetime alone, for example, his armies repelled two Greek invasions.

The revival of Hinduism during Shunga rule was perhaps as much a result of Pushyamitra's religious proclivities—he performed the **ashvamedha** twice during his reign—as it was a political reaction against Buddhism, and a ploy to gain the support of the Brahmans. The resurgence of Hinduism under Pushyamitra was not continued by later Shunga rulers, who instead favored Buddhism. Hinduism, however, was the religion of the Shungas' successors, the Kanvas (72-28 BCE). Unfortunately, almost nothing is known about their reign, and Magadhan history after 28 BCE is vague until the advent of the Guptas in 320 CE.

One of the many areas formerly under Mauryan control which became independent following the empire's disintegration was Central India, where in Deccan the Shatavahanas (c. 235?/50? BCE-225 CE) came to power. Historians are divided on the date of the rise of the Shatavahanas, but it seems probable that the latter took advantage of the fall of the Mauryan Empire in establishing their kingdom, and later enlarged the kingdom from its western Deccan core state into an empire which included all of Deccan and Malwa.

At its height, c. 25 CE, the Shatavahana empire was quite prosperous, with a thriving internal trade based on the great market cities of Pratishthana, Nashik, Govardhana, Vejayanti, and Dhanyakataka. The maritime trade with Europe and East Asia flourished as well. After barely surviving a series of invasions launched against them by the Western Satraps (Western Kshatrapas or Shakas), c. 35-90 CE, the Shatavahanas experienced a century-long resurgence beginning with the reign of Gotamiputa Siri-Satakani (c. 70-95 CE). By 225 CE, however, weakening central control over the empire led to a struggle among the provincial governors who subsequently founded their own independent kingdoms. In the end, these centrifugal forces proved too powerful and the empire of the Shatavahanas disintegrated.

Among the many states in South Asia during this period, two were formed by invaders: the Shakas and the Kushanas. The Shakas were driven from their homeland in Sogdiana and into South Asia c. 170 BCE by the Great Yüeh-chi, a nomadic people originally from Mongolia. Earlier, the Great Yüeh-chi themselves had been driven from east Central Asia after the Great Wall was built to stop their predatory raids into China c. 150-100 BCE. After destroying the last of Indo-Greek kingdoms c. 50 BCE, the Shakas consolidated their gains and established an empire with an administrative system modeled on that of the Achaemenid and Seleucid governments, in which the empire was divided into large provinces or satraps, each ruled by a military governor or mahakshatrapa. Although the Shakas ruled over a large area of northwestern India, their power was weakened by internal struggles among the many governors, and by attacks from both the **Indo-Parthians** and the Kushanas during the first century CE. The Western Satraps survived these attacks, but were later destroyed by the Guptas c. 400 CE.

Like the Shakas, the Kushanas were invaders from Central Asia who built an empire in South Asia. A century and a half after the Great Yüeh-chi forced the Shakas to migrate into South Asia, one of the five Yüeh-chi tribal leaders, Kujala Kadphises, leader of the Kushana tribe, conquered the others, and founded the first Kushana kingdom in the early first century CE. Of all the Kushana emperors, however, Kanishka (r. c. 78/144-? CE) is the most famous. Under Kanishka, the Kushana Empire (c. 1-225 CE) reached its largest extent, apparently stretching from Kashmir to Malwa, and from Kashi to Sogdiana. Kanishka is remembered as a patron of Buddhism (to which he converted), and of the arts. He was a formidable warrior and maintained a huge army to defend his territory. The Kushana economy was vigorous and materially prosperous because the empire was well-located to profit from both internal as well as foreign trade via the northern and central trade routes, which linked China and Southeast Asia to Europe via South Asia. Like their many predecessors, the Kushanas later weakened and fell prey to invasions; they lost control of their South Asian provinces c. 225.

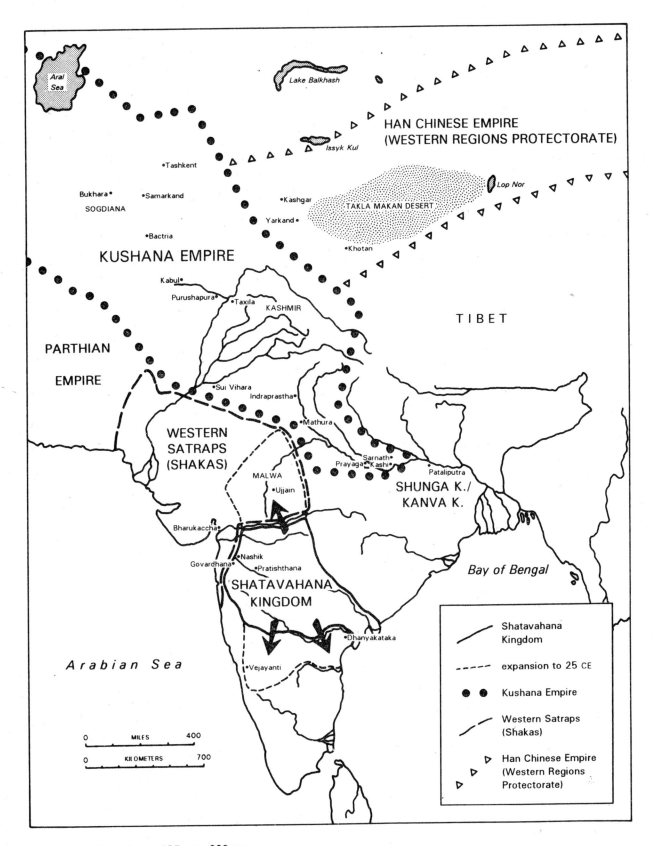

Map 9 South Asia, c. 185 BCE-320 CE

10   Growth and Decline of the Gupta Empire, 320-550

The creation of the Gupta Empire, one of the largest in South Asian history, represented the struggle of the Gupta monarchs for political dominance over the various kings and rulers of northern India. The Guptas won this struggle through a combination of direct military conquest and territorial absorption, as well as the implementation and maintenance of a feudalist system in which "lesser" rulers were allowed to retain their kingdoms but had to submit tribute and owe their loyalty to the Gupta emperor.

Upon inheriting the Gupta throne, Chandragupta I (318-30) drew upon the material and military resources of his own territory and that of his **Lichchavi** wife, Kumaradevi, to become founder of the Empire. By the end of his reign, Chandragupta I had, through direct conquest, added Awadh, Prayaga, and Bihar to his core state in what is now eastern Uttar Pradesh (Goyal 1967; A. Agrawal 1989).

After Chandragupta I's death, Samudragupta (330-75) was faced with the task of consolidating his hold over the territory given to him by his father and with the desire of extending Gupta imperial control over additional territories. During the early part of his reign, Samudragupta seems to have reduced several of his northern neighbors (Ahicchatra, Mathura, and Kota) to vassal status, exacting tribute from them, but allowing them to retain their thrones in a subordinate role. The **Allahabad pillar inscription** records that Samudragupta next extended Guptan imperial rule in Deccan and even farther south. Following his earlier pattern, Samudragupta forced vassal status upon a dozen different states, apparently as far south as Kanchi. Before he could complete his conquest of the south, however, Samudragupta was forced to return to the north to quell a growing resistance to his overlordship among the Naga rulers in an area known as Aryavarta. Once he had destroyed the resistance of the Naga kings, Samudragupta conquered the Shakas of Eran, followed by a successful campaign in Bundelkhand. Samudragupta's military conquests brought him great power and prestige and enabled him to exact tribute and subservience from a number of frontier states in the east, north, and northwest, all of whom feared having their territories annexed, and who were content to serve as vassals of the Gupta Empire.

Chandragupta II **Vikramaditya** (375-415) acceded to the Gupta throne apparently after a brief dynastic struggle in which Samudragupta's eldest son (and Chandragupta's brother) was overthrown (A. Agrawal 1989). This struggle for power weakened the Empire in the eyes of many of the rulers of the eastern and southern frontier states; they subsequently rebelled. To quell this defiance, Chandragupta II embarked on a series of campaigns of conquest to reassert Gupta control over the recalcitrant states, to extend his control over Malwa and Saurashtra, and to destroy the Shaka kingdom in the west. The conquest of the Shaka kingdom was extremely important because it enabled Chandragupta II to control the lucrative South Asian trade with the West as well as eliminate what had been a lingering problem in imperial defense. At his death, Chandragupta II left his son, Kumaragupta I, an empire at its apex of economic prosperity and military power.

Upon assuming the throne, Kumaragupta I (415-54) did not have to face the problems of imperial consolidation and expansion as had his predecessors. During his reign no enemies dared question his authority. His son and heir was not so fortunate.

When Skandagupta (454-67) assumed the throne, he almost immediately faced an internal conflict with the Pushyamitras whose challenge to the new Gupta emperor was crushed only after a bloody fight. Externally, the Hunas (Huns) presented another challenge. From their base at Herat in Afghanistan, the Hunas had invaded Persia and began to encroach on Gupta territory. Skandagupta fended off their attacks and forced them to abandon their plans of conquest for the next fifty years.

Although it would exist for another century, the Gupta Empire slowly declined after Skandagupta's death. Until the late 1960s, historians believed that a new wave of invasions by the Hunas caused the destruction of the Gupta Empire c. 550, but new historical theories (Goyal 1967; A. Agrawal 1989) suggest that the Hunas only aided in the final disintegration which was largely precipitated by internal dissension. A series of relatively weak Gupta rulers after Skandagupta apparently could not maintain the stability of the empire, and, as a result, power began to devolve onto smaller political entities, i.e., individual kingdoms and other former vassal states. This devolution led ultimately to the collapse of the empire.

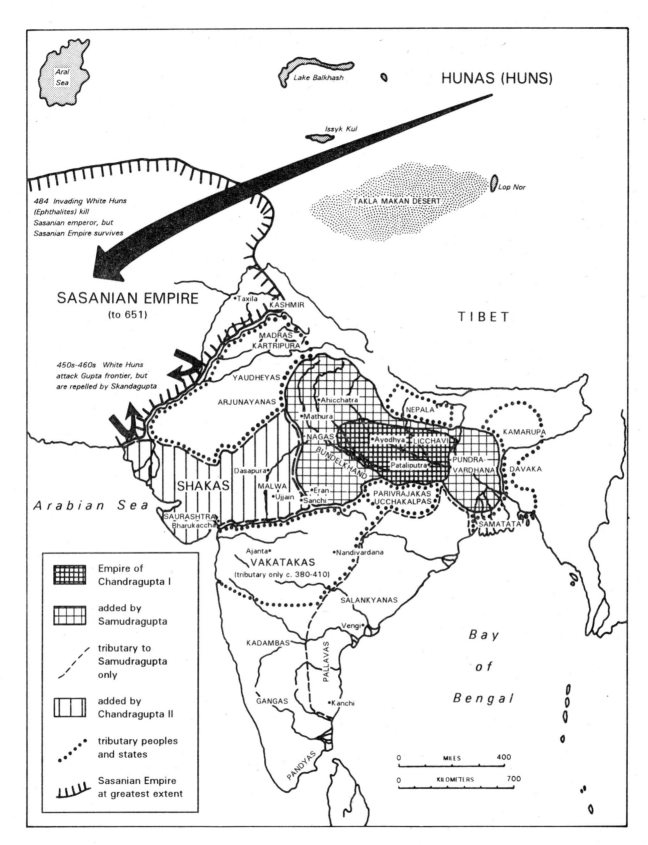

Map 10 contents (labels within the map):

Aral Sea

Lake Balkhash

HUNAS (HUNS)

Issyk Kul

Lop Nor

TAKLA MAKAN DESERT

484 Invading White Huns
(Ephthalites) kill
Sasanian emperor, but
Sasanian Empire survives

SASANIAN EMPIRE
(to 651)

450s-460s White Huns
attack Gupta frontier, but
are repelled by Skandagupta

Taxila

KASHMIR

TIBET

MADRAS
KARTRIPURA

YAUDHEYAS

ARJUNAYANAS

Ahicchatra

NEPALA

KAMARUPA

Mathura

NAGAS

Ayodhya LICCHAVI

BUNDELKHAND

Pataliputra

PUNDRA-
VARDHANA

DAVAKA

Dasapura

SHAKAS

MALWA

Eran

PARIVRAJAKAS
UCCHAKALPAS

Arabian Sea

Ujjain

Sanchi

SAURASHTRA
Bharukaccha

SAMATATA

Ajanta

Nandivardana

VAKATAKAS
(tributary only c. 380-410)

SALANKYANAS

KADAMBAS

Vengi

Bay
of
Bengal

PALLAVAS

GANGAS

Kanchi

PANDYAS

Legend:

Empire of
Chandragupta I

added by
Samudragupta

tributary to
Samudragupta
only

added by
Chandragupta II

tributary peoples
and states

Sasanian Empire
at greatest extent

0   MILES   400

0   KILOMETERS   700

Map 10 Growth and Decline of the Gupta Empire, 320-550

11 Northern India, 550-606

With the collapse of the Gupta Empire in c. 550, imperial unity in India disappeared in favor of the diversity of regionalism. This change should not, however, be interpreted to mean that India plunged into chaos. Instead, one could interpret this new situation as a period in which ruling families in India, many of whom chafed under the yoke of the Imperial Guptas, were able to reexert their independence.

One of the many royal families which began to exert itself after the demise of the Gupta Empire was that of the Maukharis (c. 500-606). Two branches of the Maukhari family served as vassals to the last important Gupta emperor, Buddhagupta (r. c. 467-97), from their homes in what are now eastern Uttar Pradesh and southern Bihar. They subsequently gained their independence. The first Maukhari ruler for whom there is any detailed historical information, Ishana-varman (r. c. 550-76), built an extensive kingdom for himself in eastern Uttar Pradesh by filling part of the political vacuum created by the waning Gupta Empire. After Ishana-varman's death, three more kings ruled over the Maukhari dominions from their capital at Kanauj until the last of them, Graha-varman (r. c. 600-606), died and the Maukhari kingdom merged with that of Harsha Vardhana (see Map 12).

Another family that gained power at approximately the same time as the Maukharis was what historians have unfortunately and rather inaccurately called the Later Guptas (r. c. 500-600?). The succession of rulers which make up the Later Guptas have not been proven to be related to the Imperial Guptas and, indeed, seem to form an entirely different family altogether. Historical evidence relating to the Later Guptas is scanty, but historians of this period have suggested that the Later Guptas supplanted Imperial Gupta rule over Magadha after the collapse of the Empire. What followed was a power struggle (c. 575-80) between Mahasena-gupta, one of the Later Gupta monarchs, and his enemies: the Maukhari king, Sharva-varman, on the west and the King of Kamarupa, Supratishthita-varman, on the east. Mahasena-gupta also faced yet another foe, the king of Tibet, Srong Tsan. Weakened by this three-pronged attack, as well as by the defection of his erstwhile vassal, Shashanka (who subsequently founded his own kingdom in Gauda), Mahasena-gupta was forced to abandon his core state in Magadha for the safe haven of his western territories in Malwa. Later, King Harsha Vardhana restored the son of Mahasena-gupta, Madha-va-gupta, to the throne of Magadha as a vassal.

After abandoning his overlord and reestablishing independent rule over the Kingdom of Gauda, a former vassal state under the Imperial Guptas, Shashanka (c. 580-637) sought to enlarge his holdings in eastern India. From his capital at Karnasuvarna, Shashanka planned the conquest of his neighbors' territories, and launched a series of attacks. His armies quickly occupied Magadha, and then turned to the conquest of Gauda's neighbor to the south, Orissa, including Kongoda. At the height of his power, the King of Gauda ruled over an extensive area including all of Bengal, Magadha, and much of Orissa, and paved the way for later Palas rule in Bengal.

In Assam, under the Varman royal family (c. 355-650), another kingdom gained its independence after the fall of the Guptan Empire: Kamarupa. A long-time vassal of the Imperial Guptas, Kamarupa had been a small tributary state under Samudragupta (330-75). The tenth ruler of Kamarupa, Sthita-varman (r. c. 565-85), was responsible for the kingdom's new independence and had, in the process, angered the Later Guptas. Not deterred from his imperial pretensions, Sthita-varman performed the ashvamedha twice during his lifetime, and maintained a firm hold over his kingdom, despite Later Gupta attempts to dislodge him from Kamarupa. His son, Susthita-varman (r. 585-95), was not so fortunate: the Later Gupta monarch, Mahasena-gupta, invaded Kamarupa and defeated the Varman ruler. The task of rebuilding Kamarupa fell to Susthita-varman's younger son, Bhaskara-varman (r. 595-650), under whom Kamarupa flourished, both economically and culturally.

Indigenous kings were not the only ones who extended their rule over northern India following the disintegration of the Guptan Empire; the Hunas (Huns) did so as well. By 520, the Hunas, under Mihirakula, had carved out an empire extending from Persia to Eran in Central India, and ruled from the city of Sakala. Over the next four decades, first the Imperial Guptas and, later, the other indigenous rulers of northern India kept the Hunas at bay. Finally, c. 565, after suffering an onslaught by both Persian and Western Turk armies, the power of the Hunas in South Asia declined dramatically. Their decline, however, led to the rise of the Pushyabhuti dynasty, under which northern India would later be reunited under one imperial overlord: Harsha Vardhana.

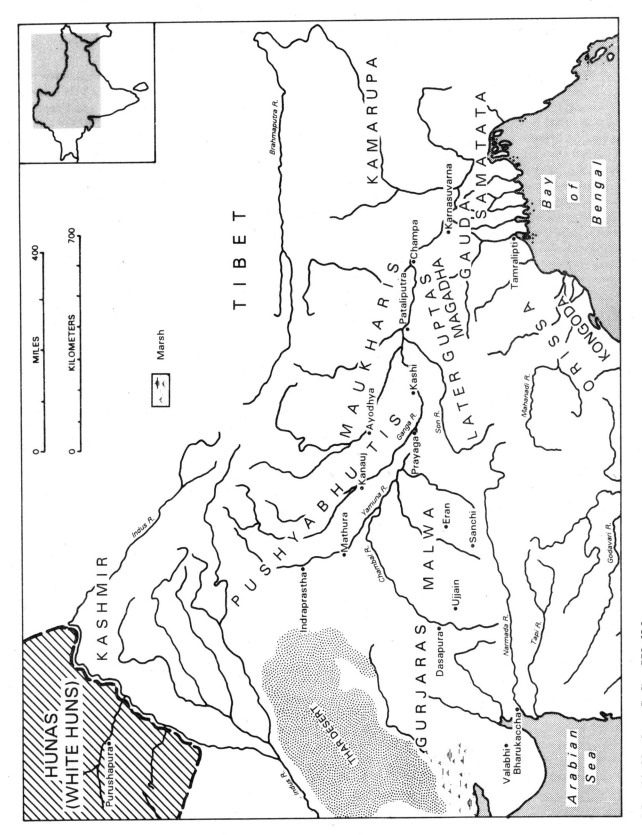

Map 11 Northern India, 550-606

27

12   Growth of Empire under Harsha Vardhana, 606-647

Harsha Vardhana became king of Thaneswar at the tender age of sixteen after his elder brother, Rajya Vardhana, was killed by Shashanka, the king of Gauda in 606. When he inherited the throne, Harsha's kingdom was limited to a small area in Panjab, which extended from the eastern bank of the Sutlej River to the upper Ganga River valley. The events which transpired after Harsha's royal ascension are the subject of much controversy and division among scholars of ancient South Asia. According to most of the scholars of this period, Harsha moved his capital from Thaneswar to Kanauj (the capital of the Maukhari Kingdom) soon after inheriting the throne by agreeing to share power with his sister, the widowed queen of the Maukharis.

Devahuti (1970) and Tripathi (1967) assert that once he had gained control of Maukhari and had consolidated his power, Harsha used Kanauj as a staging area from which to launch his expansionist plans of conquest over northern India. His first goal was to avenge the murder of his brother. Using what appears to be a prime example of Kautilyan statecraft, e.g., "the enemy of my enemy is my friend," Harsha allied himself with King Bhaskaravarman of Kamarupa. Once assured of that king's allegiance and military assistance, Harsha set out to engage King Shashanka in battle. On his push eastward across the North Indian Plain in c. 618, Harsha encountered no resistance and even gained the allegiance of several minor kings. Scholars again disagree on the ultimate outcome of this eastward movement by Harsha and his army of some 50,000 foot soldiers, 20,000 cavalry, and 5,000 elephants, or indeed, if a battle between him and Shashanka even took place. Most agree, however, that Shashanka did forfeit some territory in Pundra-vardhana and that Harsha and his ally, Bhaskaravarman, divided up this gain between them. With Shashanka's death c. 620, Harsha incorporated the rest of that king's lands into his burgeoning empire, which had grown to include much of northern and eastern India.

According to estimates from the Chinese Buddhist pilgrim, Hsuan Tsang, who visited India during Harsha's reign, the emperor of Thaneswar's army now consisted of some 100,000 cavalry and 60,000 elephants and a correspondingly enlarged infantry. The most re-cent study of this period (Devahuti 1970) indicates that Harsha used this augmented force to attack the western kingdom of Dhruvasena II of Valabhi, and compelled that king to ally himself with Harsha c. 630.

Strengthened and buoyed by his most recent conquest, Harsha next turned to launch an attack c. 633 against Pulakeshin II of the Western Chalukya kingdom, who controlled most of the Deccan Plateau south of the Narmada River. Harsha's attack was repulsed by Pulakeshin. Harsha never again attempted to incorporate the Deccan into his empire; indeed, rulers in the south would continue to fend off attacks by northern invaders until the sultan of Delhi, Muhammad Tughluq, incorporated almost all of the southern peninsula into his empire in the early fourteenth century.

Harsha's last military campaign was directed against the provinces of Udra (Orissa) and Kongoda along the southeastern coast of India c. 636. That region's ruler, Madhavaraja II, had died and left a power vacuum which Harsha undertook to fill. According to Devahuti (1970), Harsha's army occupied the northern and central sections of Udra, as well as the Ganjam district of Kongoda. Even this last event is awash in scholarly controversy. R. D. Banerjee (1980) denies that Harsha ever incorporated Orissa into his dominions. He believes that the chief extant source of information about Harsha's life, the *Harshacharita* ("Deeds of Harsha"), written by Bana, Harsha's court biographer, is inaccurate on this point.

While most scholars present the image of Harsha's absolute control over all of his territorial empire, Devahuti alone puts forth the theory that Harsha's imperial administration was, in part, based upon the principle of suzerainty. She asserts that while he had direct control over most of the empire, some areas within the empire were governed by local monarchs who owed their allegiance to the emperor and were, in turn, supported by him.

Whatever the controversies surrounding the conquests and long reign of Harsha Vardhana (606-647), he remained the last indigenous empire-builder in northern India. Subsequent empires in the north would be built not by indigenous Indian rulers, but by invaders from Central and Southwest Asia as well as from Europe.

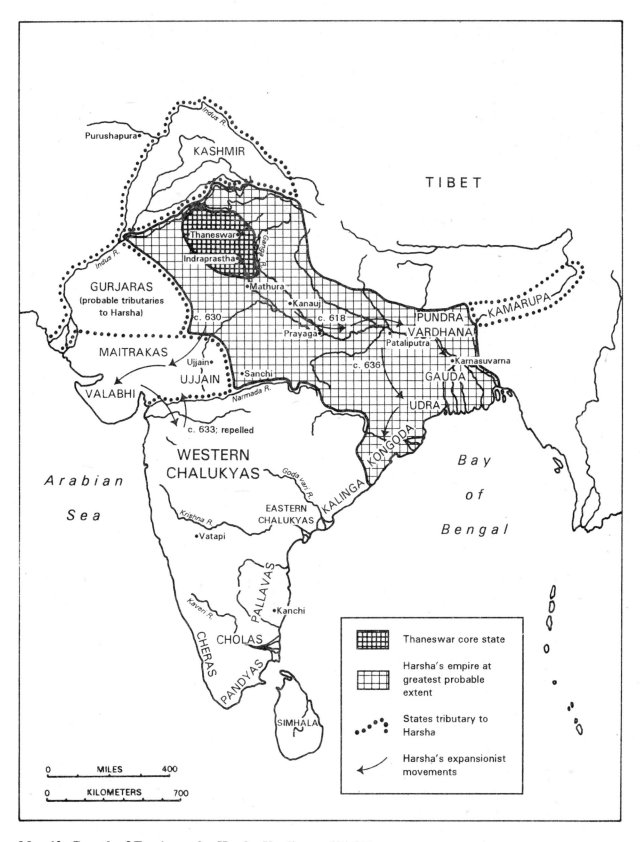

Map 12 Growth of Empire under Harsha Vardhana, 606-647

13 The Struggle for Power in Southern India, 550-850

Beginning in the mid-sixth century, three powerful kingdoms, the Chalukyas of Vatapi (later replaced in the tripartite conflict by the Rashtrakutas of Malkhed c. 750), the Pallavas of Kanchi, and the Pandyas of Madura, arose and began a contest for power in India south of the Narmada River.

The largest of the three kingdoms was Chalukya. Its dynasty was founded by Jayasimha (r. c. 500-520), who established his rule over a small kingdom in Deccan. Jayasimha's great-grandson, Kirttivarman I (r. 567-92/3), first led the dynasty to prominence. Kirttivarman I built upon the small kingdom bequeathed to him and extended it on all sides through military conquest. When Kirttivarman I died, his brother, Mangalesha (r. 592/3-610) agreed to serve as regent until Kirttivarman I's son, Pulakeshin II (r. 610-42/3), attained a majority. Mangalesha, however, usurped the throne, and only after a bloody fratricidal war did Pulakeshin II gain it back. For all his treachery, Mangalesha did leave his nephew a much-enlarged kingdom which Pulakeshin II immediately sought to consolidate once in power. Under Pulakeshin II, the Chalukya empire reached its greatest extent. In western Deccan, he exterminated the Kadambas, and retained the Alupas and Gangas as vassals. In northern Deccan, he launched his naval forces against Puri, the capital of the Mauryas of Konkana, captured the city, and incorporated Konkana into the empire. Pulakeshin II also gained the voluntary submission to his overlordship of the Latas, the Malvas, and the Gurjaras. All three were probably vassals of Mangalesha; Pulakeshin II reaffirmed that status. Later, after c. 618, he forced the submission of both Koshala and Kalinga.

The Chalukyan empire survived for a little over a century following the death of Pulakeshin II (a collateral branch of the family, the Eastern Chalukyas, survived until the end of the eleventh century). Like so many other empires in India, a combination of factors led to its ultimate demise: weak rulers, imperial overextension, too many military excursions (against the Pallavas), external invasions (the Arabs), decentralization of power, and internal dissension (the Rashtrakutas).

Farther to the south, the Pallavas of Kanchi rose to prominence after their overlords, the Shatavahanas, declined in power in the early third century. Very little is known about the Pallavas until the early seventh century. At that time, Mahendravarman I (r. 600-630) controlled an extensive kingdom bounded by the Krishna and Kaveri rivers, and as a result stood in the way of Pulakeshin II's further conquests in the south. After his defeat of Koshala and Kalinga, Pulakeshin II turned south with his forces, crossed the Krishna River, and advanced on the Pallava capital at Kanchipuram. Mahendravarman I successfully defended the capital, but was forced to cede substantial northern territories to Pulakeshin II. During the reign of Narasimhavarman I (r. 630-68), the greatest of the Pallava rulers, Pulakeshin II launched another attack against the Pallavas, but suffered a number of defeats at the hands of the Pallava monarch. Narasimhavarman I carried the war deep into Chalukya territory, and even laid siege to Vatapi itself. Pulakeshin II was killed during the conflict and Vatapi was captured by the Pallavas. Narasimhavarman I captured large portions of Chalukya territory until Pulakeshin II's son, Vikramaditya I (r. 655-81), forced the Pallava ruler, after several battles, to return them. Conquest of the Pallava kingdom seemed to be an obsession with the Chalukya monarchs: after Narasimhavarman I's death, a series of Chalukya rulers unsuccessfully made the attempt. The Pallava dynasty survived until the early tenth century when the last Pallava monarch, Kampavarman (r. 870-912?), died.

The third major kingdom of South India, the smallest of the three, was that of the Pandyas of Madura. The Pandyas began their dynasty at approximately the same time as the Pallavas, but almost nothing is known about the first few rulers. The Pandyas had traditionally been enemies of the Pallavas, and apparently allied themselves initially with the Chalukyas in a bid to gain additional territory. Once the Chalukyas had grown too powerful, however, the Pandyas became allies of the Pallavas, the Cholas, and the Cheras, forming a loose confederacy which stood in opposition to the Chalukyas. This confederacy of southern powers was not strong enough to overcome the Chalukyas; by the late seventh century, the Pandyas and their allies had reconciled themselves to the new state of affairs until the reign of the Pandya monarch, Koccadaiyan (r. c. 700-730). Also known as Ranadhira, Koccadaiyan conducted wars of territorial aggression and expanded his kingdom to include Kongu. The Pandyan kingdom survived until 920, when it was finally overrun and absorbed by the Cholas.

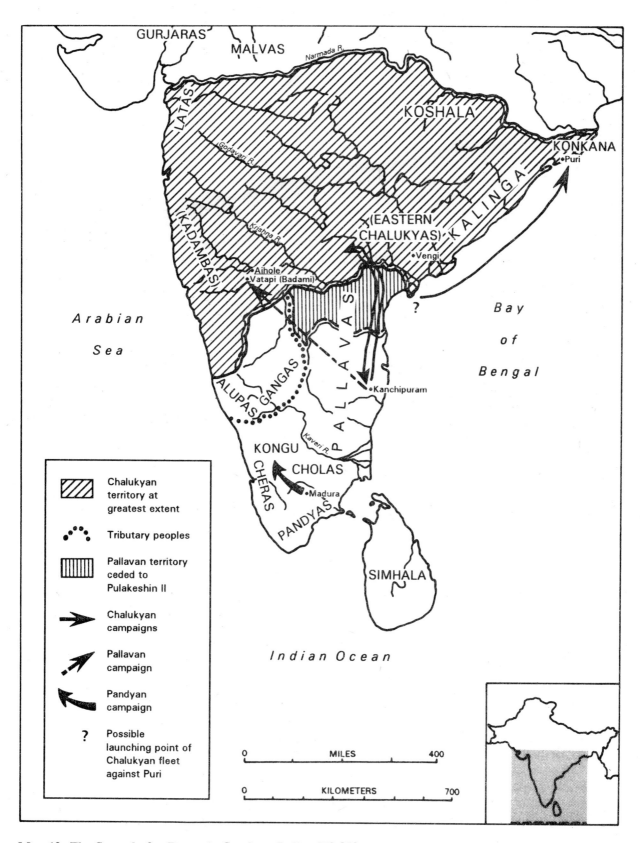

GURJARAS

MALVAS

Narmada R.

KOSHALA

KONKANA

•Puri

LATAS

Godavari R.

(KADAMBAS)

Krishna R.

(EASTERN
CHALUKYAS) K A L I N G A

Arabian

Sea

•Aihole
•Vatapi (Badami)

•Vengi

P
A
L
L
A
V
A
S

?

Bay

of

Bengal

ALUPAS

GANGAS

•Kanchipuram

Kaveri R.

KONGU

CHOLAS

CHERAS

•Madura

PANGYAS
PANDYAS

SIMHALA

Indian Ocean

Chalukyan
territory at
greatest extent

Tributary peoples

Pallavan territory
ceded to
Pulakeshin II

Chalukyan
campaigns

Pallavan
campaign

Pandyan
campaign

? Possible
launching point of
Chalukyan fleet
against Puri

0   MILES   400

0   KILOMETERS   700

Map 13 The Struggle for Power in Southern India, 550-850

31

14 Rise of the Cholas in the South, c. 850-1279

In approximately 850, a Chola chieftain, Vijayalaya, captured the city of Tanjavur from his rivals, the Muttaraiyars. Vijayalaya apparently attacked the city with the approval of his nominal overlords, the Pallavas, and with the critical military assistance of the Velirs of Kodumbalur. The Pallavas helped create a menace to their own power, however, as Vijayalaya soon transformed what appeared to be a minor local victory into the beginnings of an independent Chola state.

By the end of the ninth century, both the Pallavan and Pandyan states in the "far south" had begun to decline due to both internal and external threats. In response, successive Chola monarchs filled the growing political vacuum in the region and their state expanded accordingly northward and southward along the Coromandel coastal plain from its core in the Kaveri delta.

As the Chola state expanded, its rulers, in order to optimize their use of both human and natural resources, had to adapt to the region's particular socio-economic conditions. The Chola economy was based on a three-tiered system. At the local level, agricultural settlements formed the foundation. Groups of these communities were, in turn, linked to commercial towns called "nagaram," which acted as redistribution centers for externally produced items bound for consumption in the local economy and as sources of products made by nagaram artisans for the international trade. At the top of this economic pyramid were the elite merchant groups, "samayam," who organized and dominated the region's international maritime trade. The Chola economic system also affected, and was affected by, the socio-cultural structure in which it operated. Hinduism's elaborate system of social and economic hierarchies enabled increasing agricultural specialization to take place, while at the same time a greater level of economic development supported an increasing number of non-cultivators.

To take the best advantage of the wealth generated by the region, Chola expansion was apparently directed not at the physical conquest of territory, but rather at the conquest of people, to establish hegemony over the peasantry and local concentrations of power, including that of local chieftains. The Chola state was not, therefore, the **unitary state** that many historians have claimed it to be, but more likely what historian Burton Stein (1980), in drawing upon anthropologist Aidan Southall's earlier work, calls a "segmentary state." The Chola state comprised areas of localized power and authority ("segments") which were tapped by successive Chola monarchs in support of their expansionism. Expansionist activity was mutually beneficial: in addition to obvious gains for the Chola monarch, participatory local rulers and their peasant warriors also received a share of plunder derived from conquest.

Several motivations for Chola economic expansionism seem clear. As George Spencer (1983) points out, the Cholas seems to have engaged in plundering neighboring areas as a means of stimulating their own economy through the redistribution of newly acquired spoils among their own people. Another reason seems to have been that the cost of maintaining a large army during the course of any particular military excursion, without the prospect of plunder, would have been prohibitive for the monarch.

The "early Chola period" (850-985) is marked by a Chola rise to local prominence, followed in 949 by a disastrous military setback inflicted on them by the Rashtrakutas. The "middle Chola period" begins with the ascension of Rajaraja I (r. 985-1012) to the Chola throne. During his reign, Rajaraja undertook a series of military campaigns, including an overseas expedition to Sri Lanka, to restore lost Chola power and to increase its influence in the region. Rajaraja's legacy was continued by his son, Rajendra I (1012-44), who carried the Cholas' economic warfare even farther afield, including, arguably, a naval expedition to Srivijaya in 1025, to protect Chola trade with China. Under subsequent rulers, Chola hegemonic power contracted, but was revitalized once again under perhaps the most conspicuous of the Chola monarchs, Kulottunga I (1070-1122). Kulottunga I was born an Eastern Chalukya and was related to the Cholas through his Chola-born mother. Upon ascending the throne, he founded the Chalukya-Chola dynasty which ruled over the kingdom until its extinction in 1279. By the early thirteenth century, deep into the "late Chola period," the Pandyan dynasty had experienced a resurgence and posed an enormous threat to the Cholas. A succession of battles with the Pandyas as well as with the Hoysalas in the northwest left the Chola kingdom severely weakened. In 1279, the last Chola monarch, Rajendra IV (1246-79), died and the Chola dominions were, ostensibly, incorporated into the Pandyan kingdom.

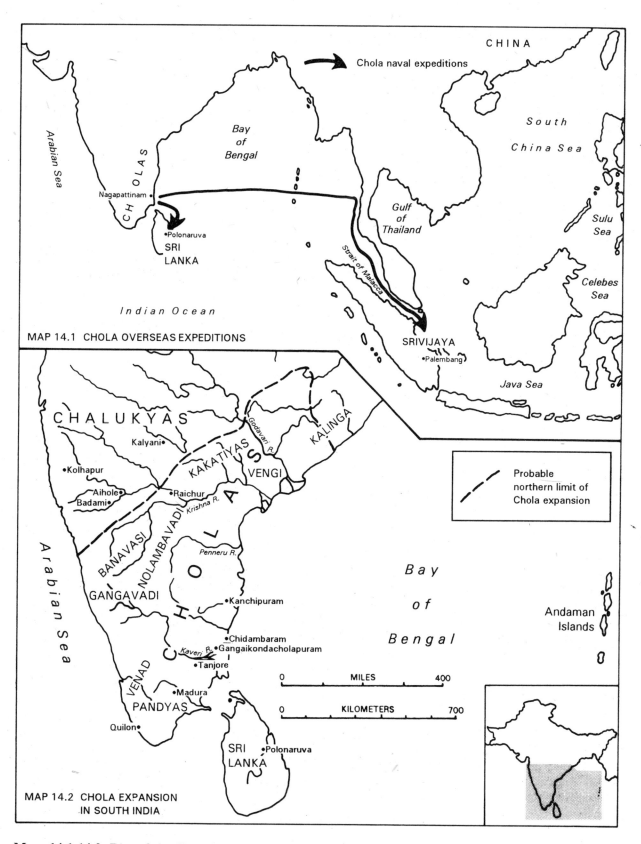

MAP 14.1 CHOLA OVERSEAS EXPEDITIONS

MAP 14.2 CHOLA EXPANSION
IN SOUTH INDIA

Maps 14.1-14.2 Rise of the Cholas in the South, c. 850-1279

15 Northern and Central India, c. 700-1200

Several regional kingdoms rose to political importance in northern and central India between the eighth and thirteenth centuries. These included the Pratiharas of Gujarat, the Paramaras of Malwa, the Chauhanas of Ajmer and Delhi—all Rajput clans—as well as the Palas of Bengal.

Although some historians claim that the Gurjaras were descendent of a tribe of invading Hunas (Huns), most believe that they were of Indian origin. In either case, the Pratiharas, a royal Gurjara family in western India, rose to prominence under Nagabhata I (c. 730-60) after he drove away Arab invaders in the eighth century. Nagabhata I's two successors suffered a number of defeats at the hands of the Rashtrakutas, and the Pratihara kingdom waned both in power and in size. The fourth Pratihara king, Nagabhata II (c. 795-833), reversed this decline, and extended the kingdom eastward to the frontier of Bengal and northward to the southern edge of Kashmir. Nagabhata II captured the city of Kanauj, and he subsequently moved his capital to that city from Ujjain. In just three years, Nagabhata II's son, Ramabhadra (c. 833-36), lost much of his father's empire, and it fell to Bhoja I (c. 836-90), Ramabhadra's son, to restore the empire.

The empire of the Gurjara-Pratiharas reached its greatest extent and power under the next three monarchs, Bhoja I, his son, Mahendrapala I (c. 890-907), and his grandson, Mahipala I (c. 907-24/25). During the nearly ninety years of their combined reigns, these three kings ruled over most of northern India. With the death of Mahipala I, Gurjara-Pratihara power began to decline. Subsequent rulers were unable to maintain so large an empire against internal and external threats. In 1019, Mahmud of Ghazni captured and plundered Kanauj. Thereafter, the Pratiharas were reduced to the status of minor chiefs until their final extinction in the second quarter of the eleventh century by the Rathor Rajputs.

Malwa originally formed part of the domain of the Gurjara-Pratiharas, but was overrun c. 812 by the Rashtrakutas under Govinda III (c. 793-814). Malwa subsequently changed hands twice more, reverting to the Pratiharas c. 836-860, and then back to the Rashtrakutas c. 915/18. After 949, the Paramara king of Malwa, Siyaka II (c. 949-72/74), attempted to proclaim his total independence, but was subdued by the Rashtra-kuta emperor, Krishna III (c. 939-67). With the collapse of the Rashtrakuta empire in 973, Malwa became independent and the Paramaras rose to prominence. At its apex, under Bhoja (c. 1018-60), the Paramara kingdom comprised considerable territories in central India, but after Bhoja's death, it declined to a mere local power and finally succumbed to outside invasions at the beginning of the thirteenth century.

The Chauhanas established a new dynasty in east-central India in the eleventh century and rose to prominence after they defeated the Paramaras in the early twelfth century. From their capital at Ajmer, successive Chauhana kings waged war against their neighbors, expanding the kingdom at the expense of the Solankis in Kathiawar, the Tomaras in north-central India, and the Central Asian Muslims in Panjab. The Chauhana kingdom reached its greatest extent under Prithviraja III (1178-1192), who died in battle fighting the armies of Muhammad Ghuri. After the establishment of the Delhi Sultanate, the Chauhanas retired to Ranthambhor, where their dynasty later ended at the hands of Alauddin Khalji in 1301.

In Bengal, the Palas rose to prominence c. 750 with the establishment of their new dynasty. Gopala (750-70), the founder of the dynasty, was, according to tradition, elected by local leaders to serve as monarch in order to stabilize the country following the collapse of Kanaujan control of Bengal under Yasovarman (c. 700-40). Gopala's son, Dharmapala (c. 770-810), transformed the Palas into a major regional power. Despite an initial setback at the hands of the Rashtrakutas early in his reign, Dharmapala extended the kingdom to Kanauj and maintained his new frontiers against attacks from both the Pratiharas and the Rashtrakutas. In turn, his son, Devapala (c. 810-50), conquered additional territories and transferred the Pala capital from Pataliputra to Monghyr. The Palas were Buddhists and patronized Buddhist centers of learning, including the great university at Nalanda. They also maintained diplomatic and religious ties with the Buddhist kingdoms of Southeast Asia. As always, the pressures of maintaining a large kingdom proved too great: the Palas lost power after the Senas seized Bengal in the mid-twelfth century and the dynasty finally ended after its remaining territory was captured by Central Asian invaders under Iktiaruddin in 1199.

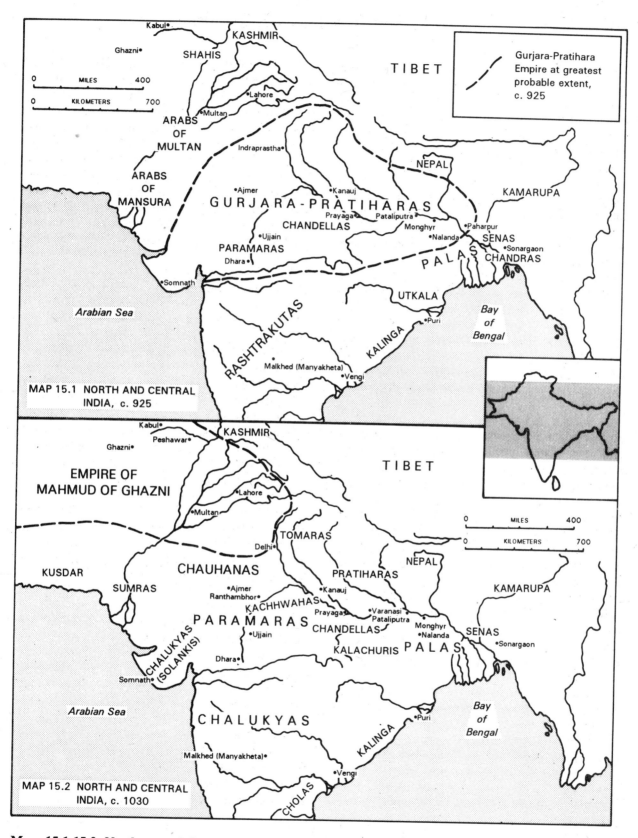

MAP 15.1 NORTH AND CENTRAL INDIA, c. 925

MAP 15.2 NORTH AND CENTRAL INDIA, c. 1030

Maps 15.1–15.2 Northern and Central India, c. 700–1200

16   Growth of Islam in South Asia, c. 700-1206

Contact between the Arab world and South Asia predated the advent of Islam in Arabia in 622. Arab merchants, plying the waters of the Arabian Sea, had earlier established regular commercial contact with South Asia. Beginning in 636, however, as conditions and motivations among many of the Arabs had changed, a group of Arab adventurers attacked Thana (a town near modern Bombay), but failed in their attempt to capture it. Several additional attacks on different towns followed, but all met with failure, until an Arab group under Ibn al-Harri al-Bahitti successfully captured Makhran (what is now Baluchistan) c. 700-10. Islam had permanently arrived in South Asia.

From their newly established bridgehead, an Arab army, led by Muhammad bin Qasim, the governor of Iraq's son-in-law, launched attacks against Sind in 712, and Multan in 713, both of which were successful. King Dahir of Sind, a poor ruler who was already experiencing internal administrative troubles, was unable to defend his realm against the Arab onslaught; he perished in battle and his kingdom was absorbed by the Arabs.

Historians have debated the causes of the Arab offensive against Sind for many years, alternatively proposing that the attack was in retaliation for the plundering of Arab ships by Sindhi pirates, or a prelude to general territorial conquest and religious conversion. Whatever the reasons, the result was clear: the Arabs had established a firm foothold in South Asia—an Islamic state—and attempted to use it as a springboard for additional conquests. Strong Indian kingdoms, however, such as those of the Gurjara-Pratiharas, Chalukyas, and Rashtrakutas, repulsed subsequent Arab attacks and prevented them from making large inroads into South Asia in the eighth century. In 871, the Arab governors of Sind and Multan broke away from the central control of the **kaliph**, established independent kingdoms, and apparently maintained a policy of partial religious toleration. Because of their inherent political and economic weakness, however, these Arab kingdoms did not serve as staging areas for the further spread of Islam in South Asia.

During the seventh century, Arab armies also advanced on Persia and had conquered it by 643. Subsequently, the Arabs launched repeated attacks against the Hindu kingdoms of Kabul and Zabul in Afghanistan—alternately conquering territory and later losing it—throughout much of the next century. During the ninth and tenth centuries, under the leadership of the Samanids, a Persian Sunni dynasty, Persia became part of another kingdom, one independent of the kaliph. The subsequent decline of the Saminids in the tenth century enabled the ambitious leader of the Saminid bodyguards, Alptigin, a Turkish slave from Central Asia, to carve out a kingdom for himself in Ghazni, thus founding the Ghaznivid empire of Afghanistan. When Alptigin's grandson, Mahmud (998-1030), gained the throne, he used the empire bequeathed to him as a base from which to launch a series of devastating raids into South Asia.

The first of Mahmud of Ghazni's raids on India came in 1000. Sixteen additional raids took place over the next twenty-five years. Mahmud led his raiders as far east as Kanauj, and as far south as Gujarat. By 1025, Mahmud had defeated the Gurjara-Pratiharas, the Chandellas of Khajuraho, the Rajputs of Gwalior, and even the the Arab ruler of Multan. As each enemy was defeated, Mahmud carried its treasures back to Ghazni. Mahmud especially delighted in looting and destroying Hindu temples, such as those at Thaneswar, Mathura, and Kanauj. On his last raid into India, Mahmud looted and destroyed the famed Shiva temple at Somnath, reportedly killing 50,000 Hindus in the process.

Although Mahmud never claimed any territory in South Asia during his raids, preferring only to destroy, kill, and loot, his raids did highlight the military and political weakness of the indigenous Hindu kingdoms of the time: the Hindus used inferior strategy and tactics, their armies were disabled by caste distinctions, and their rulers never seemed able to unite to repel the invaders, relying instead on their own individual efforts—a policy which, in the end, proved disastrous.

In 1151, the Ghaznivids were replaced by the Ghurids, a ruling family from western Afghanistan. The most famous of the Ghurid rulers was Muhammad (1173-1206) who, beginning in 1175, made a concerted effort to conquer India and to annex its territory to his own. Within twenty years, Ghurid armies, led in most cases by slave-generals, had captured Delhi, Kanauj, Varanasi, Gwalior, Ajmer, and Anhilwara. At his death in 1206, Muhammad Ghuri's empire encompassed most of northern India; his pursuit of territory laid the foundation for Islamic rule in South Asia which would last for the next 600 years.

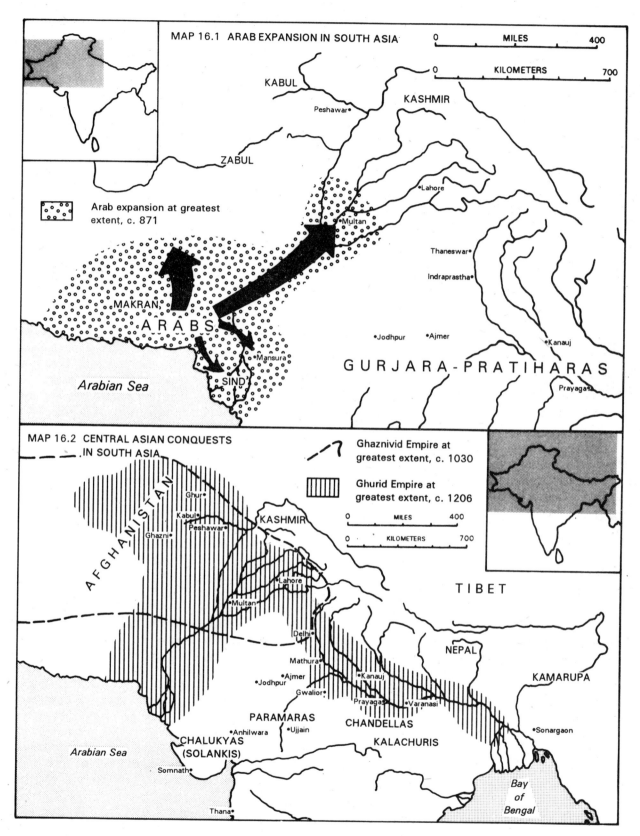

Maps 16.1-16.2 Growth of Islam in South Asia, c. 700-1206

37

17   Growth of the Delhi Sultanate, 1206-1526

Upon the death of Muhammad Ghuri in 1206, Qutbuddin Aibak, one of three slave-generals left in charge of Muhammad Ghuri's possessions in South Asia, became the first sultan of Delhi. Qutbuddin (1206-10) founded the first of a series of five unrelated dynasties which ruled over the Delhi Sultanate, a Muslim kingdom, for the next 320 years.

The first of the five dynasties, usually called the Slave dynasty (1206-90) because of the slave origins of its rulers, encompassed the reigns of nine other early Turkish sultans beyond Qutbuddin, whose own short reign as sultan was spent maintaining control over his kingdom rather than expanding it. Subsequent rulers did extend the frontiers of the Sultanate, but faced a constant struggle in trying to maintain those gains against indigenous rebel forces trying to reclaim their lost lands. Iltutmish (1211-36), for example, captured territories in Bengal, Bihar, Rajasthan, and Sind, but parts of Rajasthan were lost almost immediately after his death. His successor, Raziya (1236-40)—the only female ruler of the Delhi Sultanate—was left with the task of trying to recapture those areas; faced with stubborn resistance and guerrilla warfare, her armies failed in their attempt. The sultans faced other internal threats as well. Provincial governors often sought power at the expense of the sultans, forcing the latter to expend vital military and administrative resources defending their imperial interests. A final threat came from the Mongols, who had been a constant source of consternation to the dynasty since the reign of Iltutmish; later, the Mongols even successfully prevented Balban (1266-86) from expanding his empire.

In 1290, the last of the "slave" sultans, Qaiqabad (1286-1290), was assassinated and his throne usurped by the Khaljis (1290-1320), who established a new dynasty. Six Khalji sultans ruled over the Sultanate; the most important of them was Alauddin (1296-1316). During his reign, Alauddin was drawn into conflicts with the Mongols who had invaded India on four different occasions (1299, 1303, 1305, and 1306). On each occasion, the sultan's forces defeated the Mongols, who were compelled to retreat and who, as a result of their last defeat, did not again threaten India until 1398. In pursuit of empire, Alauddin conquered several neighboring, independent kingdoms. The kingdom of Gujarat was forcibly annexed (1299), the kingdoms of Deccan were made tributaries (1310), as were those of Rajasthan (1311). Under Alauddin, the Delhi Sultanate had reached its greatest extent to date.

Alauddin's successors were weak and, in 1320, the Khaljis were replaced by a rival family, the Tughluqs (1320-1413). Under the second Tughluq emperor, Muhammad (1325-51), the Delhi Sultanate reached its greatest extent ever, encompassing an area stretching from Panjab to Bengal and from the Himalayas to almost the southern tip of the subcontinent. Despite his skill as a general, Muhammad bin Tughluq faced serious difficulties in attempting to maintain so large an empire: effective administration was hindered by geography and by the ambitions of local rulers. Numerous rebellions erupted throughout the Sultanate, a devastating famine struck, and an outbreak of bubonic plague ripped through the empire, incapacitating the sultan's army for nearly a decade. All of these factors proved too much to control. Not long after Muhammad's death, the Sultanate again shrank to the boundaries of Alauddin Khalji's days, leaving behind a number of independent kingdoms, including Bahmani in Deccan and Vijayanagara in the far south. The Tughluq dynasty was weakened again in 1398, when Timur, the Mongol leader, invaded India, and occupied and sacked Delhi before finally retreating. The Tughluqs never recovered from Timur's attack and they were replaced by the Sayyids (1413-53).

Of the five dynasties to rule the Sultanate, the Sayyids were by far the weakest. The Sayyids were unable to stop the centrifugal forces already in play and, under the last Sayyid ruler, Alauddin Alam Shah (1445-51), the once-mighty Delhi Sultanate had shrunk to only the city of Delhi and environs.

The Sultanate fared better, at least initially, under the Lodi dynasty (1451-1526), the last to rule the Sultanate. Bahlul (1451-89), the first Lodi sultan, expanded the tiny area left by Alam Shah to include all of Panjab and what is now Uttar Pradesh, as well as parts of Rajasthan. Building from that base, Sikandar Lodi (1489-1517), Bahlul's son, extended the Sultanate to include Bihar and additional areas in Rajasthan. Sikandar regained some of the Sultanate's past glory, but his eldest son, Ibrahim (1517-26), quickly lost control over what had been left to him. External clashes along the western frontier coupled with conflicts with his own nobles led Ibrahim Lodi down a path of disaster which ended with his death at the Battle of Panipat (1526). With him died the Delhi Sultanate and the throne of Delhi passed to the Mughals under Babur.

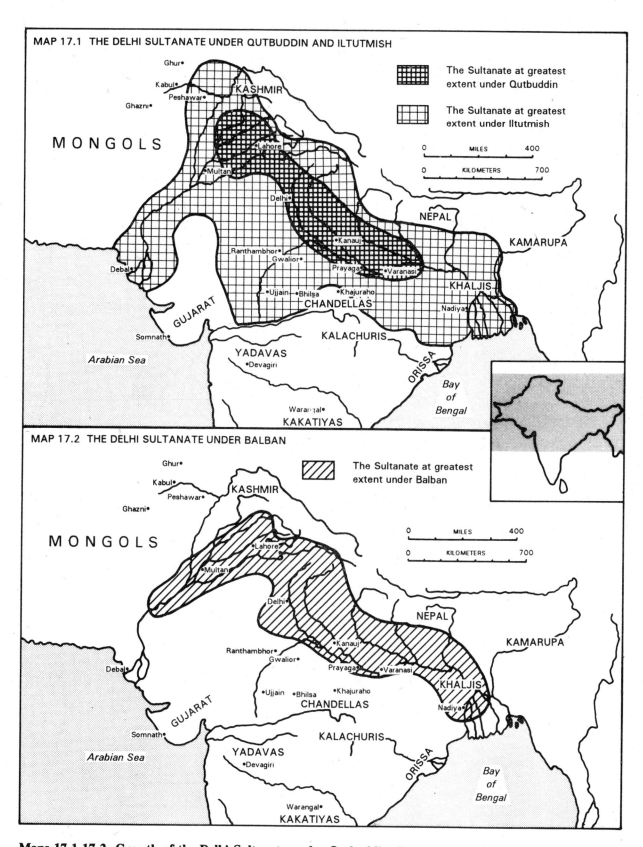

Maps 17.1-17.2 Growth of the Delhi Sultanate under Qutbuddin, Iltutmish, and Balban

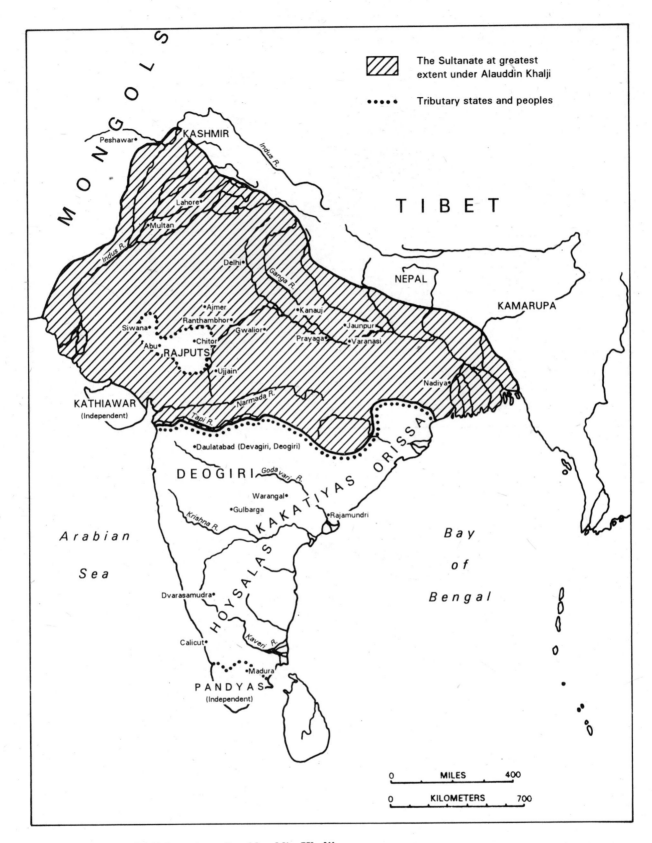

Map 17.3 The Delhi Sultanate under Alauddin Khalji

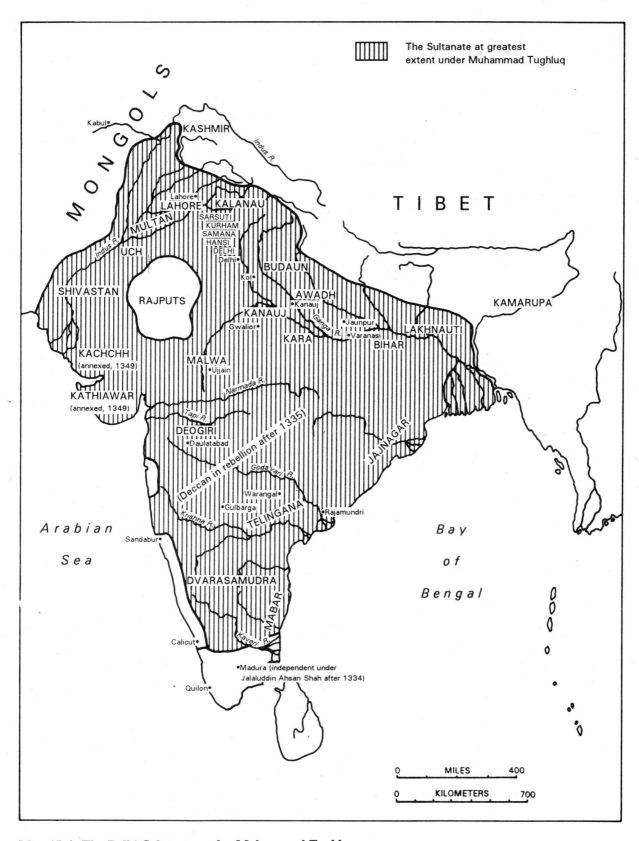

Map 17.4 The Delhi Sultanate under Muhammad Tughluq

41

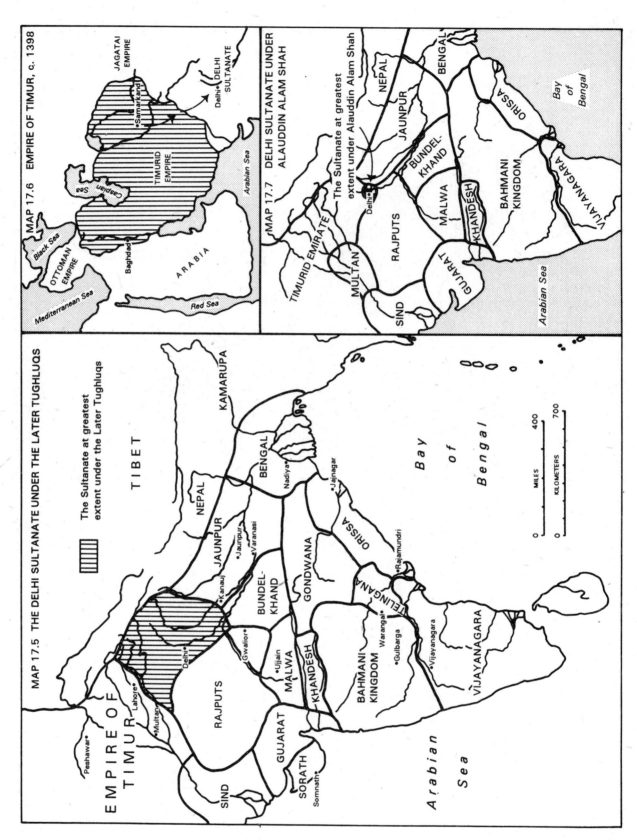

MAP 17.5 THE DELHI SULTANATE UNDER THE LATER TUGHLUQS

The Sultanate at greatest
extent under the Later Tughluqs

MAP 17.6 EMPIRE OF TIMUR, c. 1398

DELHI SULTANATE UNDER
ALAUDDIN ALAM SHAH

MAP 17.7 The Sultanate at greatest
extent under Alauddin Alam Shah

Maps 17.5–17.7 The Delhi Sultanate, 1352–1451

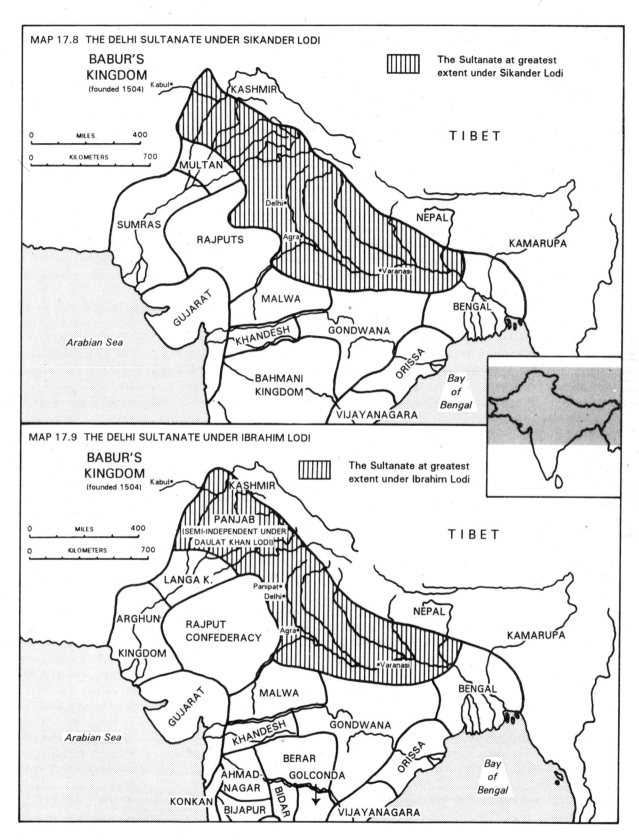

Maps 17.8-17.9 The Delhi Sultanate under Sikander and Ibrahim Lodi

18 Southern India, c. 1340-1565

Two important kingdoms, one Muslim, one Hindu, existed in South India during much of this period. The first kingdom was Vijayanagara, founded c. 1340 by two brothers of the Sangam dynasty (c. 1340-1485), Bukka and Harihara. The second was the Bahmani kingdom, founded in 1347 in Deccan by Hasan, Zafar Khan, a senior officer of Muhammad Tughluq, sultan of Delhi.

The founding of Vijayanagara seems to have been largely as a response to continued Muslim incursions into South India under the Delhi Sultanate in the early fourteenth century. The first expedition had been sent as early as the 1290s by Alauddin Khalji, but with the advent of the Tughluqs, under whom the Sultanate's power rose dramatically, expeditions into the south increased in intensity and frequency. These incursions exacerbated the already highly competitive and destructive elements within South Indian politics and forced a unifying response from the kings of South India, especially after Muhammad Tughluq moved his capital from Delhi to Devagiri (Daulatabad).

Unlike many other Indian kings, who were unable or unwilling to adapt to the new political circumstances wrought by the Sultanate's territorial ambitions, Vijayanagara's rulers adapted readily: they modified their military forces to include more cavalry, imitating the Muslims; raised a small standing cadre of forces capable of rapid expansion in time of conflict; and embarked on the construction of fortresses.

In addition to martial changes, Vijayanagara grew also in response to changing political and economic circumstances brought by the Muslims. The rulers of Vijayanagara built upon the weakening by the Muslims of older Hindu political forms, e.g., the strong interrelationship between kings and local landed aristocracy, to forge new, more king-centered power relationships. They also drew upon, and encouraged, the important shift from predominantly lowland, river-based agriculture, to a mixed agricultural base, with an increasing emphasis on upland agriculture fed by tank irrigation. Overseas trade was another important factor in the development of Vijayanagara: its western coast marked a vital nexus of the entrepôt trade between East Asia, South Asia, and Europe.

Vijayanagara reached its greatest extent and power under Krishnadevaraya (1509-29), Achyutadevaraya (1529-42), and Aliya Rama Raja (1542-65), the latter the de facto ruler under King Sadashiva. Growing Vijayanagara power and territorial ambitions posed a threat to Muslim sultanates in South India, however, and in 1565, a coalition of forces under the sultans of Bijapur, Golconda, Ahmadnagar and Bidar defeated Rama Raja's forces and destroyed his capital city. Several successor states inherited what was left of Vijayanagara, lasting another century, but they never regained the former glory of the unified kingdom.

The Bahmani kingdom, once subject to the overlordship of Muhammad Tughluq (who had established it as a base in Deccan), arose as an independent state in the same decade as its neighbor, Vijayanagara. In 1347, the Bahmani ruler, Zafar Khan, grew tired of his subordination to the Delhi sultan, took the title of Bahman Shah, and founded a dynasty which survived well over 150 years (1347-1518).

Bahman Shah spent his decade-long reign expanding and consolidating the kingdom; his successors were later embroiled in nearly constant conflict with the kings of Vijayanagara, with whom they shared a common boundary along the Krishna river. The primary dispute between them involved the possession of the Raichur **doab**: it was a fertile agricultural region, was also rich in mineral resources, and additionally had strategic value because it contained fortresses at Raichur and Mudgal. During the course of their years of mutual conflict, the Bahmanis possessed the doab more often than Vijayanagara.

The incessant fighting took its toll on the population of the Bahmani kingdom, as did a brutal factional struggle within. The kingdom's nobility was divided into two distinct groups, the Deccanis—older, and well-established—and the Pardesis, who comprised recent arrivals. The Pardesis were more prosperous than the Deccanis and this led to intense rivalry between the two groups, a rivalry which included assassinations and massacres. The conflict between the Deccanis and Pardesis gradually destabilized the kingdom internally and led to a weakening of Bahmani central authority over the nobility. Provincial governors consequently gained in power until, in 1518, the kingdom split into five smaller, independent kingdoms: Ahmadnagar, Berar, Bidar, Bijapur, and Golconda. Four of these kingdoms later destroyed Vijayanagara, but so exhausted themselves in the process that they lay exposed to an even greater danger from the north—the Mughals.

44

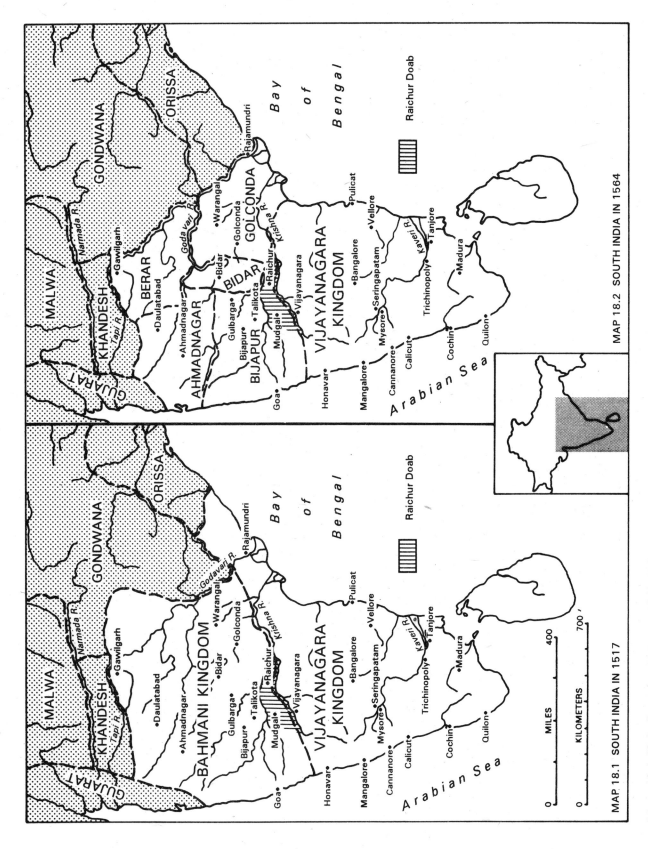

MAP 18.2 SOUTH INDIA IN 1564

Raichur Doab

Bay of Bengal

ORISSA

GONDWANA

MALWA

GUJARAT

KHANDESH

BERAR

Narmada R.

Tapi R.

Gawilgarh

Daulatabad

Ahmadnagar

AHMADNAGAR

Bidar

BIDAR

Gulbarga

Bijapur

BIJAPUR

Mudgal

Goa

Talikota

Raichur

Godavari R.

Warangal

Golconda

GOLCONDA

Krishna R.

Rajamundri

Vijayanagara

VIJAYANAGARA KINGDOM

Honavar

Mangalore

Cannanore

Calicut

Cochin

Quilon

Pulicat

Vellore

Bangalore

Seringapatam

Mysore

Trichinopoly

Tanjore

Kaveri R.

Madura

Arabian Sea

MAP 18.1 SOUTH INDIA IN 1517

Raichur Doab

Bay of Bengal

ORISSA

GONDWANA

MALWA

GUJARAT

KHANDESH

Narmada R.

Tapi R.

Gawilgarh

Daulatabad

Ahmadnagar

BAHMANI KINGDOM

Bidar

Gulbarga

Bijapur

Mudgal

Goa

Talikota

Raichur

Godavari R.

Warangal

Golconda

Krishna R.

Rajamundri

Vijayanagara

VIJAYANAGARA KINGDOM

Honavar

Mangalore

Cannanore

Calicut

Cochin

Quilon

Pulicat

Vellore

Bangalore

Seringapatam

Mysore

Trichinopoly

Tanjore

Kaveri R.

Madura

Arabian Sea

MILES

0   400

KILOMETERS

0   700

Maps 18.1-18.2 Southern India, c. 1340-1565

45

19   Arrival of the Portuguese, 1498

In July 1497, Portuguese navigator Vasco da Gama (1469?-1524) left Lisbon and set out on a ten-month journey which took his three ships around the Cape of Good Hope, into the Indian Ocean, and, ultimately, to the Indian city of Calicut on the Malabar coast. Da Gama was not the first European to visit India; Europeans had journeyed to South Asia before and there was at least one European already in Calicut when da Gama arrived.

Da Gama's historical importance lies in the fact that he led the first European expedition to make the journey to India entirely by sea. This event would have profound implications for India's future for it was now possible to move people and materials reasonably safely and expeditiously between Europe and South Asia. The vanguard of Portugal's empire-builders had arrived.

Da Gama and his men did not come to India primarily as conquerors, however, nor did they represent a state which was well-known for its maritime experience or its overseas commercial endeavors. At his departure, da Gama's Portugal was a small, poor country, with a population of approximately one million, and dependent on cereal grains and other foodstuffs imported from its newly acquired colonies in the Azores and in North Africa. Portuguese overseas expansion during most of the fifteenth century was primarily due, therefore, to the pressures of economic necessity. In addition, historians have suggested that other motives included a desire to afford the younger sons of nobles and others opportunities to obtain land, wealth, and personal distinction; and, to a lesser extent, to propagate Christianity (see Pearson 1987).

The Portuguese monarch also played a prominent role in the country's overseas expansion. Successive kings throughout the fifteenth century officially sanctioned further explorations along the western coast of Africa and the Portuguese gained much-needed maritime experience in the process. These explorations often resulted in profitable "discoveries" of benefit both to the "discoverer"—usually a merchant—and to the monarch. Until the late 1490s, most of Portugal's overseas commercial activities were limited to fishing in the North Atlantic and to trading with the states of the Mediterranean. One of the richest of these states was Venice. The Venetians recognized early that vast wealth could be derived, in large part, from acting as middlemen in the supply of spices to the rest of Europe. Witnessing this profit-making, Manuel I (r. 1495-1521) correctly anticipated that huge profits could be made from the Asian trade, principally from the spice trade, and with that in mind sent da Gama out on his voyage to India.

In the fifteenth century, the Asian spice trade with Europe was largely dominated by Muslims of Southwest Asia, though the spices themselves were often owned not by the Muslims who carried the goods on their ships, but by Hindu spice merchants who lived along the Malabar coast or in Gujarat. Despite the fact that the spice trade was dominated by Muslims and overall quite competitive, the Indian Ocean remained an open sea in the fifteenth century—no one country controlled the sea trade. This condition changed dramatically with the arrival of the Portuguese who made it their goal to establish, through force, a monopoly over the supply of spices to Europe, and to tax and regulate the rest of the Asian trade which included, among other items, textiles, rice, and precious stones and metals. By monopolizing the spice trade and regulating the trade in other goods the Portuguese gained maximum benefit and profit from that trade for themselves.

Indian reaction to the arrival of the Portuguese was one largely of unconcern. The **zamorin** of Calicut, a petty Hindu ruler of substantial wealth, was impressed by Portuguese naval armaments, but less so by the Portuguese themselves. Although the zamorin did not possess a navy (nor did any of the other rulers of India at the time), da Gama and his ships did not represent a threat to his power initially and, given da Gama's eagerness to purchase spices of whatever quality was offered to him by the spice merchants of Calicut, the zamorin and Indian spice merchants remained unimpressed. The zamorin had no idea that upon his return to Lisbon in 1499, da Gama would net a 3,000 percent profit on those poor quality spices, or that consequently da Gama's ships were to be only the first of hundreds of Portuguese ships to venture to India to engage in the highly profitable spice trade. The zamorin could not have realized that with the arrival of the Portuguese in India, he was witnessing the birth of a new era in South Asian history.

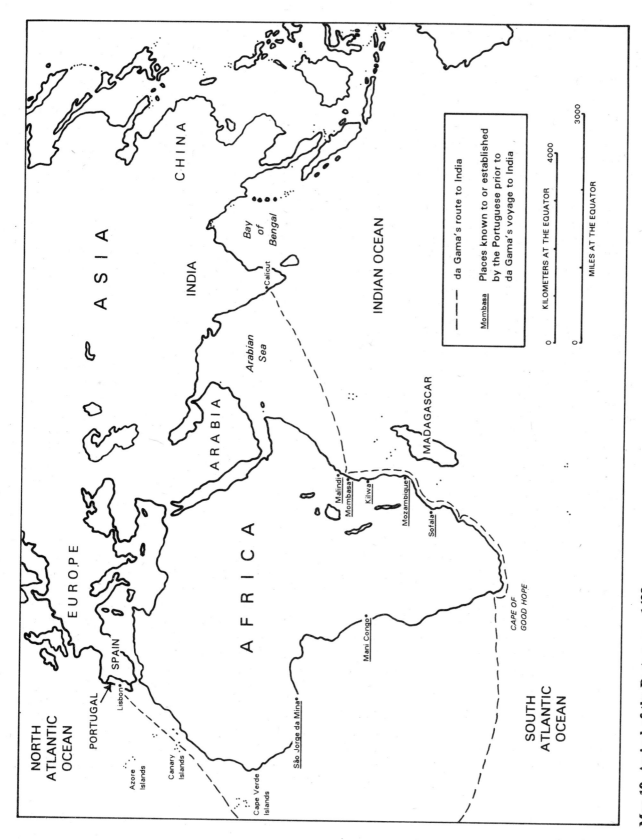

Map 19 Arrival of the Portuguese, 1498

NORTH ATLANTIC OCEAN

EUROPE

PORTUGAL
Lisbon

SPAIN

Azore Islands

Canary Islands

Cape Verde Islands

AFRICA

São Jorge da Mina

Mani Congo

SOUTH ATLANTIC OCEAN

CAPE OF GOOD HOPE

MADAGASCAR

Sofala

Mozambique

Kilwa

Mombasa

Malindi

ARABIA

Arabian Sea

Bay of Bengal

Calicut

INDIA

ASIA

CHINA

INDIAN OCEAN

da Gama's route to India

Mombasa Places known to or established by the Portuguese prior to da Gama's voyage to India

KILOMETERS AT THE EQUATOR
0   3000   4000

MILES AT THE EQUATOR

20　European Settlements in South Asia, 1498-1763

Formal European settlement in South Asia in the modern period began two years after Admiral Vasco da Gama made initial Portuguese contact with South Asia in 1498. In 1500, Pedro Alvarez Cabral arrived at Calicut with six ships and convinced the zamorin of Calicut to sign a treaty which allowed Cabral to establish a factory for the use of Portuguese spice buyers, or factors. This first factory at Calicut was destroyed by Muslim merchants, but the Portuguese established additional major factory settlements, fortified to protect themselves, at Cochin (1500), Cannanore (1501), Goa (1510), Diu (1535), and Daman (1558).

During the sixteenth century, using coercion and often force, the Portuguese dominated the spice trade from South Asia, which consisted primarily of shipments of cheaply bought pepper, off-loaded in Lisbon, and sold throughout Europe at profits of up to 3,000 percent. This near-monopoly ultimately collapsed due to the inefficiency of crown control over the trade among Portuguese spice merchants; the high cost of maintaining warships and forts to defend the trade; greater evasion of Portuguese control over the trade by other groups, including South Asians; and direct assaults on the Portuguese and their settlement network in Asia by the Dutch, the French, and the English.

Eager to share in the wealth generated by spices and other products in the South Asian trade, the newly created Dutch Vereenigde Oostindische Compagnie (United East India Company) founded a factory settlement at Petapuli on the Coromandel coast in 1606, which was later fortified and renamed Fort Geldria in 1613. Over the next few decades, the Dutch built, maintained, and expanded additional settlements and forts at Negapatam, Chinsura, Colombo, and elsewhere in India. Despite the large number of settlements, neither the Dutch presence in South Asia nor its trade volume were as pervasive or as long lasting as that of their key rivals: the Portuguese, the French, and most especially the English.

The English East India Company, granted a charter in 1600 by Queen Elizabeth I (1533-1603), dispatched three ships to India, under the command of William Hawkins. The ships arrived at Surat, the largest port of the Mughal Empire, in late summer 1608. Hawkins was largely ignored by Mughal officials as well as by the Mughal emperor, Jahangir (r. 1605-1627). This behavior was not, however, atypical. Indians of this period had little interest in trading with the English or any other Europeans. Merchants and officials at Surat were most impressed not with English manufactures, but with English military prowess. This was demonstrated when another Englishman, Captain Best, arrived in port in 1612 and opened fire on several Portuguese vessels, forcing their dispersal. By the time James I's ambassador, Sir Thomas Roe, arrived in India in 1616, he was able (after a nearly three-year delay) to negotiate for the establishment of an English factory at Surat. Thus began England's long association with South Asia.

Over the next twenty-five years, the English were busy establishing settlements at Mandaraz (Madras) on the Coromandel coast (1639), which after 1642 would be known as Fort St. George; at Hughli in Bengal (1658), at the site of a former Portuguese factory; at Bombay (1668); and at an additional site on the Hughli River, Fort William (Calcutta) (1690). These major settlements became the pillars upon which all future British expansion in the subcontinent was based.

Following the death of the Mughal emperor Aurangzeb in 1707, and the subsequent gradual decline of the Empire, the only major European rival of the British was the French. The French Compagnie des Indes Orientales (Company of the Oriental Indies) established a home base in South Asia in 1674 at Pondicherry on the Coromandel coast, south of Fort St. George. Additional factory settlements followed at Surat and Chandernagore, both near similar British settlements. Until the 1740s, British and French conflict was limited to simple economic competition, which the French, with significantly higher profit margins, were winning.

Soon, two conflicts, the War for the Austrian Succession (1741-49) and the Seven Years' War (1756-63), which hitherto had been confined to Europe, spilled over into open warfare between the French and the British in South Asia. Although French forces under Joseph François Dupleix (1697-1764) were initially victorious, a lack of support from the French monarch Louis XV and the clever connivances of Englishman Robert Clive (1725-74) ultimately led to a reversal of French fortunes in South Asia and left the British as the paramount European power in South Asia by 1763.

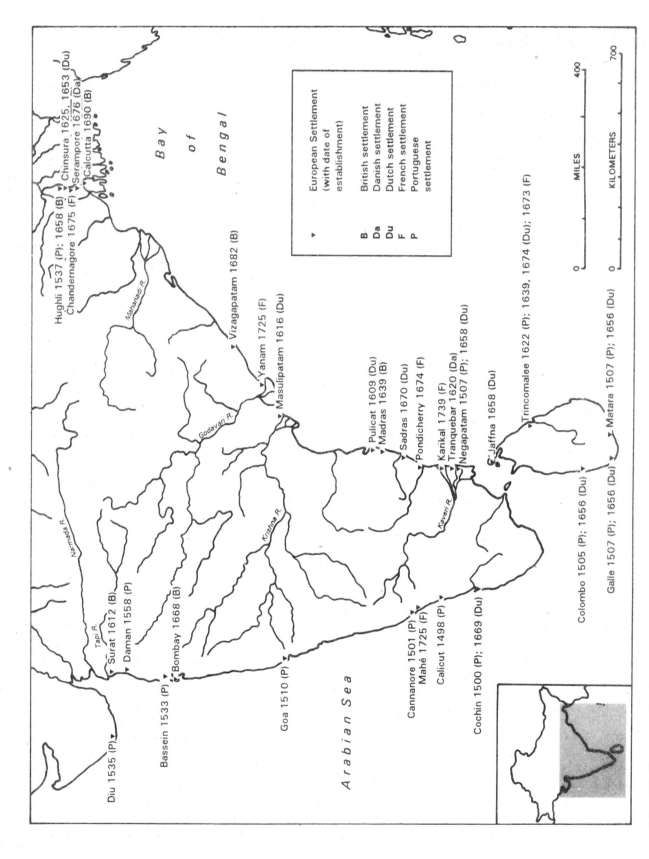

Map 20 European Settlements in South Asia, 1498–1763

European Settlement
(with date of establishment)

▼

B   British settlement
Da Danish settlement
Du Dutch settlement
F   French settlement
P   Portuguese settlement

Bay of Bengal

Arabian Sea

Diu 1535 (P) ▼

Bassein 1533 (P) ▼

Surat 1612 (B) ▼
Daman 1558 (P) ▼
Bombay 1668 (B) ▼

Goa 1510 (P) ▼

Cannanore 1501 (P) ▼
Mahé 1725 (F) ▼
Calicut 1498 (F) ▼

Cochin 1500 (P); 1669 (Du) ▼

Hughli 1537 (P); 1658 (B) ▼
Chandernagore 1675 (F) ▼
Chinsura 1625, 1653 (Du)
Serampore 1676 (Da)
Calcutta 1690 (B)

Mahanadi R.
Narmada R.
Tapi R.
Godavari R.
Krishna R.
Kaveri R.

Vizagapatam 1682 (B) ▼

Yanam 1725 (F) ▼
Masulipatam 1616 (Du) ▼

Pulicat 1609 (Du) ▼
Madras 1639 (B) ▼
Sadras 1670 (Du) ▼
Pondicherry 1674 (F) ▼
Karikal 1739 (F) ▼
Tranquebar 1620 (Da) ▼
Negapatam 1507 (P); 1658 (Du) ▼
Jaffna 1658 (Du) ▼

Trincomalee 1622 (P); 1639, 1674 (Du); 1673 (F) ▼

Colombo 1505 (P); 1656 (Du) ▼

Galle 1507 (P); 1656 (Du) ▼

Matara 1507 (P); 1656 (Du) ▼

MILES
0   400   700
KILOMETERS
0

49

21 Growth of the Mughal Empire, 1526-1605

A Chaghatai Turkish ruler, Zahiruddin Muhammad Babur (1526-30), founded the Mughal Empire in 1526, after defeating the last Delhi sultan, Ibrahim Lodi, at the first battle of Panipat in April of that year. His 12,000 troops armed with matchlocks and cannons, Babur quickly overwhelmed the numerically superior, but ill-equipped, Lodi force. After dethroning Ibrahim Lodi, Babur absorbed the Lodi kingdom, moved his capital from Kabul to Agra, and from there launched attacks against the Rajput kings of Rajasthan. At Babur's death in 1530, his kingdom stretched from Central Asia to Bihar and south to central India. The task of consolidating and expanding Mughal territories in South Asia was left to his son, Humayun (1530-56).

Upon inheriting his father's empire, Emperor Humayun was also faced with a fraternal competition for power. In keeping with tradition, Humayun's four brothers became provincial governors, but two of the four sought to increase their own power at the new emperor's expense. In addition, Humayun faced threats from disgruntled Afghans in the east who sought to restore the Lodi throne, and from Bahadur Shah, ruler of Gujarat, who sought to force the Mughals out of South Asia. After sending an army to Gujarat, Humayun was successful in destroying Bahadur Shah's plans, but the Mughal emperor later fell victim to the growing power of an Afghan ruler of Bihar, Sher Khan Sur (1539-45), who, after two victorious encounters with Humayun's armies in 1539 and again in 1540, drove the Mughals out of South Asia. Sher Khan (who assumed the title of Sher Shah in 1539 after the first battle with Humayun) became the new ruler of northern India.

In 1554, Humayun returned from his exile in Afghanistan to recapture his empire in northern India and to restore the Mughal throne. Humayun was successful, but died accidentally the following year, leaving the empire in the hands of his twelve-year-old son, Akbar.

After a regency period of four years, Akbar (1556-1605) ruled outright after 1560. For the next eleven years, Akbar was engaged primarily in military matters: his generals invaded and occupied the kingdom of Malwa, and defeated the Afghans at Chunar in Awadh, while he crushed a rebellion by his Uzbek nobles, and defeated Rajput forces at Chitor and Ranthambhor. Akbar also embarked on the construction of large imperial fortresses at Agra, Allahabad, Lahore, and Ajmer, as well as smaller ones throughout the empire. Feeling more secure, Akbar next moved his capital from Agra to Fatehpur Sikri, where it remained until 1585. From his new capital, Akbar launched a series of new campaigns of conquest. In 1572, he annexed Gujarat; in 1574, he undertook a protracted campaign to bring the rest of Bihar, as well as Bengal and Orissa, under his direct control—a task not formally completed until 1592.

Maintenance and further expansion of the empire required efficient administration. Akbar and his advisors built upon the foundations laid earlier by Sher Shah, who had favored more centralized control of his empire than had previously existed under the Delhi Sultanate. Akbar's effort to build a new imperial administrative system was quite different from that of Babur and Humayun; they had left intact the well-entrenched administrative institutions they found after supplanting the last rulers of the Delhi Sultanate (Siddiqui 1983).

Under Akbar, executive power rested with the emperor. He was assisted by four central ministers responsible for (1) budget and taxation, (2) army and espionage, (3) the legal apparatus and religious patronage, and (4) the royal household. Certain areas, like foreign relations, remained within the purview of the emperor, while lesser officials were appointed to fulfill other duties not discharged by the four central ministers. A similar system of functional administration operated in each of the empire's provinces (Richards 1993).

In 1585, Akbar again moved his capital, this time to Lahore. An important consideration in this move was the emperor's desire to quell frontier disturbances by Yusufzai Afghan tribes which threatened the lucrative caravan trade between Central and South Asia. Akbar spent the next six years battling the Yusufzai chiefs until he finally forced their submission.

While at Lahore, Akbar also sought to expand the empire northward. In 1585, he sent an invasion force into Kashmir. The Kashmiri king, Ali Shah, surrendered immediately, but his son, Yaqub, engaged in two years of valiant resistance before finally submitting to Akbar. By 1595, Akbar's armies had also occupied Multan and Sind. Akbar's last major conquest was in Deccan, where between 1595 and 1601 he defeated the sultan of Khandesh, and annexed his kingdom as well as parts of neighboring Berar and Ahmadnagar.

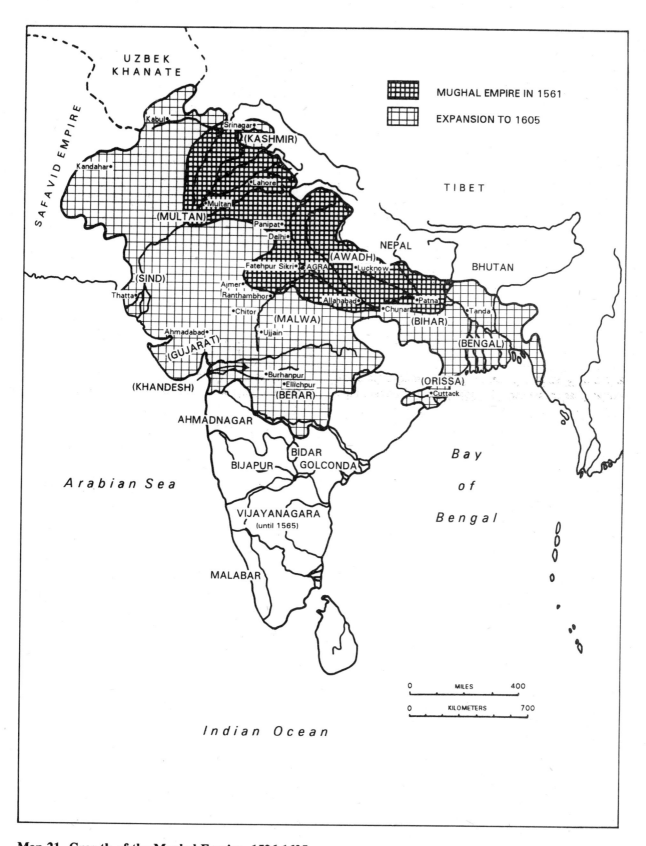

Map 21 Growth of the Mughal Empire, 1526–1605

51

22　Mughal South Asia, 1605-1707

Prince Salim, Akbar's son, after a brief struggle for power with his own son, succeeded to the Mughal throne in 1605. He took a new name, Jahangir, and immediately set about the task of consolidating and extending the empire bequeathed to him. Jahangir's first campaign of imperial extension was directed against the Rajput prince, Rana Amar Singh of Mewar, whose defeat proved elusive for many years. Only after 1613 were Jahangir's armies able to force the rana's surrender. His defeat marked an important turning point in Mughal history: it heralded the end of indigenous resistance to the Mughals for several decades to come.

Although Jahangir was less personally interested in imperial expansion than his father, he nonetheless did not neglect it. The emperor's armies continued to press deeper into northeastern India, fighting first the Afghans—thereby continuing a policy pursued by Akbar—and later, the Burmese Ahoms. The Ahoms, who had been expanding westward along the valley of the Brahmaputra for well over a century, were a formidable enemy, and successfully checked significant Mughal advances in the northeast during Jahangir's reign.

Jahangir was more successful in the foothill kingdoms of the Himalayas, where he forced Rajput kings to accept his overlordship. The emperor's major area of interest, however, lay in Deccan, where he proceeded to build upon his father's earlier conquests. Despite several initial failures, after 1616 Jahangir's armies finally succeeded in destroying the sultan of Ahmadnagar's army and subsequently annexed the rest of that state as well as the rest of Berar. The Deccan campaigns marked the last major military operations of Jahangir's reign before his death in 1627.

Following a brief tripartite struggle for the throne after his father's death, Prince Khurram was proclaimed emperor Shah Jahan (1628-58). Although Shah Jahan is perhaps best remembered for his construction of the Taj Mahal, he also excelled in military affairs. As a prince, he conducted most of the major campaigns during his father's lifetime, and was thus well trained and suited to the lifestyle of a conquering emperor. He moved decisively to punish Khan Jahan Lodi, an Afghan noble who had served under Jahangir, and who, after Shah Jahan's accession, fled south to Deccan to conspire against the emperor. After two years of fighting, Khan Jahan Lodi was captured by Shah Jahan's troops and beheaded.

Piece by piece, Shah Jahan added either actual territories to the empire or extended imperial control. Baglana in Rajasthan fell to Mughal armies in 1637, followed by campaigns in Sind, designed to crush Baluchi resistance to imperial authority. After 1634, the Mughal emperor established indirect political control over Bundelkhand and Gondwana (Chota Nagpur) in Central India. In the 1640s, Shah Jahan was less successful in regaining control over his ancestors' former territories in Central Asia; only after nearly a decade of fighting, the deaths of thousands of troops, and the expenditure of tens of millions of rupees, did the emperor abandon the effort. At his death, Shah Jahan's empire was immense, but costly. Enormous revenues, derived from agriculture, found their way into the Mughal treasury, but much of it was spent on war and monument building.

Shah Jahan's death touched off a fratricidal war of succession among his four sons; ironically, Shah Jahan's least favorite son (and third in age), Aurangzeb, was the one who won the war of succession and claimed the Mughal throne.

Aurangzeb (1658-1707), who took the regnal name, Alamgir, was an extremely devoted and orthodox follower of Islam, and a strong general, equally devoted to the expansion of the empire. His first attempts at imperial expansion during the 1660s and 1670s were of mixed success. In Assam, he forced the submission of the Ahom chief, but failed to maintain control over him and Assam once again slipped outside the imperial orbit. In Chota Nagpur, Aurangzeb defeated the raja of Palamau and annexed his kingdom. Campaigns against the Pathans of the northwestern frontier met with little success and Aurangzeb resorted to bribes and other incentives to quell the tribes' resistance.

By far the most absorbing field of conquest for Aurangzeb was Deccan. In 1685, he dispatched two large armies to the region simultaneously: one laid siege to Bijapur and the other attacked Golconda. Bijapur was annexed outright, while Aurangzeb spared the sultan of Golconda this fate, requiring him only to forfeit some of his territory. By 1689, Aurangzeb's armies had also conquered the Maratha kingdom. The Mughal empire had now reached its greatest extent, but the Marathas, unwilling to completely surrender, waged continuous warfare against Mughal control, forcing Aurangzeb to remain in Deccan until his death eighteen years later.

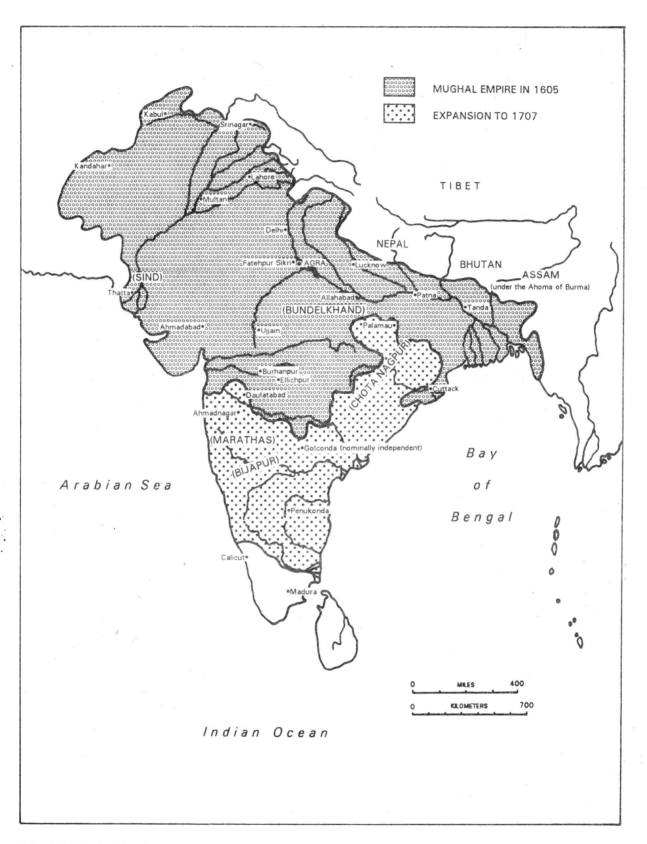

TIBET

Kabul

Srinagar

Kandahar

Lahore

Multan

Delhi

(SIND)

Fatehpur Sikri   AGRA   Lucknow

NEPAL

BHUTAN

ASSAM
(under the Ahoms of Burma)

Thatta

Ahmadabad   Ujjain

Allahabad

(BUNDELKHAND)

Patna

Tanda

Palamau

Burhanpur

Ellichpur

(CHOTA NAGPUR)

Daulatabad

Cuttack

Ahmadnagar

(MARATHAS)

Golconda (nominally independent)

Bay

(BIJAPUR)

of

Arabian Sea

Bengal

Penukonda

Calicut

Madura

0   MILES   400

0   KILOMETERS   700

Indian Ocean

Map 22 Mughal South Asia, 1605-1707

23   Growth of the Marathas, c. 1645-1720

Maratha power arose, like its counterparts in Rajasthan and Panjab, mainly in reaction to the oppression of Mughal rule. In the 1630s, Shaji, a **jagirdar** of the sultan of Ahmadnagar, attempted to rid Deccan of the Mughals by carrying on a war against them. He met with too much resistance, however, and by 1636 Shaji was forced to surrender and subsequently banished to Poona (Pune). The task of molding ongoing Maratha hostility toward the Mughals into an effective resistance movement was left to Shaji's son, Shivaji Bhonsle (1627-80).

Instilled at an early age with his mother's devotion to Hinduism and his father's hatred of "foreign" rule, Shivaji set about raising a small band of guerrilla fighters. Under his excellent leadership and martial skills, these rebels had, by 1659, become a threat to the sultan of Bijapur, who sent a force out under the command of General Afzal Khan to deal with them. After pretending to surrender at Pratapgarh, one of his many hilltop fortresses, the Maratha rebel leader murdered Afzal Khan in a face-to-face meeting; Shivaji's forces then quickly dispersed the Bijapuri general's disheartened troops.

Shivaji's victory over Afzal Khan firmly established the Marathas as a regional power. Deccani sultans learned the futility of trying to tame that power and left that task in the hands of their Mughal overlords, who within five years had forced Shivaji to surrender most of his fortresses and had made him a **mansabdar**. But Shivaji chafed under this sham imperial service and soon resumed his struggle against the Mughals. By 1670, he had recaptured the majority of his fortresses and continued his campaigns of harassment and plunder against Mughal garrisons and nearby cities. At his death in 1680, Shivaji's dominions extended the length of the Konkan coast, from north of the Portuguese enclave of Daman to just south of Goa. To the east they were bounded by the western ghats, where many of his fortresses lay. Shivaji also possessed territories in the far south, including one as far away as Tanjore. Small though they were, Shivaji's conquests had established a firm footing for Hindu nationalism in Deccan.

Shivaji's eldest son, Sambhaji (1657-89), assumed his father's fighting spirit and continued to resist the Mughals despite Aurangzeb's personal devotion to crushing all such resistance. In 1681, the Mughal emperor led a massive army into Deccan, determined to extend his direct rule throughout South India. Aurangzeb spent the next twenty-five years in Deccan and did not return to Delhi until 1705. His attempts to crush the sultanates of Deccan were initially effective and in 1689, he even captured Sambhaji, who was tortured and then hacked to death, but Aurangzeb was unable to stamp out Maratha resistance to Mughal rule completely. In addition to their well-organized military, the ability of the Marathas to successfully resist the force of Aurangzeb's attacks on their homeland was, in part, due to the unifying power of the twin ideological concepts of **swaraj** and **Maharashtra dharma**. Maratha rulers after Shivaji made repeated nationalistic and patriotic appeals to their people to defend Maratha independence in Deccan, reminding them that ultimate success or failure lay in their hands (Kulkarni 1983).

Maratha resistance experienced a resurgence after Aurangzeb's death in 1707 and his son, Bahadur Shah (1707-12), was unable to stop it. Hoping to engender Maratha goodwill, Bahadur Shah installed Shivaji's grandson, Shahu (1682-1749), as raja of Satara. This effort proved fruitless and the Marathas continued their campaigns.

Feeling the need to unify the various Maratha groups into a more effective force, in 1713 Shahu appointed a Chitpavin Brahman, Balaji Vishwanath, as **peshwa**, a position which under Shahu became hereditary. Balaji was an able administrator who not only converted the position of peshwa into one of real power, but also amplified the prestige and power of the Maratha state. In 1714, Balaji concluded a treaty with the Mughal emperor which gave the Marathas control over Shivaji's old territories and many others in Deccan in exchange for a yearly tribute and the maintenance of 15,000 cavalry for Mughal imperial service. The peshwa also obtained for the Marathas the right to collect **chauth** and **sardeshmukhi** from the six Mughal provinces, or subas, of Deccan. During the struggle between the Sayyid brothers—two highly placed Mughal officials under Bahadur Shah who were then engaged in imperial kingmaking—and other Mughal nobles in Delhi, Balaji arranged for a Maratha army to travel north to assist the Sayyids in the struggle. By his death in 1720, Balaji Vishwanath had contributed immensely to the resurgence of Maratha power in Deccan, strengthening Maratha administration and wealth, and adding to it a mantle of legitimacy.

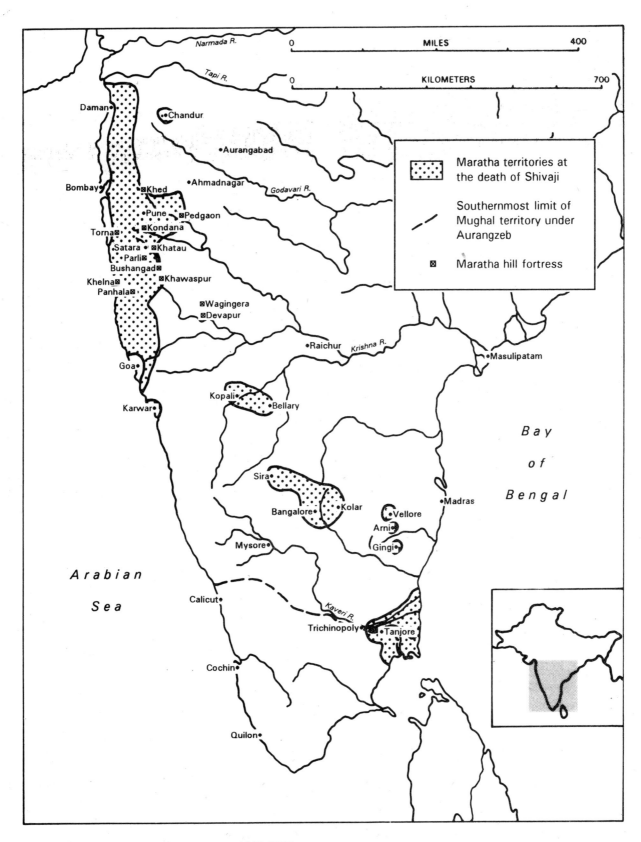

Map 23 Growth of the Marathas, c. 1645-1720

24   Anglo-French Conflict in South Asia, 1746-1763

The political stability of the Mughal Empire had been in decline since the death of Aurangzeb in 1707, and after Nadir Shah of Persia sacked Delhi in 1739, it became clear that any real Mughal central authority had collapsed. Europeans in South Asia soon realized that the regional Mughal officials with whom they had been dealing now lacked support from the center and that this weakness could be manipulated and exploited.

In 1744, the War of the Austrian Succession, a conflict between the major powers of Europe—one which found France and Britain on opposite sides—spilled over into South Asia. Initially, the directors of both the French and British trading companies were anxious to avoid a potentially disruptive and destructive conflict in South Asia. Upon learning that the British government was willing to commit naval forces to protect their investments, however, the directors of the English East India Company were ready to rid themselves of their French competition in South Asia. By the end of 1744, a Royal squadron arrived and quickly brought French commercial shipping in South Asia to a standstill. François Dupleix, governor of Pondicherry, who sought to save French fortunes as well as his own, sent a message to the governor of Bourbon and Mauritius, Admiral Mahé de la Bourdonnais, to assemble a squadron and sail to India to protect French interests. Not until late spring 1746 were his ships ready; they arrived off the Carnatic coast in June. Despite the harassment of French merchant shipping, real war between the French and British had been averted until de la Bourdonnais, acting under pressure from Dupleix, laid siege to the British town of Madras. He quickly captured it, but in doing so, sparked the First Carnatic War. De la Bourdonnais left Madras in the hands of Dupleix, who now faced the wrath of the nawab of Carnatic, Anwaruddin, whose authority Dupleix was obviously flaunting. The nawab sent a 10,000-man army to drive the French out of Madras, but Dupleix, using superior tactics, firepower, and skill, routed the nawab's forces with only 450 men. Dupleix next secured the nawab's neutrality in the French conflict with the British by offering him bribes. Free to attack without fear of intervention, Dupleix laid siege to Fort St. David, but this attack was repulsed by the British, among them a young clerk-turned-soldier named Robert Clive. British forces, in turn, laid siege to Pondicherry in 1748, but were forced to retire due to the monsoon's onset. When the war in Europe ended later that year, Madras was restored to the British by the Treaty of Aix-la-Chapelle.

Another Anglo-French conflict, the Second Carnatic War (1751-54), soon followed. Between 1748 and 1749, the deaths of both the **nizam** of Hyderabad and the nawab of Carnatic ignited a struggle of succession. Dupleix, who quickly grasped the opportunities for power and wealth this struggle provided, intervened directly to help install Indian rulers of his own choosing. The British, sensing that Dupleix's success would lead to the decline of their power in South Asia, backed opposing rulers and the succession struggle turned into an undeclared war. At war's end, after a series of French reversals, French influence in South India was limited to Hyderabad, the British had gained influence in Carnatic, and Dupleix, whose king-making activities and self-seeking intrigues had long troubled the French government, was recalled to Paris.

The Third Carnatic War (1756-63) broke out in response to the commencement of the Seven Years' War in Europe. A new French governor, Count de Lally, was able to capture Fort St. David and some smaller British possessions in Carnatic, but not Madras. In need of assistance, de Lally made the mistake of recalling Gen. de Bussy, then at Hyderabad. With de Bussy's departure, French influence at the nizam's court collapsed, never to be restored. Buoyed by their victories over the French at Chandernagore and over the nawab of Bengal, Sirajuddaulah, at Plassey in 1757, the British took the offensive and occupied the Northern Sarkars (1758), defeated a French army at Wandiwash (1760), and captured Pondicherry (1761). Pondicherry and Chandernagore were restored to the French after the war in Europe came to an end with the Peace of Paris in 1763, but French power in South Asia had been effectively eliminated.

Anglo-French conflict in South Asia had profound repercussions for the future. First, it exposed the overall weakness of the Indian political situation, enabling unscrupulous European adventurers like Dupleix and Clive to plunder and mold India to their liking. Most importantly, however, the conflict highlighted the effectiveness of European military training when applied to indigenous troops in defeating much larger, but traditionally-trained and -equipped indigenous forces. Indian troops, with European training and equipment, were later used by the British to conquer much of India.

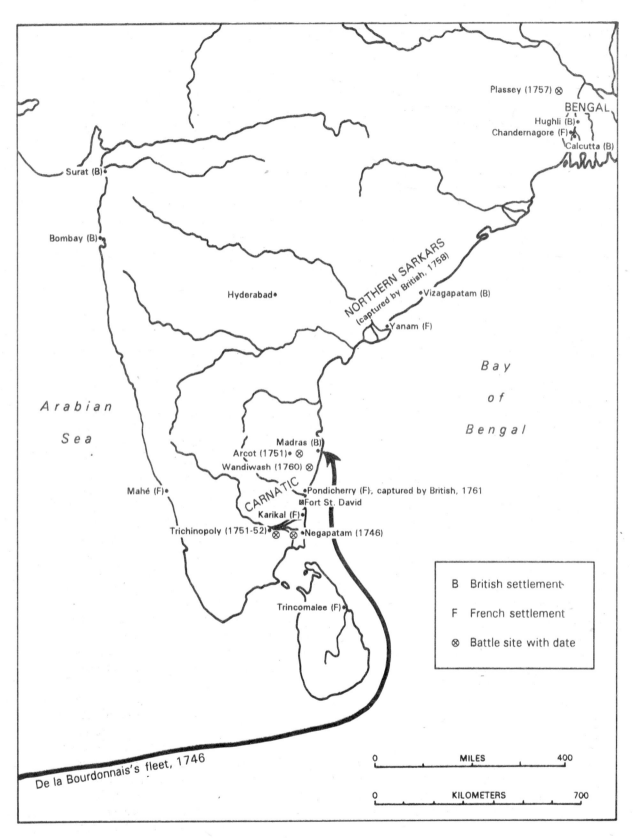

Plassey (1757) ⊗
BENGAL
Hughli (B)
Chandernagore (F)
Calcutta (B)

Surat (B)•

Bombay (B)•

NORTHERN SARKARS
(captured by British, 1758)

Hyderabad•

Vizagapatam (B)•

Yanam (F)•

B a y

o f

B e n g a l

A r a b i a n

S e a

Madras (B)•
Arcot (1751)• ⊗
Wandiwash (1760) ⊗

Mahé (F)•

CARNATIC

Pondicherry (F); captured by British, 1761
Fort St. David
Karikal (F)•
Trichinopoly (1751-52)• ⊗ ⊗ Negapatam (1746)

Trincomalee (F)•

B	British settlement
F	French settlement
⊗	Battle site with date

0 _____ MILES _____ 400

0 _____ KILOMETERS _____ 700

De la Bourdonnais's fleet, 1746

Map 24 Anglo-French Conflict in South Asia, 1746-1763

25   Growth of British Territory in South Asia, 1753-1849

By 1753, it became patently clear that the British in India were interested in more than just friendly trade. Some, like Robert Clive, realized that India's political instability could be exploited not only to amass personal wealth, but also to gain additional concessions from local and regional leaders. The British had, by 1753, established strong footholds in Bombay, Madras, and Bengal. These three areas served as springboards from which the East India Company soon expanded its territorial holdings in South Asia.

The Battle of Plassey (1757) marked a critical juncture in the growth of British territory in South Asia. After an East India Company army, led by Robert Clive, defeated the army of the nawab of Bengal, Sirajuddaulah, the Company became the de facto master of Bengal. In 1765, the Mughal emperor formally conferred on the Company the rights of **diwani**. The British thus established a permanent bridgehead in India. The relative ease with which they acquired the massive wealth of Bengal spurred further attempts to increase land holdings in South Asia through a combination of conquest, intrigue, and subterfuge, often with the active collaboration of Indian merchants, the landed gentry, and others who saw advantages for themselves in helping the British expand in India (Bayly 1988).

After seizing the Northern Sarkars from the French in 1758, British efforts were concentrated initially in South India and directed at Mysore (see Maps 27.1-27.4), with whom the British fought an unsuccessful war (1767-69). Undeterred, the British found their attention soon drawn elsewhere. After assuming the direct collection of diwani as well as the direct administration of Bengal in 1772, the British, under Governor-General Warren Hastings (1732-1818), began to once again interfere in Indian politics. Hastings' support of the nawab of Awadh in his dispute with the Rohillas led to the Rohilla War (1774), in which the nawab of Awadh used a British brigade to help him conquer and annex Rohilkhand. Despite Parliament's outrage at this misuse of British power in India and the arrival of four councillors mandated to curb the governor-general's powers as prescribed by the Regulating Act (1773), the British were soon involved in yet another conflict: British designs on the island of Salsette and support for Raghoba, a Maratha claimant to the peshwaship, led them to war with the Marathas in 1775 (see Map 28).

While still embroiled in the war with the Marathas, British authorities in Madras again attempted to destroy the power of Mysore. Only on the fourth attempt, in 1799, did the British finally succeed (see Maps 27.1-27.4). In the end, British victory over Tipu Sultan resulted in substantial territorial gains in South India.

In addition to direct military occupation and control of territory in South Asia, the Company also engaged in indirect control. Upon becoming governor-general in 1798, Richard Colley Wellesley (1760-1842) skirted the provisions of **Pitt's Act of 1784** by creating a system of **subsidiary alliances** which reduced many Indian princely states, including Hyderabad, Mysore (after 1799), Travancore, and Awadh, to the status of British clients. States which refused to agree to subsidiary alliances faced coercion, or even destruction, at the hands of Wellesley's armies. In some cases, Indian territories were annexed outright: Tanjore met this fate in 1799; as did Surat in 1800; and Nellore, North and South Arcot, and Trichinopoly in 1801. Wellesley stripped Awadh of two-thirds of its area after first forcing it to become a subsidiary ally in 1801.

In 1813, a new governor-general, Lord Hastings, assumed office. Hastings was determined to continue the expansion of British holdings in South Asia and, within a year of arriving in India, embarked on his first war of conquest, the Anglo-Nepalese War (1814-16), after which Nepal became another client state (see Map 64). During his tenure, Hastings also launched wars against the Pindaris (1817-19) and the Marathas (1817-19), securing huge territories in Central India for the Company. Five years later, Lord Amherst started the first of what became three British wars of conquest against Burma in the nineteenth century, annexing Arakan and Tenasserim in 1826 (see Map 30).

After the British dispatched their most serious rivals to paramountcy in South Asia, the Marathas, in the 1817-19 war, and annexed Sind in 1843, they were left with only one obstacle to complete control over the subcontinent: the Sikh kingdom in Panjab. For many years, the British and the Sikhs had maintained fairly cordial relations. In the wake of Ranjit Singh's death (1839), however, Anglo-Sikh relations became increasingly strained as the British maneuvered to take advantage of the succession struggle and the consequent political disturbances which overtook Panjab. Ultimately, the British fought two wars with the Sikhs (1845-46 and 1848-49). Like many states that preceded it, the Sikh kingdom also fell to the British; it was their last major acquisition in South Asia (see Maps 31.1-31.2).

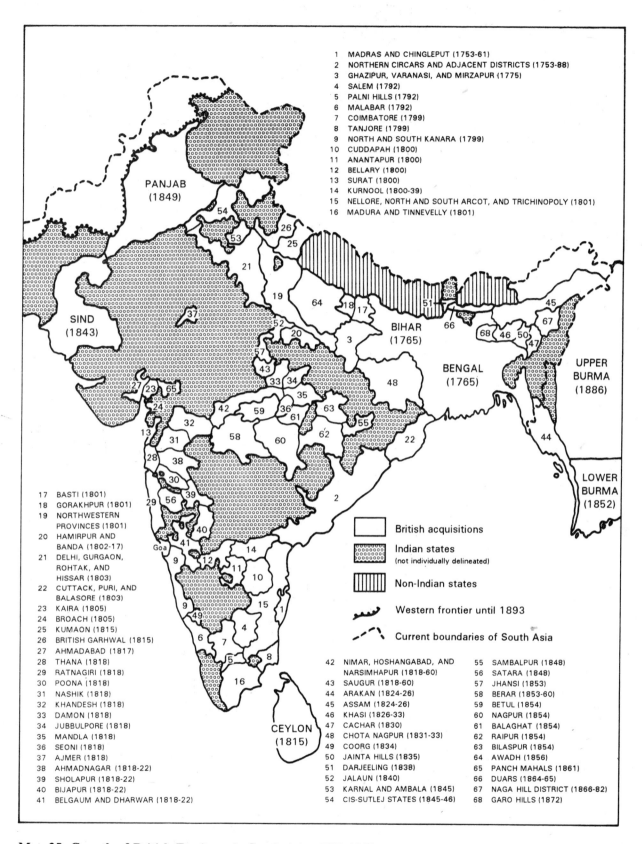

1 MADRAS AND CHINGLEPUT (1753-61)
2 NORTHERN CIRCARS AND ADJACENT DISTRICTS (1753-88)
3 GHAZIPUR, VARANASI, AND MIRZAPUR (1775)
4 SALEM (1792)
5 PALNI HILLS (1792)
6 MALABAR (1792)
7 COIMBATORE (1799)
8 TANJORE (1799)
9 NORTH AND SOUTH KANARA (1799)
10 CUDDAPAH (1800)
11 ANANTAPUR (1800)
12 BELLARY (1800)
13 SURAT (1800)
14 KURNOOL (1800-39)
15 NELLORE, NORTH AND SOUTH ARCOT, AND TRICHINOPOLY (1801)
16 MADURA AND TINNEVELLY (1801)

17 BASTI (1801)
18 GORAKHPUR (1801)
19 NORTHWESTERN PROVINCES (1801)
20 HAMIRPUR AND BANDA (1802-17)
21 DELHI, GURGAON, ROHTAK, AND HISSAR (1803)
22 CUTTACK, PURI, AND BALASORE (1803)
23 KAIRA (1805)
24 BROACH (1805)
25 KUMAON (1815)
26 BRITISH GARHWAL (1815)
27 AHMADABAD (1817)
28 THANA (1818)
29 RATNAGIRI (1818)
30 POONA (1818)
31 NASHIK (1818)
32 KHANDESH (1818)
33 DAMON (1818)
34 JUBBULPORE (1818)
35 MANDLA (1818)
36 SEONI (1818)
37 AJMER (1818)
38 AHMADNAGAR (1818-22)
39 SHOLAPUR (1818-22)
40 BIJAPUR (1818-22)
41 BELGAUM AND DHARWAR (1818-22)

42 NIMAR, HOSHANGABAD, AND NARSIMHAPUR (1818-60)
43 SAUGUR (1818-60)
44 ARAKAN (1824-26)
45 ASSAM (1824-26)
46 KHASI (1826-33)
47 CACHAR (1830)
48 CHOTA NAGPUR (1831-33)
49 COORG (1834)
50 JAINTA HILLS (1835)
51 DARJEELING (1838)
52 JALAUN (1840)
53 KARNAL AND AMBALA (1845)
54 CIS-SUTLEJ STATES (1845-46)

55 SAMBALPUR (1848)
56 SATARA (1848)
57 JHANSI (1853)
58 BERAR (1853-60)
59 BETUL (1854)
60 NAGPUR (1854)
61 BALAGHAT (1854)
62 RAIPUR (1854)
63 BILASPUR (1854)
64 AWADH (1856)
65 PANCH MAHALS (1861)
66 DUARS (1864-65)
67 NAGA HILL DISTRICT (1866-82)
68 GARO HILLS (1872)

British acquisitions

Indian states (not individually delineated)

Non-Indian states

Western frontier until 1893

Current boundaries of South Asia

Map 25 Growth of British Territory in South Asia, 1753-1849

59

Following the precipitous decline of the Mughal Empire after the death of Aurangzeb in 1707, the English East India Company found itself in the position of having to defend Company interests militarily against the French in South Asia. This necessity marked the origins of the British Army in India. By 1757, the Company had established armies at each of the three Presidencies: Bombay, Madras, and Bengal.

Initially, British forces in India consisted of only Europeans: either King's troops (British Crown troops paid by, and in service to, the Company), or Europeans recruited directly by the Company. The demand for European troops in India soon outstripped supply, and in 1693 the first Indian **sipahis (sepoys)** were enlisted to serve in the Company's army, under the command of British officers. Army service proved popular among Indian recruits due to the relatively high status and regular pay such service offered.

In its early years, the Army in India was rather haphazardly organized, but in 1796 the Company implemented a reorganization plan, drafted largely by Charles Cornwallis, then governor-general, which resulted in an improved command structure and greater efficiency. After 1796, the magnitude of the Army in India's role increased as well: in addition to defending the Company's investments in India, its mission was to help support Britain's political, economic, and strategic interests throughout the rest of Asia. The size of the Army in India also experienced dramatic changes. The relatively small three-Presidency Army in India of roughly 18,000 troops in 1763 had grown almost six-fold to over 102,000 troops in 1796. By 1857, the size of the Army had increased to over 271,000 troops. The ratio of European troops to indigenous Indian troops in 1796 was 1:4.69; in 1857, this figure climbed to 1:5.86, reflecting the increasing British dependence on indigenous troops to support their position in South Asia and beyond.

The end of the War of 1857 brought many changes to the British Army in India. Like all other East India Company possessions, the Army in India was transferred to British Crown control in 1858. In addition, the Army underwent a dramatic restructuring: more European troops were posted in India than before the War, the ratio of European troops to Indian troops was decreased to 1:2 for Bengal and 1:3 for Bombay and Madras, and all "scientific branches" of the Army, including artillery, were placed under the exclusive control of the British. The British government reshaped the Army in India's mission to include the following goals: to protect British India from external attacks and future internal rebellions; to make available troops for overseas operations; and finally, to maintain law and order in British India.

Further changes took place near the turn of the century. In 1902, Lord Kitchener, then commander-in-chief of the Army in India, implemented several army reforms, both in mission and in structure. The Army's new chief role was to defend against an attack from the northwest. In addition, the four regional armies which had supplanted the three Presidency Armies in 1894 were themselves superseded by just two armies: the Northern and the Southern. Finally, Kitchener established a Staff College at Quetta to train army staff officers.

The outbreak of war in 1914 placed an enormous and unexpected strain on the Army in India. Although Indian troops had seen overseas service on numerous occasions prior to the war, the British authorities in India never anticipated having the Army in India fight in a protracted, large-scale, overseas war. As a result, the Army was underequipped and undertrained, but nevertheless overcame its many handicaps and, on the whole, performed well (see Map 34).

During the interwar period, politically conscious Indians demanded increased "Indianization" of the Army in India, especially within the officer corps. The Government of India made some effort in this direction, but progress was exceptionally slow, and by 1939, Indianization affected only a small number of army units. Despite the obvious lessons of the First World War, the Army in India was still underprepared at the outbreak of the Second World War. On the eve of war, the New Delhi and London governments still defined the Army in India's mission as one limited mostly to internal and regional defense, and very little of the army had been mechanized. Political exigencies of the interwar period, coupled with the economic turmoil of the Great Depression, inhibited the large increases in military expenditures that would have been necessary to modernize the Army in India. The Second World War ultimately forced modernization upon the Army (see Map 36).

Upon Partition in 1947, the Army in India was divided between India and Pakistan to form the basis of their own independent armies.

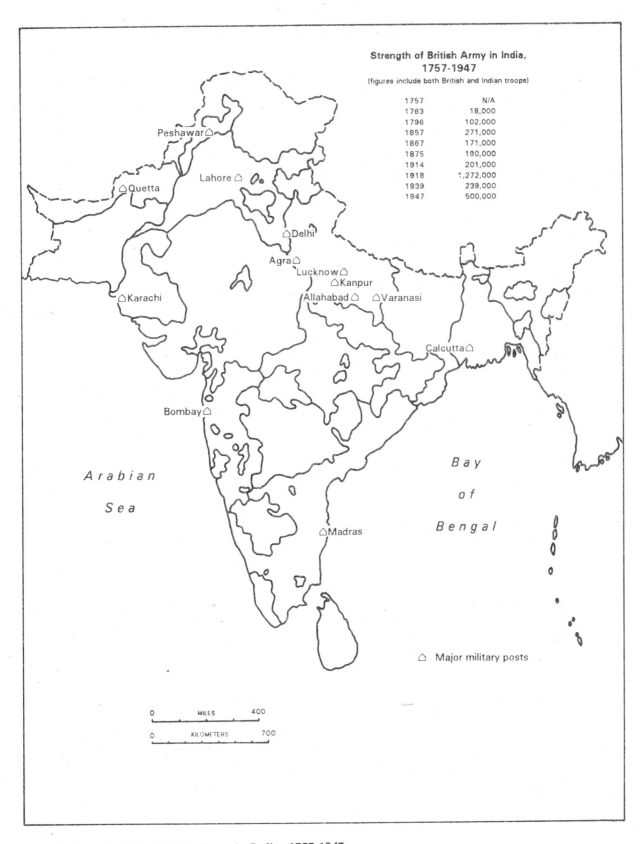

Strength of British Army in India,
1757-1947
(figures include both British and Indian troops)

1757	N/A
1763	18,000
1796	102,000
1857	271,000
1867	171,000
1875	190,000
1914	201,000
1918	1,272,000
1939	239,000
1947	500,000

Peshawar△

Quetta△ Lahore △

△Delhi

Agra△

Lucknow△

△Kanpur

Allahabad △ △Varanasi

△Karachi

Calcutta△

Bombay△

Arabian

Sea

Bay

of

Bengal

△Madras

△ Major military posts

0	MILES	400
0	KILOMETERS	700

Map 26 Growth of the British Army in India, 1757-1947

27   Mysore and the Wars of 1767-69, 1780-84, 1790-92, and 1799

Until the second half of the eighteenth century, Mysore was an independent Hindu kingdom. In 1761, Haidar Ali, a Muslim mercenary in the service of the dalwai or chief minister of Mysore, usurped the throne, and became ruler. Haidar Ali sought to extend the territorial limits of his new kingdom, but his designs threatened the Marathas, the nizam of Hyderabad, and the territorial expansion of the British.

The British began the First Anglo-Mysore War (1767-69) in an effort to take advantage of Haidar Ali, who was then engaged in a conflict with both the Marathas and the nizam. Haidar Ali was a shrewd diplomat, however, and quickly made peace with the Marathas and the nizam—who had both become coalition partners of the British—and thus freed himself to focus his full attentions on the British. After two years of warfare, with Haidar on the verge of conquering Madras, the British quickly agreed to his dictated peace. The treaty with the British called for mutual restoration of conquered territory and a defensive alliance between Haidar Ali and the British.

In 1780, the Second Anglo-Mysore War broke out after Haidar Ali sent 90,000 troops into the Carnatic. Haidar's attack was not unprovoked, however, as the British at Madras had reneged on the treaty of 1769 by refusing to assist Ali after Mysore was attacked by the Marathas that year. The British had also attacked Mahé, a French settlement on the Malabar coast under Ali's protection, after the outbreak of war between the French and the British during the American War for Independence. The final offense came when British troops attempted to traverse a portion of Haidar's territory without his permission. Thus sufficiently provoked, Haidar Ali formed a tripartite alliance with the Marathas and the nizam and proceeded to punish the British. At the first major battle, at Conjeveram, Ali's forces decimated most of Gen. Hector Munro's force of 3,800 men and captured the few that remained. Despite a lack of assistance from Haidar's so-called allies (the nizam quit the conflict in 1780; the Marathas dropped out in 1782, after making peace with the British; the French were unwilling to help), and Haidar's own death in December 1782, his son, Tipu Sultan, carried on the war and compelled the Madras government to surrender in 1784. The Treaty of Mangalore provided for mutual restoration of territory.

Despite, or perhaps because of, their twin defeats at the hands of Mysore, the British continued to conspire against that kingdom, continually failing, in the process, to honor their treaty obligations.

In 1788, Lord Cornwallis, who was then governor-general, attempted to establish a defensive alliance with the nizam, offering to restore parts of former Hyderabadi territory then held by Mysore to him. In addition, Cornwallis pursued a policy of allying himself with Tipu Sultan's other enemies in an effort to isolate Mysore. The following year, Tipu Sultan attacked the kingdom of Travancore, which had entered into a hostile alliance with the British against Mysore. Cornwallis, determining that he was now freed from the constraints placed on him by the **India Act of 1784**, entered into an alliance with the Maratha peshwa and the nizam, and precipitated the Third Anglo-Mysore War. After an initial setback at the hands of Tipu's forces in 1791, the British and their Indian allies defeated Tipu Sultan after British forces laid siege to his capital at Seringapatam in the spring of 1792. The Treaty of Seringapatam (1792), which concluded the war, forced Tipu to surrender two of his sons to the British as hostages, and to pay reparations. He also lost one-half of his territory, including much of the western seacoast, to the British and their allies.

After Tipu Sultan's humiliating defeat, he sought to establish alliances with France, Turkey, and Afghanistan. Only the French, under Napoleon, were eager to assist, but it seems doubtful that they would have been able to offer much. The Turks and Afghans, like Tipu, were concerned about growing British power in the subcontinent, but felt too threatened to send aid. Despite his lack of success at securing foreign assistance, Tipu Sultan after 1792 embarked on a policy of rebuilding his shattered kingdom. This effort, combined with British perceptions that Tipu was successful in securing foreign aid, led the British governor-general, Lord Wellesley, to launch a preemptive war against Mysore in 1799. This Fourth Anglo-Mysore War lasted only three months and resulted in the death of Tipu Sultan, who fell bravely defending his fortress at Seringapatam. After the war, Wellesley reduced the size of Mysore, shared the spoils with the Marathas and the nizam (the British took the Mysorean seacoast—Mysore was thereafter land-locked), and installed a Hindu raja on the throne of Mysore, enlisting him in the British subsidiary alliance system.

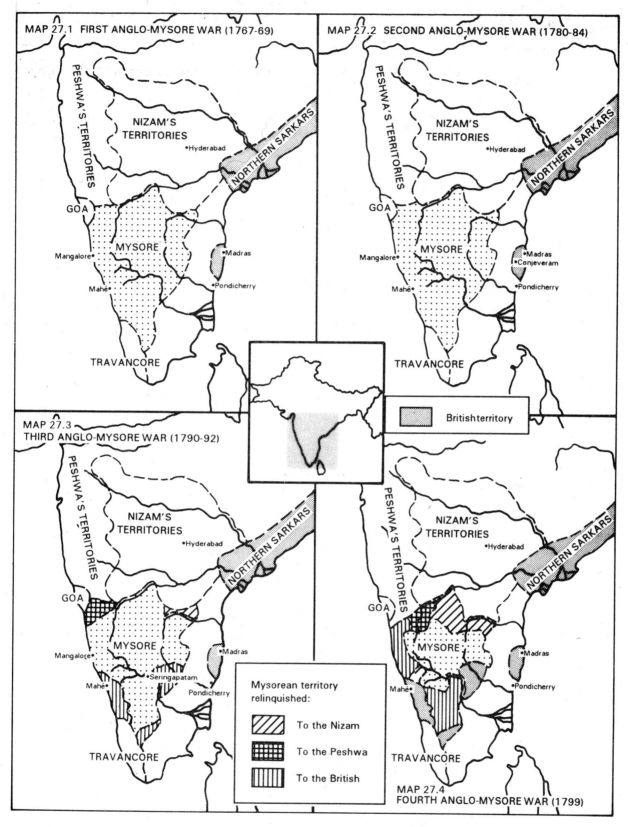

Maps 27.1-27.4 Mysore and the Wars of 1767-69, 1780-84, 1790-92, and 1799

63

28   Maratha Confederacy and the Anglo-Maratha Wars

An important accomplishment of the second peshwa, Bajirao I (1720-40), son of Balaji Vishwanath, was the creation of a Maratha Confederacy. The large territories that the Marathas had come to possess by 1720 required firm administration and military control, and while Bajirao was ably capable of providing the former, he relied on four Maratha military leaders, Raghuji Bhonsle, Damaji Gaekwar, Malhar Rao Holkar, and Ranoji Sindhia, to provide the latter.

By 1722, both of the Sayyid brothers were dead, murdered by their opponents. The Marathas thus lost significant support for their claims in Deccan. These claims were soon challenged by the nizam, who declined to honor the 1719 agreement between the Maratha peshwa, Balaji, and the Mughal emperor which gave the Marathas rights to revenue in Deccan. The nizam, however, unwilling to fight both the Marathas and a Mughal army sent by the emperor's viceroy in Deccan, Mubariz Khan, made peace with the Marathas and then proceeded to destroy Mubariz Khan's army in 1724. The nizam ultimately reconciled with the emperor, but his victory over Mughal forces compelled the emperor to recognize the nizam as viceroy of Deccan; the nizam thus became an independent ruler in all but name.

Meanwhile, despite their lack of support from Delhi, the Marathas under Bajirao were gaining in power, and by 1737 became a threat to Delhi itself when Maratha light cavalry entered the city and carried off some plunder. The emperor, Muhammad Shah, appealed to the nizam for assistance against the Marathas in exchange for a grant of more territory and ten million rupees. The nizam readily agreed, but his forces were humbled by those of the Marathas near Bhopal in December that year and he was forced to cede to them additional territories and pay reparations. As shrewd a peshwa as his father, Bajirao was quick to fill the power vacuum in Central India left by the rapid disintegration of the once-mighty Mughal Empire, thereby elevating the Marathas to the status of the single most powerful group in South Asia.

Following the death of peshwa Balaji Baji Rao (1740-61) in the wake of the humiliating defeat at Panipat (1761), at the hands of a combined force of Afghan, Mughal, and Rohilla Afghan troops, the solidarity of the Maratha Confederacy began to erode. This decline was due to a succession dispute over the peshwaship, and the ambitions of its military leaders,

especially Sindhia and Holkar. In 1775, Raghoba, the great-uncle of the minor peshwa Madhav Rao Narayan (1774-96), seeking to usurp the peshwaship for himself, conspired with the British for their support in exchange for ceding them territories at Salsette and Bassein. The British, under Governor-General Warren Hastings, satisfied their greed by agreeing to support Raghoba's bid. The Anglo-Maratha War which followed (1775-82) was virtually a stalemate; neither side was able to defeat the other. The two parties concluded the Treaty of Salbai (1782) and maintained an uneasy peace for another two decades, thanks in large measure to the diplomatic skill of Nana Fadnavis. Nana, a Maratha Brahman minister, was the real power behind the peshwa, and was able to keep the crumbling Maratha Pentarchy galvanized in the final decades of the eighteenth century. This situation, however, soon changed. After Nana's death in 1800, the Pentarchy began to collapse as two of its members, Yeshwant Rao Holkar and Daulat Rao Sindhia, let their struggle for power explode into violence. In 1801, Holkar attacked Poona, causing the peshwa, Baji Rao II (1775-1851) to flee to the safety of a British warship. At Bassein, in 1802, Baji Rao, fearing his own loss of power, signed a treaty with the East India Company; he thus became a subsidiary ally of the British. This action touched off the Second Anglo-Maratha War (1803-5). Bhonsle and Sindhia were unwilling to accept Baji Rao's betrayal of their sovereignty to the British and fought to save it. Their armies were soundly defeated by Governor-General Wellesley's brother, Arthur (later Duke of Wellington), by the end of 1803. In 1804, Holkar attempted to defeat the British armies on his own, but he, too, was defeated. As a result, he and the other Maratha chiefs all lost territories to the British.

In 1817, Baji Rao II, unhappy with his diminished status and power, led his equally disgruntled Maratha chiefs against the British one last time, beginning the Third Anglo-Maratha War (1817-19). It proved a disaster for the Marathas. British armies quickly surrounded Sindhia's forces in late 1817 and forced him to surrender. Bhonsle was defeated after two major battlefield losses for him at Sitabaldi and Nagpur (1817). Holkar lost at Mahidpur (1817). The peshwa suffered a similar fate. The war was a resounding British success. By 1819, they had put an end to all significant indigenous resistance to their rule and had become the paramount power on the subcontinent.

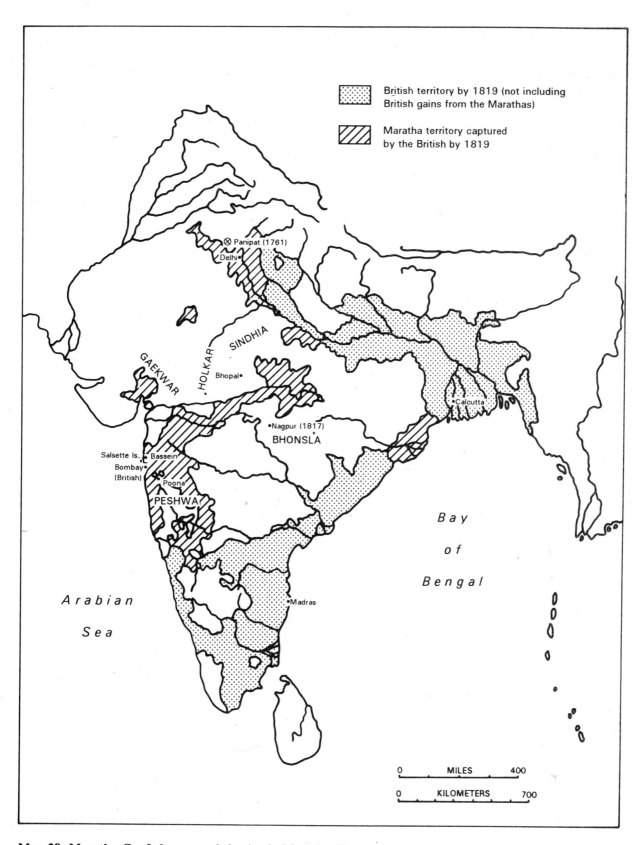

Map 28 Maratha Confederacy and the Anglo-Maratha Wars

65

29 Panjab under Ranjit Singh, 1799-1839

In the 1790s, Panjab consisted of fourteen independent principalities whose rulers had no sense of unanimity even when faced with a series of invasions from Afghanistan. During their third invasion of Panjab in five years, Zaman Shah Durrani (r. 1793-99), the Afghan king, and his troops had precipitously abandoned the city of Lahore upon hearing that their country had been invaded by Persia.

Ranjit Singh (1780-1839) was only nineteen when, in the summer of 1799, he rose to prominence in Panjab by occupying Lahore following the Afghan army's retreat. The Sikh ruler came to Lahore not as a liberator—the city had already been abandoned by Zaman Shah for six months—but as a benevolent conqueror. He restored order, encouraged the resumption of business and trade, and quickly set about consolidating his control over the city. Lahore was not his first territorial conquest in Panjab, but by possessing the provincial capital he became the most powerful ruler in all of northern India.

Over the next ten years, Ranjit Singh engaged himself in a series of battles with other Sikh rulers in an effort to expand his rule throughout Panjab. In the course of four years, he had attacked Jammu and Gujrat, occupied Akalgarh, subdued Kasur, attacked Kangra, formed a military alliance with Fateh Singh Ahluwalia, forcibly occupied Chaniot, and laid siege to Multan. In 1805, Ranjit Singh forced Mai Sukhan, the ruler of Amritsar, to evacuate the city. Ranjit Singh's occupation of Amritsar added significantly to his power as he had added the Sikh religious capital to his already long list of conquests. By the time of his death, Maharaja Ranjit Singh had conquered, occupied, and absorbed dozens of territories until Panjab was strong and united under his rule. His empire covered an area as large as France, stretching from Sind to the Himalayas and from the Sutlej River to the Sulaiman Range beyond the Indus.

Administering such a large empire was a difficult task, but the maharaja took a very active role in government and surrounded himself with able and intelligent ministers who ran the affairs of state. Ranjit Singh always took an active interest in his empire and the people he ruled. He kept a close watch on the civil administration of Panjab and set high standards for all of his top officials. He dictated policy and often toured his dominions to discourage corruption and collusion among his officials and to ensure that his orders were carried out.

The business of maintaining the empire against the threat of both internal and external enemies was a costly one and, not surprisingly, the largest single expenditure each year, roughly 40 percent of the total budget, was on the defense establishment. Ranjit Singh's armies, divided into infantry, cavalry, and artillery units, were a blend of traditional and modern elements. The maharaja was an ardent admirer of European military training and techniques and employed several Europeans (including two who had earlier served in Napoleon Bonaparte's armies) as high-ranking officers to train his troops. Infantry, cavalry and artillery troops that received modern, European-style training formed Ranjit Singh's regular army, while those troops that retained traditional training methods were styled irregulars. In addition, there was a second grouping, the jagirdari forces, who were troops trained and maintained by those subordinate chiefs to whom Ranjit Singh had granted a **jagir**. The overall quality of Ranjit Singh's troops was high and even British observers remarked that his regular troops were as good as those of the British Army in India.

Under Ranjit Singh's rule, the rural economy of Panjab flourished. Agricultural productivity was arguably the highest in all of India and the bulk of the people were employed as farmers. Wheat was the main crop, but some areas within Panjab were known for their production of rice, barley, sugarcane, fruit, and cotton. Agriculture provided the primary revenue base for government. Modeled on the Mughal system which it replaced, Ranjit Singh's land revenue system typically extracted fully one-half of each cultivator's total yield, an amount not uncommon nor considered unreasonable for the time. It was adjusted or even eliminated in times of famine or drought. Some of the revenues were returned to the cultivators in the form of state-built agricultural improvements such as irrigation wells and canals. In contrast to agriculture, industry was not well developed. Several mining operations extracted iron ore, salt, coal, lead and other metals, but not in large quantities. Large-scale manufacturing did not exist. Small-scale industries produced both cotton and silk textiles, paper, and armaments.

Ranjit Singh's forty-year reign marked a high point in Sikh history: Panjab prospered, and the people enjoyed peace and a relative freedom which they had not previously known.

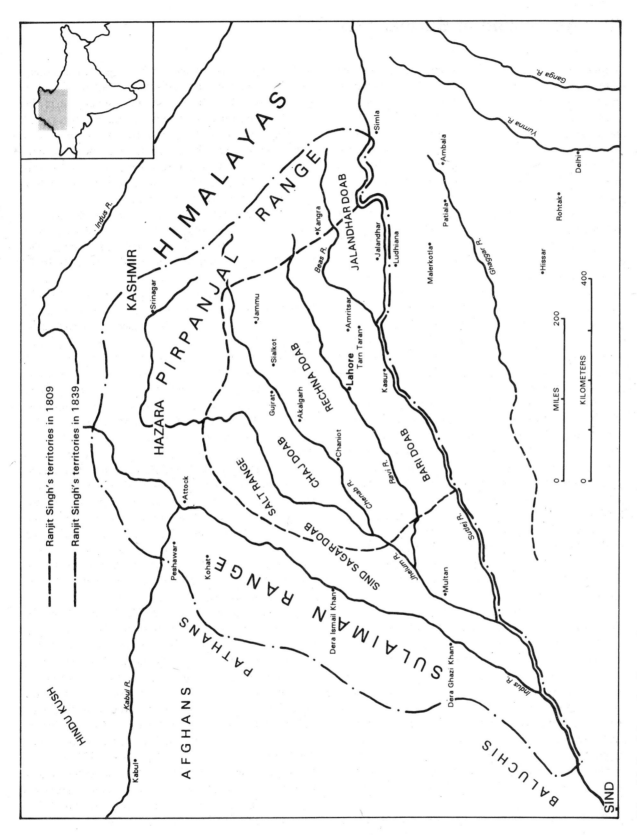

Map 29 Panjab under Ranjit Singh, 1799-1839

Ranjit Singh's territories in 1809
Ranjit Singh's territories in 1839

HIMALAYAS

PIRPANJAL RANGE

KASHMIR

HAZARA

JALANDHAR DOAB

RECHNA DOAB

CHAJ DOAB

BARI DOAB

SIND SAGAR DOAB

SALT RANGE

SULAIMAN RANGE

HINDU KUSH

AFGHANS

PATHANS

BALUCHIS

SIND

Indus R.

Ganga R.

Yumna R.

Kabul R.

Beas R.

Chenab R.

Ravi R.

Jhelum R.

Sutlej R.

Ghaggar R.

Indus R.

Srinagar

Jammu

Sialkot

Gujrat

Akalgarh

Chaniot

Kangra

Jalandhar

Ludhiana

Amritsar

Tarn Taran

Lahore

Kasur

Simla

Ambala

Patiala

Malerkotla

Rohtak

Delhi

Hissar

Attock

Peshawar

Kohat

Dera Ismail Khan

Dera Ghazi Khan

Multan

Kabul

MILES   200   400

KILOMETERS

0

67

During the same decade that Robert Clive won the battle at Plassey, dramatic events were unfolding in nearby Burma. King Alaungpaya (r. 1752-60) founded a new dynasty, the Konbuang (1752-1885), and set about uniting Upper and Lower Burma into one kingdom. Alaungpaya's successors, chiefly Bodawpaya (r. 1782-1819), were responsible for stabilizing Burma's internal politics and for largely eliminating outside threats to its sovereignty. These rulers also extended indirect Burmese control to the coastal areas of Arakan and Tenasserim. By 1816, King Bodawpaya's troops were, in the British view, dangerously close to British possessions in India.

While the Burmese king saw these frontier areas as within his sphere of influence, he declined to take responsibility for any raids the inhabitants of those areas might launch against British-controlled settlements. In addition to the raids, the British also objected to the way their traders were treated in Burma and expected the Burmese king to intercede; in both instances, British protests were ignored.

After 1819, the new Burmese king, Bagyidaw (r. 1819-37), insisted on pressing his claims along the Indo-Burmese frontier. Burmese forces occupied Manipur, annexed Assam, and, in January 1824, attacked the small frontier state of Cachar, then under British protection. After their victory over British-Indian troops, the Burmese retreated to Manipur. Within days, Burma's king, buoyed by his easy victory, gave the order to attack British India proper; the order proved disastrous. Bagyidaw underestimated the resources the British had at their disposal, and plunged his country into a war for which it was largely unprepared.

Lord Amherst, the British governor-general, declared war in early March, and the first troops left for Burma two months later. The British had decided to take the capital, Mandalay, and to there force a surrender of the Burmese. A fleet of British warships and troop transports filled with over 10,000 soldiers navigated the 960 kilometers (600 miles) of the Irrawaddy River northward to the capital city. British naval power easily overcame Burmese defenses at Mandalay and, despite logistical problems and bouts with tropical diseases, by early 1826 British troops had crushed Burmese resistance throughout Lower Burma and in Assam.

The First Anglo-Burmese War officially ended with the signing of the Treaty of Yandabo (24 February 1826): the Burmese relinquished control over Arakan and Tenasserim to the East India Company, paid the British an indemnity of 10 million rupees, recognized the independence of Manipur, agreed not to interfere in Assam and the other border areas, and, finally, permitted the British to station a **Resident** at Ava. In November 1826, King Bagyidaw was forced to conclude a commercial treaty with the Company.

For twenty-five years, King Bagyidaw and his successors, Tharrawaddy (r. 1838-45) and Pagin Min (r. 1845-52), chafed under the stipulations and humiliation of the Yandabo treaty. Obsessed with the desire to exact revenge on the British, Burma's rulers allowed their own governments to deteriorate and become corrupt. Some of this corruption affected British trading interests in Burma, who often exacerbated the conditions in which they operated by exaggerating their own plight to British authorities. In this environment, Lord Dalhousie (1812-60), the Indian governor-general, ordered Commodore Lambert to sail to Rangoon to investigate. Lambert, an advocate of gunboat diplomacy, disregarded Dalhousie's instructions to do his best to avoid an open conflict; the commodore did everything he could to insult the Burmese and to provoke a war. By February 1852, Dalhousie, himself an ardent expansionist, had decided on war. He issued an ultimatum to Pagin Min, knowing the Burmese king could not comply and still retain the throne. By early April the Second Anglo-Burmese War was under way. The British were successful, but rather than fight a protracted war in the jungles of Upper Burma, Dalhousie declared a cease-fire, and subsequently annexed Lower Burma to British India.

The outbreak of the Third Anglo-Burmese War was the result of two events: an enormous fine imposed by the Burmese government under King Thibaw (r. 1878-85) on a British trading firm for allegedly exporting more teak timber than they had paid for, and Thibaw's machinations to secure French support. With pressure mounting from outraged merchant groups and fearful of a Franco-Burmese alliance in Southeast Asia, the Indian governor-general, Lord Dufferin, began the Third Anglo-Burmese War in early November 1885. The war lasted only twenty days. King Thibaw was deposed, and in January 1886, the rest of Burma was annexed by British India, of which it remained a part until 1937. Burma regained its independence in 1948.

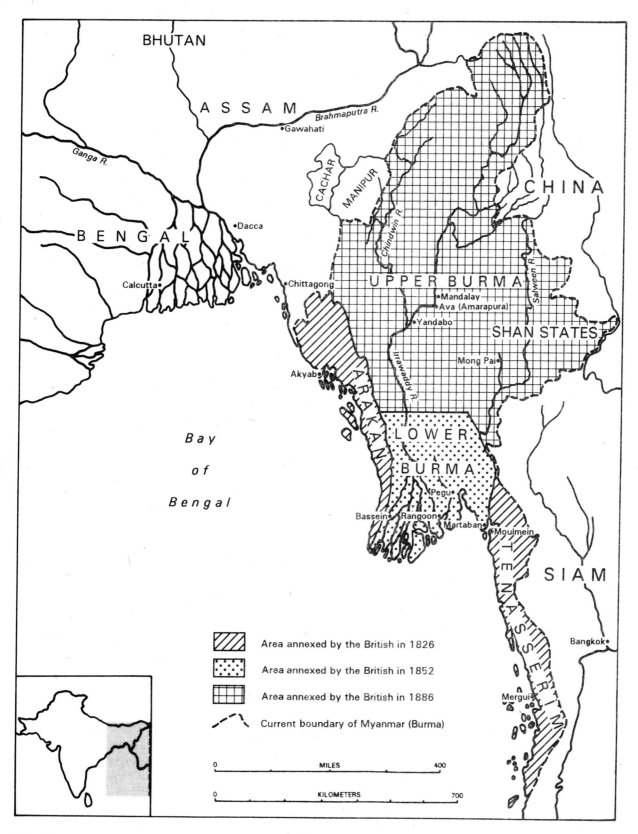

BHUTAN

ASSAM

Brahmaputra R.

•Gawahati

Ganga R.

BENGAL

•Dacca

Calcutta•

CACHAR

MANIPUR

Chindwin R.

CHINA

•Chittagong

UPPER BURMA

•Mandalay

Ava (Amarapura)

•Yandabo

Salween R.

SHAN STATES

Akyab•

Irrawaddy R.

•Mong Pai

A R A K A N

Bay

of

Bengal

LOWER

BURMA

•Pegu

Basseine• •Rangoon

•Martaban

•Moulmein

SIAM

T E N A S S E R I M

•Bangkok

Mergui•

▨ Area annexed by the British in 1826

⬚ Area annexed by the British in 1852

▦ Area annexed by the British in 1886

— — Current boundary of Myanmar (Burma)

0   MILES   400

0   KILOMETERS   700

Map 30 Absorption of Burma, 1824–86

69

31 Anglo-Sikh Wars of 1845-46 and 1848-49

Before his death in 1839, Maharaja Ranjit Singh did not adequately provide for an orderly succession. Consequently, when Ranjit Singh's eldest son, Kharak Singh, ascended to the throne of the Sikh state, he was met with considerable opposition. Kharak was unpopular and was quickly ousted in favor of his own son, Nao Nihal Singh. When Nihal Singh died in a suspicious accident in 1840, he was replaced first by his mother, Maharani Chand Kaur, and then by his uncle, Sher Singh, who had earlier ordered Chand Kaur assassinated.

To gain their support, Sher Singh had made promises to the **Khalsa** that he could not keep. When the promises were not forthcoming, he, too, was assassinated, as was his chief minister, the **Dogra** Dhian Singh. Finally, in 1843, Rani Jhindan, mother of Dalip Singh, Ranjit Singh's grandson, became regent, enlisting the aid of her brother, Jawahar Singh, as advisor. The Khalsa, determined to gain control, killed Jawahar Singh, and assumed de facto control over the affairs of state. The army's **panchayat** soon began to issue orders on its own authority.

Viewing this chaotic political environment, the British, already eager to rid themselves of this last rival on the subcontinent, began to mass troops along the Panjab frontier. In 1838, only 2,500 British troops were stationed along the frontier; by the autumn of 1845, they had over 40,000 troops and ninety-four pieces of field artillery in place. The British also contributed to the chaos by surreptitiously fueling the aspirations of a host of claimants to the Sikh throne.

Angered by the growing power of the British, the Khalsa put pressure on the rani to take action. Unable to exert control over the Khalsa and to enforce restraint, Rani Jhindan authorized them to attack the British across the frontier in December 1845. The outbreak of war was thus caused as much by British provocation as it was by the impetuosity of the Sikh army and the weakness of Rani Jhindan.

The First Anglo-Sikh War lasted only three months. Numerically, the two opposing forces were roughly equivalent in strength, but in the end, British forces proved superior. Four pitched battles took place over the course of the war at Mudki (18 December), Firozshah (21-22 December), Aliwal (28 January 1846), and Sobraon (10 February). Despite their valiant efforts, each battle was a Sikh loss, and by 12 February, it was clear that the war was over. On 9 March 1846, the Sikhs signed the Treaty of Lahore. The Sikhs were forced to cede the Jalandhar Doab (an area of nearly 18,500 kilometers/11,500 square miles) to the British; pay a war indemnity of 15 million rupees, 10 million of which was paid by the cession of Kashmir and Hazara (the British subsequently sold Kashmir to the Jammu maharaja, Gulab Singh, for cash); reduce the Khalsa to 20,000 infantry and 12,000 cavalry—a reduction of over 50 percent; and accept the stationing of a British Resident (Sir Henry Lawrence), with a force of British troops, at Lahore. Fearing a quagmire, the British avoided outright annexation, favoring instead to allow Panjab to retain its independence, but with greater British influence over its affairs.

Peace did not last long. The Royal Court at Lahore resented the treaty settlement and the sale of Kashmir to Gulab Singh. The Khalsa, too, were unhappy; despite their initial defeat, and partial disbandment, the Khalsa maintained their fighting spirit and planned to take revenge on the British. The greatest problem for the British was the rising discontent of recently demobilized Sikh soldiers. With many unable to find suitable employment, they posed a serious threat to Panjab's new status quo.

In April 1848, Mulraj, who had been recently replaced as governor of Multan, attacked and killed two British envoys who were escorting his successor to his new post. Rallying a force of malcontented Sikhs to his cause, Mulraj occupied the fortress at Multan. The British collected a small local force, laid siege to Multan, and awaited the arrival of Sikh reinforcements from Lahore. When the reinforcements arrived, their commander, Sher Singh, took the rebels' side and led his troops against the British instead. The local rebellion at Multan became the Second Anglo-Sikh War.

This second war, like the first, lasted only a few months. By February 1849, the Sikhs had been defeated. This time, however, Sikh independence was permanently destroyed. Indian governor-general Lord Dalhousie pensioned off Maharaja Dalip Singh, then a minor, and sent him to live in England. Dalhousie then ordered the total annexation of Panjab.

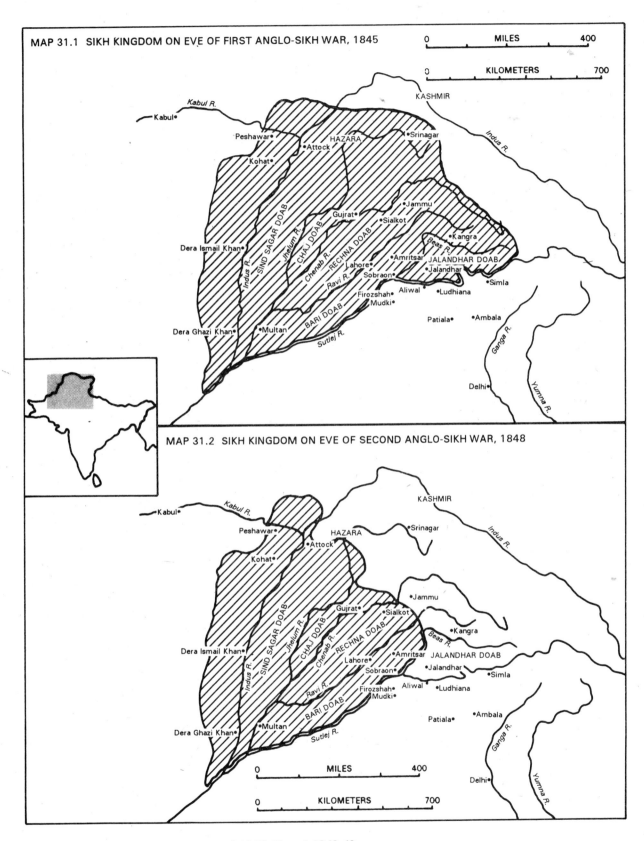

Maps 31.1-31.2 Anglo-Sikh Wars of 1845-46 and 1848-49

71

32   India During the War of 1857-58

On Sunday, 10 May 1857, sepoys of the Meerut Cantonment rose in rebellion against their British officers. The spark which ignited this rebellion (or Indian "mutiny" as it is still called by some) was sepoy anger over some eighty-five of their comrades having been punished for refusing to use their new Enfield rifles. The British introduced the Enfield because it was more accurate and effective than the old smooth-bore muskets which most sepoys had been using, but a rumor had spread within the cantonment that the rifle's cartridges, whose paper ends had to be bitten off prior to loading, were packed in a mixture of beef and pork tallow. As cows were sacred to Hindus and pork abhorred by Muslims, any such mixture of fats would have been offensive to members of both religions. To the sepoys, the rumor seemed to confirm many of the horrible suspicions they had about the British: in their minds, the British were attempting to destroy their religions and their society.

The rebellion of the sepoys at Meerut was only symptomatic of deeper grievances many Indians had against British rule. Many Indians, both Hindus and Muslims, objected to the political high-handedness of Britons like Clive, Wellesley and, more recently, Dalhousie. In 1849, Dalhousie annexed Jaitpur and Sambalpur; in 1850, Baghat; in 1852, Udaipur; in 1853, Jhansi; in 1854, Nagpur; and in 1856, Awadh. These states were all taken under the **doctrine of lapse**, a policy considered unjust by many Indian rulers.

For many Indians, economic and social conditions had also worsened under British rule. New revenue systems impoverished many cultivators, while the sudden loss of their lands due to "lapse" forced many prosperous jagirdars into penury as well. Many Indians were angered by British interference in the social order. The abolition of female infanticide, thuggee, and sati, while beneficial, raised concerns among Indians that the British would not stop there in their efforts to "reform" Indian society.

Increased Christian missionary activity in India after 1839 began to take its toll. Missionaries often denounced Indian religious beliefs while trying to gain converts. Missionary schools imparted Western knowledge, but did not restrict that knowledge to non-religious subjects. Proselytization also took place in prisons and in military cantonments. Finally, many sepoys suspected that in being asked to participate in the East India Company's overseas expeditions, such as to Burma in 1852, the British were attempting to make them **outcastes**.

After leaving Meerut, the rebellious sepoys marched south to Delhi to convince the Mughal emperor, Bahadur Shah II—who had no real power and was living on a Company pension—to lead them against the British. Unfortunately for the sepoys, Bahadur Shah II proved an ineffective and reluctant leader and much momentum was lost. Nevertheless, news of the rebellion did spread quickly throughout the Gangetic plain, prompting similar rebel outbreaks among the sepoys at Lucknow and Cawnpore (Kanpur), and among the peasant population in the rural Gangetic plain. By the end of the summer of 1857, the British had lost control over much of northern India, and the rebel leadership had passed into the hands of Nana Sahib (the adopted son of the ex-peshwa, Baji Rao II) and Rani Lakshmi Bai of Jhansi. Despite such capable leadership, the rebels suffered from a lack of unity. Some rebels rallied to Bahadur Shah II, some to the newly proclaimed peshwa, still others to the rani of Jhansi. No attempt was made at concerted action among the rebel forces; this lack of unity and of purpose proved to be their undoing. On 14 September, Delhi was recaptured, followed by Lucknow in November and Cawnpore in December. Fresh British troops arrived from overseas, and from South India, an area which had been untouched by the rebellion. Indian allies, such as the Sikhs and Gurkhas, also supported the British in their efforts to regain control of northern India.

As the British began to recapture areas in northern India, the rebellion began to collapse due to the defeat of its leaders: Bahadur Shah II was captured at Delhi and deported to Rangoon. His sons and grandsons were brutally executed without trial, thus effectively ending the Mughal dynasty; the rani of Jhansi was killed in battle; Tantia Tope, the peshwa's general, was captured and later executed, while the peshwa himself fled to Nepal and disappeared. By July 1858, the war was at an end; the British had won. The war was not, however, without long-term effects. Company rule in India was replaced by Crown rule—the British parliament now assumed full control over British Indian affairs. Atrocities committed by both sides dramatically and permanently altered Indo-British relations: Britons, for example, became more aloof from Indian society, an attitude which persisted until Indian Independence in 1947.

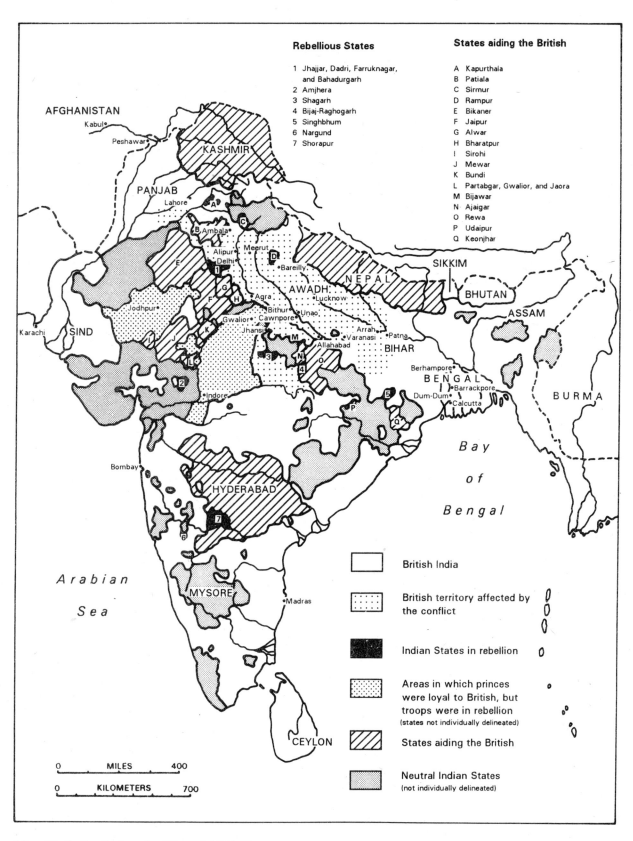

Rebellious States

1 Jhajjar, Dadri, Farruknagar,
and Bahadurgarh
2 Amjhera
3 Shagarh
4 Bijaj-Raghogarh
5 Singhbhum
6 Nargund
7 Shorapur

States aiding the British

A Kapurthala
B Patiala
C Sirmur
D Rampur
E Bikaner
F Jaipur
G Alwar
H Bharatpur
I Sirohi
J Mewar
K Bundi
L Partabgar, Gwalior, and Jaora
M Bijawar
N Ajaigar
O Rewa
P Udaipur
Q Keonjhar

AFGHANISTAN

Kabul

Peshawar

KASHMIR

PANJAB

Lahore

Ambala

Alipur

Meerut

Delhi

Bareilly

NEPAL

SIKKIM

BHUTAN

AWADH

Lucknow

Agra

Bithur

Unao

Gwalior

Cawnpore

Jhansi

Arrah

Varanasi

Patna

Allahabad

BIHAR

ASSAM

Jodhpur

Karachi

SIND

Berhampore

BENGAL

BURMA

Barrackpore

Dum-Dum

Calcutta

Bay

of

Bengal

Bombay

HYDERABAD

Arabian

Sea

MYSORE

Madras

CEYLON

British India

British territory affected by
the conflict

Indian States in rebellion

Areas in which princes
were loyal to British, but
troops were in rebellion
(states not individually delineated)

States aiding the British

Neutral Indian States
(not individually delineated)

0   MILES   400

0   KILOMETERS   700

Map 32 India during the War of 1857-58

33 Britain, Russia, and the Great Game

Once the British established a solid foothold in South Asia, they began to worry about losing it. By the end of the eighteenth century, the British most feared the French who, under Napoleon Bonaparte (1769-1821), twice attempted—in 1798 and again in 1801, with the aid of Russia—to send an invasion army to India. Both attempts failed, but the willingness of the Russians to contemplate an attack on India, coupled with continued Russian expansion in Asia, made the British reevaluate their thinking. After 1819, when Britain became the paramount power on the subcontinent, and Russia had expanded into Central Asia, bringing it even closer to India, the Bear began to loom large in the minds of British strategic planners. Thereafter, all Russian actions in the Central Asian region, whether military or diplomatic, tended to be interpreted as part of a concerted Russian effort to unseat Britain from South Asia. The British saw their struggle with Russia as a "Great Game," a zero-sum competition in which a win for one side was a loss for the other; it was a game Britain was determined to win.

According to historian Malcolm Yapp, the primary motive of London-based British foreign policymakers in dealing with Persia, Afghanistan, and Sind until 1849 was not the external defense of India, as most historians have long since claimed, but rather an attempt to use India as a pawn in maintaining the balance of power on the continent. By using India in this way, Britain hoped to avoid the need for continued military intervention in Europe by drawing away first French, and later Russian, attention from Europe. Meanwhile, British rulers in Calcutta were faced with the very real difficulty of reconciling their own genuine desire to defend India from external attack with this new aspect of British foreign policy. Knowing that London would be unsupportive of any external attack thesis, however, British strategists in India disguised their external defense efforts by drawing upon London's fears of possible increased Russian involvement in Europe (Yapp 1980). Following a well-heeled London policy of encouraging the establishment of "buffer states" as a means of maintaining the balance of power, British planners in India sought to develop Afghanistan as just such a buffer state; it could then serve as a check on further Russian expansion in Central Asia.

After the Russo-Persian War (1826-28), the Persian government for the first time allowed Russian diplomats to attend the court in Teheran, leading to British-Indian fears that Persia would aid the Russians in extending their dominion to Afghanistan. These fears were exacerbated after 1835, when Persia launched an abortive attempt to capture the Afghan city of Herat. The Government of India eventually retaliated against Persia in 1838, but British-Indian policy now sought to ensure the independence of Afghanistan. Rather than engage the Afghans in a treaty, however, Lord Auckland, the governor-general, chose to make threats instead—threats which led ultimately to the disastrous and costly First Anglo-Afghan War (1838-42).

In the 1870s, further Russian expansion, seemingly in the direction of Afghanistan, and the Russian invasion of the Balkans (1877) led **Forward School** advocates in India to attempt to reassert British influence in Afghanistan. Meanwhile, the Afghani amir, Sher Ali, was busy playing the British against the Russians, a game which the British in India did not appreciate. In late 1878, the viceroy, Lord Lytton, sent an invasion force into Afghanistan, precipitating the Second Anglo-Afghan War (1878-80). British forces were victorious, and Sher Ali was deposed. His nephew and successor, Abdur Rahman Khan (r. 1880-1901), became amir. In response to British action in Afghanistan, Russia annexed additional Central Asian territories.

By the 1890s, the authorities in Calcutta were anxious to establish firmly demarcated boundaries for Afghanistan to discourage further Russian encroachment to the north and to legitimize their own annexation of territory along the Indo-Afghan frontier. The amir agreed, grudgingly, and Afghanistan was constituted as a geographically definable "state" (1893).

Russia continued its push southward, but avoided encroaching on Afghanistan. With the signing of the Anglo-Russian Convention (1907), a diplomatic arrangement which divided Persia into spheres of British and Russian influence and in which Russia recognized Afghanistan as a British client state, the perceived "Russian menace" faded. One element of the Great Game, however, remained: British machinations in Afghanistan. These intrigues ended only after another Afghani amir, Amanullah Khan, initiated the Third Anglo-Afghan War (1919). Although the war was fought to a stalemate, Britain forever renounced its interventionist policy in Afghanistan. The Great Game was at an end.

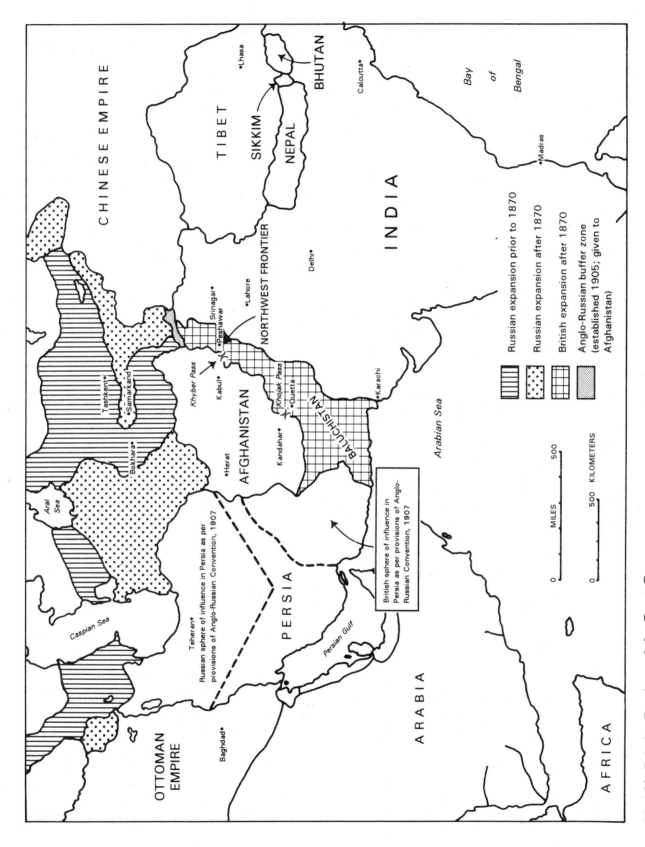

Map 33 Britain, Russia, and the Great Game

34   India and Its Contributions to the First World War

India's contributions to Great Britain's war effort during the First World War, both in men and matériel, were immense. On August 4, 1914, Britain declared war on Germany and in less than four weeks, the Government of India sent abroad the first of what would become many hundreds of thousands of Indian troops to take part in the war. During the next four years, Indian troops saw action on the battlefields of Belgium; northern France; Gallipoli and Salonika; Aden, Mesopotamia, the Gulf of Oman, Palestine and Persia; and Cameroon, East Africa, and Somaliland. By 1918, over one million Indians had served overseas as enlisted men or officers. Massive recruitment drives and a radical change in recruitment policy in 1917 resulted in a dramatic increase in the size of the Army in India from its pre-war level. In 1914, the Army in India consisted of only 155,423 combat troops and 45,660 non-combat troops. By 1918, the Army in India had swelled to 826,855 combat troops and 445,582 non-combat troops, an increase of over 530 percent. In terms of the number of personnel contributed from all parts of the British Empire, India ranked second only to the British Isles.

The great majority of Indian troops sent overseas—over one-half million by 1918—were involved in the Mesopotamian theater. The British had three main objectives in attacking the Ottoman Empire from the southeast. First, the British believed that an attack in Mesopotamia would divert Ottoman forces from a potentially damaging attack on Egypt and the Suez Canal; second, the British hoped to secure the Anglo-Persian Oil Company's pipeline; and third, they hoped to stimulate the Arabs to attack their Ottoman overlords. The campaign began in early November 1914 and, after initial quick victories at Basra, Qurna, Amara, Nasiriya, and Kut, an Anglo-Indian expeditionary force was poised to strike at Baghdad. The attack on Baghdad, which came in late October 1915, proved a disaster and Anglo-Indian forces were forced to retreat back to Kut where they, in turn, were besieged by the Turks. After five months, and high casualties, the Anglo-Indian force was forced to surrender. A renewed campaign began in October 1916 and Baghdad was eventually captured by the Anglo-Indian expeditionary force in March 1917. Although Anglo-Indian military activities in Mesopotamia were ultimately successful, the campaign resulted in the highest death tolls among Indian troops during the war—29,555 of the war total of 53,486 killed.

In addition to personnel, India contributed huge amounts of war matériel and supplies to the British war effort. Immediately prior to the war, India imported from the United Kingdom, the Austro-Hungarian Empire, Belgium, Germany, the United States, and Japan most of the manufactured items it needed. Cotton textiles, wool textiles, machinery and millwork, iron and steel, as well as railway plant and rolling stock, comprised India's principal imports. As might be expected, the United Kingdom was the single largest supplier of finished goods to India. When the United Kingdom declared war on Germany, it found itself not only unable to export to India the volume of goods it had supplied in the past, but it also required that India increase its overall economic output of manufactured goods in order to meet wartime demand. Because the Indian economy was purposely not structured to produce mass quantities of manufactured items, it took nearly two years for it to develop that capability. Once it had, by early 1917, India was able to supply a greater percentage of its own wartime needs and also help supply goods for the overall British war effort. To help coordinate, control, and promote greater efficiency in war production, the Government of India established the Indian Munitions Board in March 1917. Under the direction of the board, India produced military ordnance, clothing, and leather goods for troops overseas; shipped railway locomotives, cars, and track to theaters in East Africa and Mesopotamia; provided nearly 250,000 tons of timber for construction and aircraft use; and managed pig-iron and steel products from the Tata Iron and Steel Works in Jamshedpur, India's largest, for use in war production.

India's contributions aided the Allied war effort considerably. In addition to the £229 million in direct military contributions and loans, Britain's largest dependency provided £367 million in war debt financing to Great Britain. India's total contribution to the Allied war effort was £596 million or over 7.5 percent of the £7,852 million the Allies spent on the war. In recognition of its significant contributions to the Allied war effort, the British Cabinet afforded India a place at the Paris Peace Conference of 1919; Indian delegates signed the Treaty of Versailles and, as a result, India became a founding member of the League of Nations.

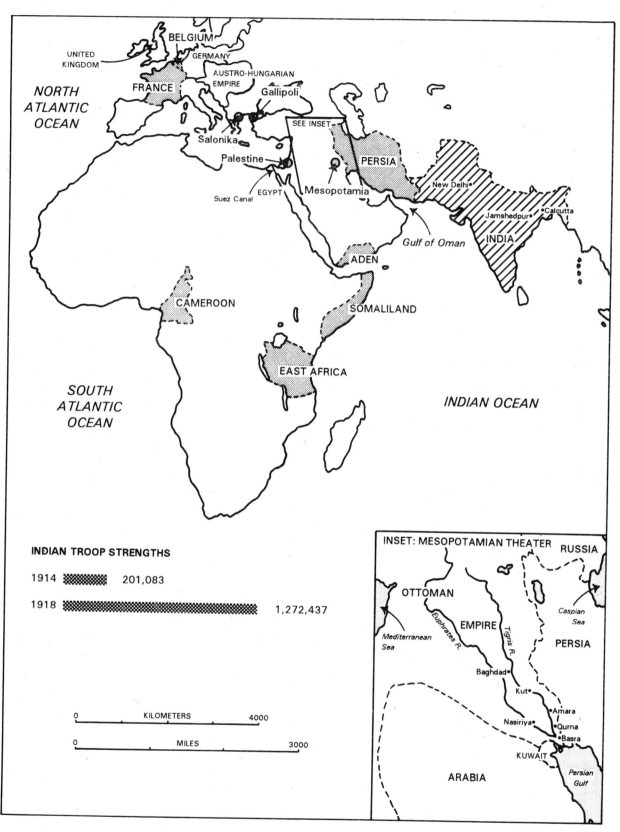

Map 34 India and Its Contributions to the First World War

Within the map:

NORTH ATLANTIC OCEAN

UNITED KINGDOM

BELGIUM

GERMANY

FRANCE

AUSTRO-HUNGARIAN EMPIRE

Gallipoli

Salonika

Palestine

Suez Canal

EGYPT

SEE INSET

PERSIA

Mesopotamia

New Delhi

Jamshedpur

Calcutta

INDIA

Gulf of Oman

ADEN

SOMALILAND

CAMEROON

EAST AFRICA

SOUTH ATLANTIC OCEAN

INDIAN OCEAN

INDIAN TROOP STRENGTHS

1914   201,083

1918   1,272,437

0   KILOMETERS   4000

0   MILES   3000

INSET: MESOPOTAMIAN THEATER   RUSSIA

OTTOMAN

Mediterranean Sea

Euphrates R.

EMPIRE

Tigris R.

Caspian Sea

PERSIA

Baghdad

Kut

Amara

Nasiriya

Qurna

Basra

KUWAIT

Persian Gulf

ARABIA

35   Princely India, 1858-1947

Following the end of the War of 1857-58, the Parliament of Great Britain passed the Government of India Act (1858), which abolished the East India Company's charter and transferred control over all Company possessions in South Asia to the British Crown. Later that year, Queen Victoria's proclamation informed Indians of the change in the structures and policy of British administration in India.

One of the most important changes involved India's princes. So long as they remained loyal to the British Crown, the queen proclaimed, the rights, privileges, and traditions of the princes would be "scrupulously maintained." Earlier treaty obligations which forced Indian states to surrender their sovereignty over external affairs, such as foreign policy, also protected them from future British interference in their internal affairs. British fears of another rebellion thus effectively secured princely positions and authority.

British retention of the Indian princes also made economic, strategic, and political sense. First, conquering the remaining princely states would have been an expensive venture, one whose high cost would not have been offset by any potential increase in land revenues. Second, the princely states offered the British military support in times of need. This idea would later be formally embodied in the formation of the Imperial Service Corps in the late 1880s. Third, the Indian princes, their loyalty pledged to the suzerain British power, served to legitimize that power. Finally, the personal behavior and rule of some of the more despotic princes served as useful comparisons to "benevolent" British rule in India.

Numbering nearly six hundred, the Indian states varied tremendously in size, location, terrain, and wealth. Their rulers also varied. Hindu Rajput princes dominated the deserts of Rajputana, while Muslim rulers, such as the nizam of Hyderabad, controlled the highlands of the Deccan Plateau. These same princes—Hindus, Muslims, and Sikhs, Rajputs, Marathas, and ex-Mughal mansabdars—also represented a multitude of personal interests and political attitudes, which prevented the British from dealing with them in any systematic or uniform manner. While some rulers were most concerned with their treaty rights and their own preceptions of internal sovereignty, many others squabbled over seemingly mundane matters, such as the honors bestowed upon them by the British, most especially over the number of gun salutes each ruler received during formal and semi-formal occasions.

Until the First World War, Indian states maintained considerable political isolation from British India. Most contact was largely through interaction at formal heads-of-state gatherings and with local Political Agents, or through correspondence between the individual princes and the Government of India. After the outbreak of the war, however, Indian princes became directly involved in the affairs of greater India. Nearly all of the Indian princes pledged their support for the Empire in its conflict with Germany, and over two dozen of the largest Indian states offered the Government of India the use of their own Imperial Service Corps troops.

This princely involvement continued unabated throughout the war. The maharaja of Bikaner, perhaps the most visible of the Indian princes at that time, was selected by Britain's prime minister, David Lloyd George, to serve in a consultative capacity on the War Cabinet; the maharaja also took part in the Paris Peace Conference of 1919 and was even one of the Indian delegation signatories of the Treaty of Versailles.

With the war's conclusion, the Indian princes continued their political activity by establishing, under British auspices, the Chamber of Princes in early 1921. The Chamber consisted of representatives of the princely states and had the British viceroy as its president. The Chamber of Princes had no executive powers of its own and acted largely as a consultative body to the Government of India. Despite its lack of specific effectiveness, the Chamber proved its overall worth in drawing the Indian princes into the turbulent political arena of India during the interwar period.

Once India and Pakistan gained their independence in 1947, each of the native Indian states were offered the choice of acceding to either India or Pakistan. For the most part, these accessions took place without incident, although notable exceptions exist in the case of Hyderabad, whose accession took place only after the Indian army invaded that state, and of Kashmir, which became a victim of conflicting claims by both India and Pakistan.

Although the Indian states were alternately requested or forced into union with either India or Pakistan, the real death of princely India came when the Twenty-sixth Amendment Act (1971) abolished the princes' titles, privileges, and privy purses.

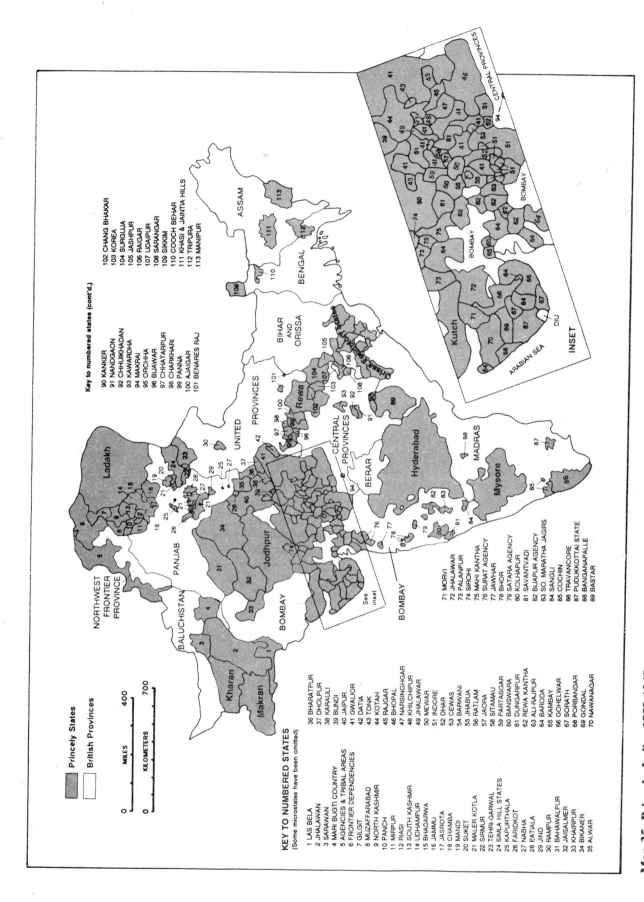

Map 35 Princely India, 1858-1947

Princely States

British Provinces

MILES 0 400

KILOMETERS 0 700

KEY TO NUMBERED STATES
(Some microstates have been omitted)

1 LAS BELA
2 JHALAWAN
3 SARAWAN
4 MARI BUGTI COUNTRY
5 AGENCIES & TRIBAL AREAS
6 FRONTIER DEPENDENCIES
7 GILGIT
8 MUZAFFARABAD
9 NORTH KASHMIR
10 PANCH
11 MIRPUR
12 RIASI
13 SOUTH KASHMIR
14 UDHAMPUR
15 BHADARWA
16 JAMMU
17 JASROTA
18 CHAMBA
19 MANDI
20 SUKET
21 MALER KOTLA
22 SIRMUR
23 TEHRI-GARWAL
24 SIMLA HILL STATES
25 KAPURTHALA
26 FARIDKOT
27 NABHA
28 PATIALA
29 JIND
30 RAMPUR
31 BAHAWALPUR
32 JAISALMER
33 KHAIRPUR
34 BIKANER
35 ALWAR

36 BHARATPUR
37 DHOLPUR
38 KARAULI
39 BUNDI
40 JAIPUR
41 GWALIOR
42 DATIA
43 TONK
44 KOTAH
45 RAJGAR
46 BHOPAL
47 NARSINGHGAR
48 KHILCHIPUR
49 JHALAWAR
50 MEWAR
51 INDORE
52 DHAR
53 CEWAS
54 BARWANI
55 JHABUA
56 RATLAM
57 JAORA
58 SITAMAU
59 PARTABGAR
60 BANSWARA
61 DUNGARPUR
62 REWA KANTHA
63 ALI-RAJPUR
64 BARODA
65 KAMBAY
66 GOHELWAR
67 SORATH
68 PORBANDAR
69 GONDAL
70 NAWANAGAR

71 MORVI
72 JHALAWAR
73 PALANPUR
74 SIROHI
75 MAHI KANTHA
76 SURAT AGENCY
77 JAWHAR
78 BHOR
79 SATARA AGENCY
80 KOLHAPUR
81 SAVANTVADI
82 BIJAPUR AGENCY
83 SO. MARATHA JAGIRS
84 SANGLI
85 COCHIN
86 TRAVANCORE
87 PUDUKKOTTAI STATE
88 BANGANAPALLE
89 BASTAR

Key to numbered states (cont'd.)

90 KANKER
91 NANDGAON
92 CHHUIKHADAN
93 KAWARDHA
94 MAKRAI
95 ORCHHA
96 BIJAWAR
97 CHHATARPUR
98 CHARKHARI
99 PANNA
100 AJAIGAR
101 BENARES RAJ

102 CHANG BHAKAR
103 KOREA
104 SURGUJA
105 JASHPUR
106 RAIGAR
107 UDAIPUR
108 SARANGAR
109 SIKKIM
110 COOCH BEHAR
111 KHASI & JAINTIA HILLS
112 TRIPURA
113 MANIPUR

36   South Asia and the Second World War

On 3 September 1939, the viceroy, Lord Linlithgow, announced that India, like Great Britain, was at war with Germany. Educated Indian opinion was divided on the issue. Many did not support Great Britain as openly—or at all—as they had at the outbreak of war in 1914. The Indian National Congress, for example, was outraged that it had not been consulted prior to India's declaration of war. Although in principle they supported Britain's war effort, Congress leaders refused to cooperate with the Government of India unless India was granted independence. The British government was unwilling to grant that concession, however, and in October 1939, Congress showed its displeasure by withdrawing from all provincial ministries. In September 1940, Congress, under Gandhi's direction, launched a **satyagraha** to agitate against the British. Thousands of satyagrahis were arrested over the next year, including Jawaharlal Nehru. Subhas Chandra Bose, who favored the violent overthrow of British rule in India, was also arrested, but he later escaped and fled to Germany. On 3 December 1941, the Government of India released the Congress protestors in the hope that they would now support the British war effort; this hope took on greater urgency after Japan entered the war on 7 December. By mid-February 1942, the Japanese had conquered much of East Asia, including the "impregnable" British fortress at Singapore, and were on the verge of attacking India itself. Fearing further disasters in Asia, Winston Churchill authorized Sir Stafford Cripps to undertake a mission to India to negotiate with the Congress. Cripps could make only postwar promises, and after Congress rejected his offer as insufficient, it launched the "Quit India" movement; soon thereafter, its leaders and some 60,000 followers were jailed—this time, for the rest of the war.

Despite domestic civil unrest in India, the all-volunteer Army in India was still loyal to the British and willingly chose to aid Britain in the war. But India's armed forces faced serious difficulties. Army expansion required an increase in officer candidates, the majority of which would have come from the class of Indians who were by then supporting Congress; therefore, officers were drawn from Britain, a process which took some time. In addition, during the interwar period, the army had not been modernized, i.e., mechanized, and was thus at a disadvantage at the outbreak of war. In 1939, the Army in India totaled less than 240,000 troops, including British units. A force of this size was appropriate for maintaining internal peace and for fending off the initial attack of a foreign power, but was woefully inadequate for imperial defense, especially in light of recent technological developments which made just sheer numbers of troops, without proper equipment, virtually useless. Moreover, the British government failed to take full advantage of the lull in the fighting in Europe between October 1939 and May 1940—a period called the "Phony War"—to expand and modernize the Army in India. Only after Hitler resumed his attacks in Europe, and the consequent fall of France in June 1940, did it become clear to Britain that the rapid expansion and modernization of the Army in India was not only necessary, but vital.

During the war, South Asian troops saw action in several theaters, including Europe, East and North Africa, and Southwest and Southeast Asia. There were nearly 180,000 casualties, including over 24,000 killed. The bulk of Indian forces (over 700,000) fought in Southeast Asia, mostly in Burma; they comprised nearly 75 percent of all Allied forces in that theater. As Japanese forces drove westward into Southeast Asia, British and French forces crumbled. Over 60,000 Indian troops captured by the Japanese at Singapore became the core of Subhas Bose's Indian National Army, a force which aided the Japanese against the British. By mid-1942, Japanese forces had captured all of Burma and the Allies were compelled to retreat to Imphal, India. In addition to the tens of thousands of retreating troops, nearly 500,000 Indians fled Burma—over 50,000 did not survive the rigors of the trip.

From May 1942 until November 1943, when the second Arakan campaign began, Allied efforts in the China-Burma-India theater were stifled by the inability of the Allies to develop an adequate plan for renewing the fight against the Japanese. Finally, in November 1943, after that year's monsoon, Allied forces pushed into Burma, capturing large portions of Arakan. In February 1944, the Japanese, bent on invading India, tried to outflank Allied forces by maneuvering around them to the north. After making good progress northward, and into Assam, Japanese forces were suddenly stopped and routed by Indian troops. Although the war in Burma was far from over, the defeat of Japanese troops in Arakan foretold a chain of further Allied (and Indian) successes in that theater. By early summer 1945, Anglo-Indian forces had recaptured the rest of Burma; the Japanese threat to India was over.

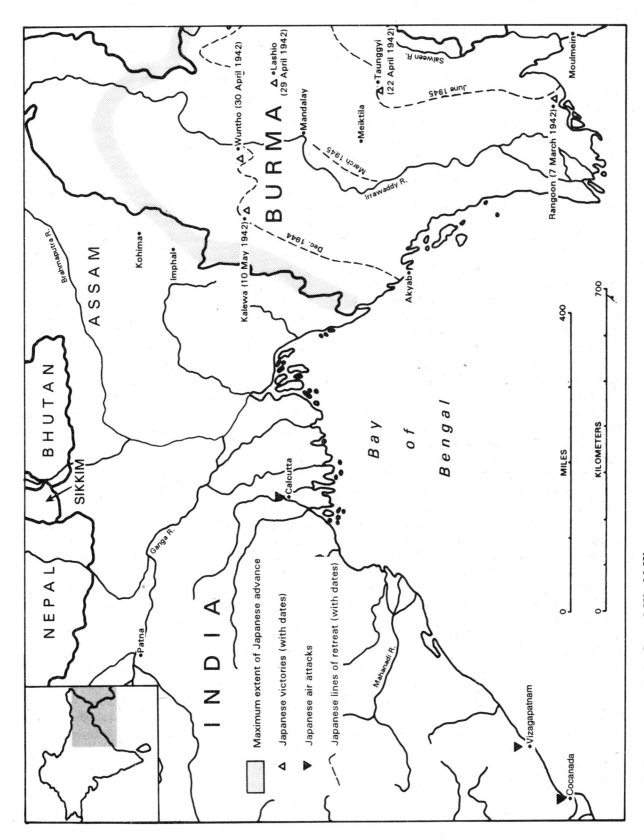

Map 36 South Asia and the Second World War

81

37 Partition of India, 1947

On August 15, 1947, the British Raj ended, British India became independent, and two new dominions, Pakistan and India, were born. Two days later, a special boundary commission, which had been appointed only one month earlier, publicly announced the final form the partition of the subcontinent would take. None of the parties involved, neither the Indian National Congress, the Muslim League, nor the communities and areas affected by the partition awards, were satisfied with the results.

The division of the subcontinent into two separate dominions had been the goal of Muhammad Ali Jinnah (1875-1948), president of the Muslim League. Jinnah, a prominent Bombay barrister and politician, ironically began his career as a champion of Hindu-Muslim unity, but the post-World War I growth of the Indian National Congress and the rise of Mohandas Gandhi as its leader made Jinnah skeptical about that unity. He believed that the Indian National Congress under Gandhi's leadership had become a Hindu-oriented organization and could not, therefore, address the needs of Muslims. By 1940, Jinnah was convinced of the irreconcilable differences between Hindus and Muslims; he believed that the two groups were really two nations and that a unified, post-Independence India would only mean the replacement of the British Raj with a Hindu Raj. From 1940 until Independence in 1947, Jinnah worked tirelessly, gaining more and more support among Indian Muslims for his goal of creating Pakistan. In the end, he was influential enough to compel both the British and the Indian National Congress to accept a partitioned India.

If Jinnah was responsible for the birth of Pakistan, then the man responsible for its peculiar geography was Sir Cyril Radcliffe, a British legal expert. Sir Cyril was selected to head the boundary commission based on the fact that he knew virtually nothing of India, had never before been to the sub-continent, and that he would, accordingly, be impartial in the final partition of British India. The various parties knew in advance that the main criterion of the awards would be to grant those areas of India with Muslim majorities to Pakistan; the rest would remain part of a truncated India. Pakistan would, therefore, consist of two wings, East and West, separated by over 1,400 kilometers (over 860 miles) of Indian territory between them.

The great bulk of the two wings of Pakistan were fairly easily delineated because they consisted mainly of districts containing Muslim majorities. The critical problem facing the Radcliffe Commission, however, was where to draw the boundaries between India and Pakistan in those provinces and districts where there was no clear-cut **communal** majority. This issue was especially dire in Panjab, where many districts and communities were interspersed with Hindus, Muslims, and Sikhs; where no awarded dividing line would be satisfactory to all; and where bloody, and often brutal, communal violence had already erupted in the months preceding the anticipated Radcliffe announcement.

Eight Indian High Court jurists aided Sir Cyril on the commission, but the responsibility of making the final dispensations of territory in Panjab fell on his shoulders alone. His decisions resulted in a divided Panjab: 62 percent of the land area and 55 percent of the total Panjabi population were awarded to Pakistan. Overnight, Hindus, Muslims, and Sikhs found themselves trapped on both sides of the border in countries potentially hostile to their respective religions. An estimated 10 to 15 million people crossed the border in the two months following Partition. Many Hindus inside Pakistan gathered their families and a few possessions and sought safe haven in India. Indian Muslims did the same before joining their Islamic compatriots in Pakistan. Sikhs faced the task of deciding which of the two countries would be the least antipathetic toward their religion.

Huge columns of refugees streamed over the border in both directions, often within sight of each other. The mass migration of millions of people during that blistering summer of 1947 was accompanied also by another, more terrible human tragedy. Thousands of Hindus, Muslims, and Sikhs, who for decades had lived fairly peacefully together in Panjab, were suddenly motivated by their anger and frustration over partition to maim, rape, and kill in brutal and, often, horrifying ways. The border was patrolled by a police force of only 50,000 men—insufficient to protect the refugees from the terror and inhumanity they inflicted on one another. As a result, an estimated one million people were killed in communal clashes in the wake of Partition.

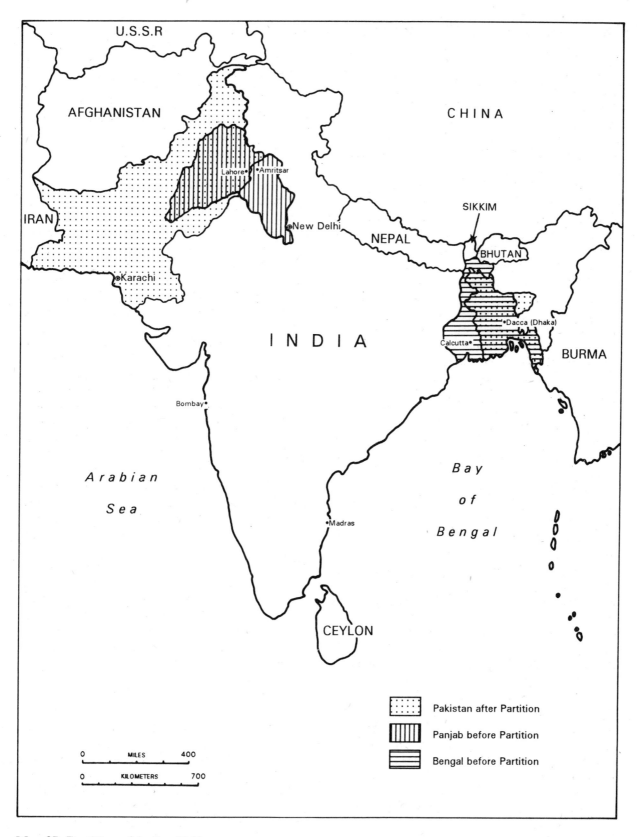

Map 37 Partition of India, 1947

38 Military Conflict and Rivalry in South Asia since 1947

Four major military conflicts have occurred in South Asia since the partition of the subcontinent in 1947. Three have involved India and Pakistan; a fourth, India and China.

The First Indo-Pakistani Conflict began in 1947, just weeks after Partition. The proximate cause of the conflict was a dispute over Kashmir. The maharaja of Kashmir, Hari Singh, was a Hindu, but 75 percent of his subjects were Muslim. When the time came for the maharaja to accede to either Pakistan or India, he wavered, hoping to remain independent. An internal rebellion, aided by Pakistani tribesmen, forced his hand; he quickly acceded to India and asked for military support. Indian forces intervened and prevented the capture of Srinagar, but could not force the Pakistanis out; the conflict ended in stalemate in 1949 and the military "line of control" has become the de facto boundary. Kashmir remains a continuing point of friction between India and Pakistan.

In 1962, India fought a short war with the People's Republic of China (PRC). Tensions between the two countries over their disputed border had been building for over three years. The war was initiated by the Chinese, who struck along India's northeastern border as cover for the seizure of territory in Ladakh where, unbeknownst to the Indians, the Chinese had built a strategic highway, linking the provinces of Tibet and Xinjiang. The attack shocked Nehru, who believed that India and the PRC could resolve their differences peacefully. The Chinese obviously did not share Nehru's idealism. In their view, India was the inheritor of a boundary unfairly thrust upon China by the British. The Chinese also resented India's position as advocate for the developing world—a position which the Chinese felt was rightly theirs. Chinese aspirations quickly became reality as their troops easily defeated Indian forces in engagement after engagement. Not until the PRC had proven its point did Chinese forces withdraw to pre-1959 lines of control and end the war. Subsequent efforts to resolve the Indo-Chinese border dispute have failed, but since 1962 it has remained peaceful, with only occasional minor border incidents (in a partial attempt to strengthen its strategic position along its eastern wing, India in 1975 formally annexed and made a state of Sikkim, an Indian protectorate since 1947).

In early 1965, a dispute over the demarcation of the Indo-Pakistani border through the **Rann** of Kutch, led to the outbreak of open conflict. After U.S.-built Pakistani tanks penetrated more than ten miles into what India claimed as its own territory in the Rann, Pakistan's prime minister, Muhammad Ayub Khan, asked for a ceasefire to settle the boundary dispute under United Nations auspices. Over the next few months, the ceasefire was violated over 2,000 times and each side exchanged volleys in a heated war of words. At the end of August 1965, Indian forces crossed into Pakistan-held Kashmir, a move reciprocated by Pakistan farther south. The Second Indo-Pakistani Conflict had begun; it did not last long. By the end of September, with both sides running low on U.S.-made ammunition, Indian tanks lay just three miles east of Lahore. Although Pakistan had captured more territory than had India, the overall military victory belonged to India. By late February 1966, Soviet mediation brought the conflict officially to an end.

The Third Indo-Pakistani Conflict erupted in late November 1971, when India intervened militarily in East Pakistan as West Pakistan attempted to crush a bid for Bangladeshi independence (see Map 41). India's intervention proved decisive. By mid-December, Pakistani forces in the east surrendered and the new state of Bangladesh was born. Pakistan's defeat was a major blow: with the severance of its east wing, Pakistan lost nearly 15 percent of its total land area, and slightly over half of its population. In addition, the war took a heavy toll on its economy and armed forces. For India the conflict was a victory: it became the dominant power on the subcontinent.

In addition to open conflict, military rivalry between India and Pakistan has also been exacerbated by their respective defense policies and by the disparity of size between them. Pakistan has sought to balance India's power on the subcontinent by maintaining an outside military alliance with the United States, by fostering friendly relations with the PRC, and, recently, by developing a nuclear capability. This latter move was precipitated by India's explosion of a nuclear device in 1974, after which, in Pakistan's view, India represented an even greater threat to Pakistan's security. In apparent deference to Pakistan, India has foregone attempts to construct nuclear weapons, but retains the ability to do so; it still worries about not only Pakistan's intentions, but China's as well. China exploded its first nuclear device in 1964 and has since amassed a considerable nuclear arsenal—a fact which commands the continuing attention of India's strategic planners.

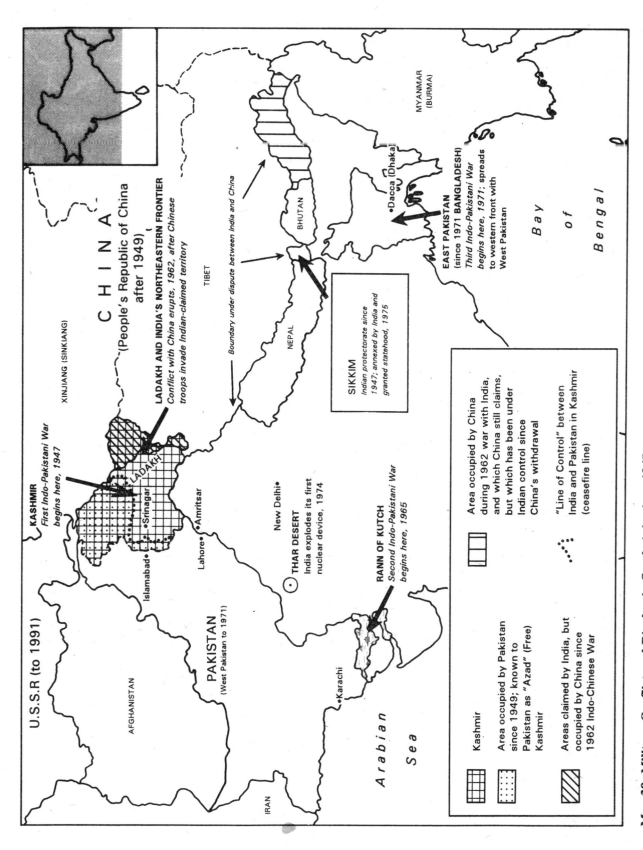

KASHMIR
*First Indo-Pakistani War
begins here, 1947*

LADAKH AND INDIA'S NORTHEASTERN FRONTIER
*Conflict with China erupts, 1962, after Chinese
troops invade Indian-claimed territory*

C H I N A
"(People's Republic of China
after 1949)"

XINJIANG (SINKIANG)

U.S.S.R (to 1991)

AFGHANISTAN

PAKISTAN
(West Pakistan to 1971)

Islamabad•

Lahore• •Amritsar

•Srinagar

LADAKH

IRAN

•Karachi

*A r a b i a n
S e a*

THAR DESERT
India explodes its first
nuclear device, 1974

New Delhi•

RANN OF KUTCH
*Second Indo-Pakistani War
begins here, 1965*

TIBET

NEPAL

Boundary under dispute between India and China

BHUTAN

SIKKIM
*Indian protectorate since
1947; annexed by India and
granted statehood, 1975*

•Dacca (Dhaka)

EAST PAKISTAN
(since 1971 **BANGLADESH**)
*Third Indo-Pakistani War
begins here, 1971; spreads
to western front with
West Pakistan*

MYANMAR
(BURMA)

*B a y
o f
B e n g a l*

Kashmir

Area occupied by Pakistan
since 1949; known to
Pakistan as "Azad" (Free)
Kashmir

Areas claimed by India, but
occupied by China since
1962 Indo-Chinese War

Area occupied by China
during 1962 war with India,
and which China still claims,
but which has been under
Indian control since
China's withdrawal

"Line of Control" between
India and Pakistan in Kashmir
(ceasefire line)

Map 38 Military Conflict and Rivalry in South Asia since 1947

85

39   Separatism and Irredentism in South Asia since 1948

Issues of separatism (the desire of a national, ethnic, or religious group to gain independence from the country in which it lives) and irredentism (the desire to incorporate a neighboring population and territory inside the boundaries of a country with which that neighboring population has a historical affinity) have plagued South Asian politics since Independence.

Of South Asia's six countries, separatist and irredentist challenges have been most pronounced in India and Pakistan mainly because of the historical precedent of Partition (see Map 37): subnational groups in both countries saw that it was possible to challenge the unity and territorial integrity of the state. Probably the most visible, and longest-lasting, challenge to national unity has been the Kashmir dispute. Kashmir's troubles began in 1947 and have defied resolution ever since. Both India and Pakistan claim all of Kashmir—Pakistan on religious grounds (the bulk of Kashmiris are Muslim) and India on political grounds (Kashmir's ruler legally acceded to India)—but since 1947 both sides have had to settle for roughly half, divided along a "line of control." While for Pakistan, the Kashmir issue is one of irredentism—it seeks to unite Kashmir into a greater Pakistani state—for India, and for some groups within Kashmir who seek not union with Pakistan but independence, the issue is one of separatism. In the 1990s, violence in Kashmir escalated as militant Muslim separatists resorted to bombings and even the kidnapping of Western tourists to achieve their political goals.

As a federal state, India has faced numerous and widespread challenges to its internal unity, and since Partition has relied on accommodation (and, often, force) to prevent further disintegration. In the 1950s, pressure from separatist Tamils (who sought the creation of a "Dravidistan") and other groups led to moderate concessions such as states reorganization (see Maps 40.1-40.2).

In the 1960s, the Indian government sought to accommodate Sikh separatists in Panjab, seeking the creation of an independent "Khalistan," by dividing Panjab into two states: a predominantly Sikh state (Panjab) and a predominantly Hindu state (Haryana). But in 1982, growing militant Sikh demands for greater autonomy, led by the Akali Dal, a Sikh political party, erupted into violence and the Indian government opted to intervene militarily. New Delhi ruled the state directly from 1983 to 1985. More outbreaks of violence, including inter-Sikh conflict, led to the reimposition of central government rule over Panjab in 1987; despite this new intervention, the unrest in Panjab continues in the 1990s.

Soon after Independence, the government of India found itself facing growing resistance to central rule in the northeastern hill territories. Hill tribes, such as the Nagas, the Mizos, and others, removed from their isolation by the Second World War, began to agitate for independence. In an independent India, hill peoples feared losing their cultural identity (and religion, which for many, was Christianity—missionaries had made deep inroads into the hill areas under British rule). Some groups, such as the Nagas and the Mizos, who were bypassed during states reorganization, resorted to agitation and violence to win their independence. Moderate Naga leaders agreed to the compromise of more autonomy within India. Consequently, in 1963, the Indian government established the state of Nagaland. The Indian government refused to grant the same level of autonomy for the Mizos, however, and Mizo guerrilla groups, such as the Mizo National Army, repeatedly clashed with the Indian Army throughout the 1970s. In 1984, settlement talks between the two parties were successful, paving the way in 1986 for the creation of the state of Mizoram. The Indian government obtained similar results in elevating Tripura, Meghalaya, and Manipur to statehood (1972), but separatist movements in the northeastern region persist.

While the issue of Tamil separatism in India was resolved in the 1950s, it remained a continuous issue in Sri Lanka and even created a nascent irredentist movement in Tamil Nadu. Sri Lankan Tamils, facing repression and discrimination from the Sri Lankan government, have fought a guerrilla war in Sri Lanka since the mid-1970s (see Map 68). In the 1990s, the Tamil movement in Sri Lanka continued to test the patience of Indian Tamils, some of whom favor incorporating Sri Lankan Tamil areas into India.

Another important post-1947 separatist movement was the Gurkhaland movement (Indian Nepalis sought an independent state; the issue was resolved in 1987 when the Indian government granted them more autonomy). In Pakistan since 1947, the central government, dominated by Panjabis, has successfully fended off challenges from independence movements in the Northwest Frontier Province, Baluchistan, and Sind.

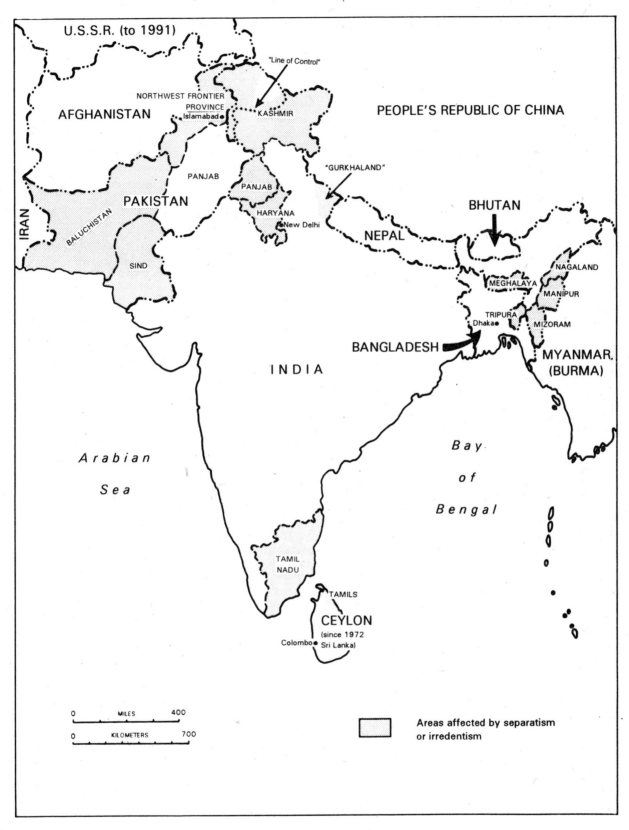

Map 39 Separatism and Irredentism in South Asia since 1948

40　India and States Reorganization, 1956 and Beyond

The question of states reorganization dates from 1920, when the Indian National Congress agreed that the linguistic reorganization of the Indian provinces was one of their political goals. The provincial boundaries of India in 1947 were the product of both some planning by the British—for military, strategic, and political reasons—and of numerous historical accidents. Some were hastily formed after the integration of the princely states. Almost none of the boundaries made sense in the context of Free India, where continued reliance on irrational boundaries would likely hinder internal and national development.

Soon after Independence, and despite earlier pronouncements, it became clear to the government that states reorganized on a strictly linguistic basis might not be suitable and might actually prove damaging to national unity by giving impetus to centrifugal forces. The Linguistic Provinces Commission (also known as the Dar Commission), a forerunner of the States Reorganization Commission, recommended in 1948 that states should be redrawn primarily in light of geographical contiguity, financial self-sufficiency, and administrative expedience. According to the Dar Commission, only after meeting these three criteria should weight be given to linguistic considerations.

The Dar Commission's findings proved unpopular with many Indians. A Congress committee, headed by Jawaharlal Nehru, arrived at the same conclusions as the Dar Commission, but suggested that some reorganization of states boundaries based on language might be appropriate on a case-by-case basis. Telugu-speaking Andhras in South India made use of the opening left by Nehru and clamored for an Andhra state. Nehru was resistant, but when the leader of the Andhra movement, Potti Sriramalu, fasted to death in 1952, the prime minister capitulated and in 1953 allowed the formation of Andhra Pradesh. The way was now paved for similar demands by other linguistic state movements.

The issue of states reorganization dominated Indian politics for three years after the formation of Andhra Pradesh. Late in 1953, Nehru appointed the States Reorganization Commission (SRC) to study the issue.

In 1955, after a thorough study, the commission recommended that India's internal boundaries be redrawn to more closely correspond with the country's linguistic divisions, but that they should be tempered with due consideration of other factors such as national unity, economics, and administrative efficiency. With some adjustments, the commission's recommendations were ultimately embodied in the States Reorganization Act, passed by the Indian parliament in 1956.

The act created fourteen states (reorganized along linguistic lines based on each area's dominant language), and six union territories (which were administered by the federal government). Following the recommendations of the SRC, the act left Bombay state untouched because to divide it into a Gujarati- and a Marathi-speaking state would have meant awarding the city of Bombay to the Marathi-speaking state, despite the fact that the city had been built upon Gujarati wealth. The act also carefully avoided any changes to Panjab because of the difficulties inherent in creating a Panjabi-speaking state which contained large non-Panjabi-speaking minorities. The parliament in 1956 also ignored the call for new tribal states such as Jharkhand and Nagaland.

Although the changes implemented by the 1956 States Reorganization Act were dramatic, the act did not satisfy all parties, nor did it prevent further agitation for additional changes. In 1960, the Nehru government finally resolved the Bombay issue, but only after rioting had broken out throughout the region. The government divided Bombay and awarded the city of Bombay to the new state of Maharashtra. Panjab was also similarly divided with the creation in 1966 of the two states of Panjab and Haryana. Bowing to pressures from the state of Bihar, the Indian government continues to ignore pleas for the creation out of Bihar of a tribal state called Jharkhand, despite the movement's longevity. After sending in troops to quash an independence movement by the Nagas in eastern India beginning in 1956, the government finally yielded to the Naga rebels by creating a separate Nagaland state for them in 1963.

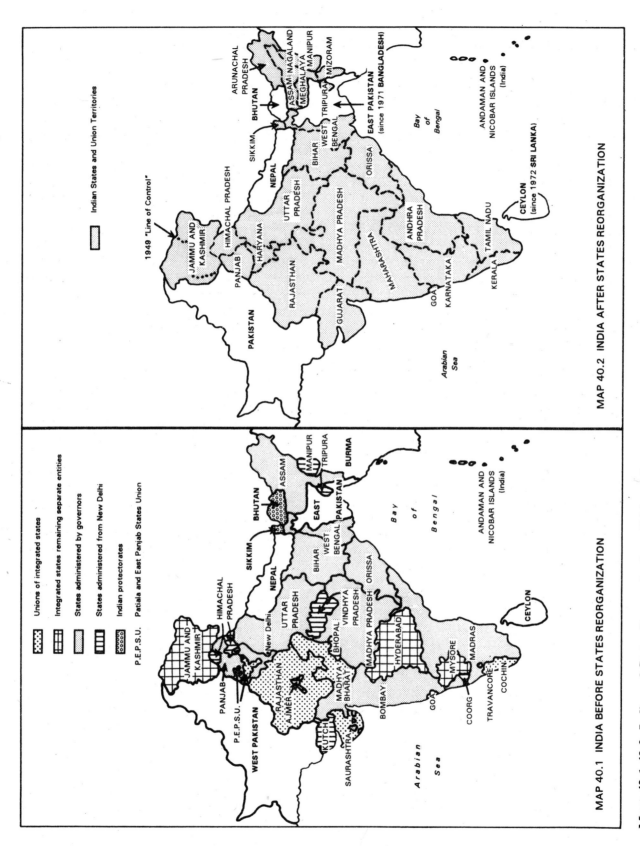

MAP 40.1 INDIA BEFORE STATES REORGANIZATION

MAP 40.2 INDIA AFTER STATES REORGANIZATION

Maps 40.1-40.2 India and States Reorganization, 1956 and Beyond

41   Bangladeshi War for Independence, 1971

Prior to the conflict of 1971, many East Pakistanis had long been dissatisfied with their political and economic condition, and viewed West Pakistan with fear and suspicion. West Pakistan dominated the twin-winged country's political processes. West Pakistan insisted that Urdu, a language not spoken by East Pakistanis, be the only national language, despite the fact that Pakistan as a whole contained fewer Urdu-speakers than it did Bengali-speakers. National economic development tended to focus on the western half of Pakistan, while the East languished. Likewise, West Pakistani political and military elites held similar fears and suspicions about the East. These elites questioned the loyalty of East Pakistanis vis-à-vis India, were dismayed over East Pakistanis' lack of interest in the Kashmir issue, and even questioned the devotion of Muslim Bengalis to Islam. These tensions had existed since the founding of the country in 1947 and finally erupted into civil war in 1971.

In 1970, a year after he had staged a coup d'etat, Gen. Agha Mohammed Yahya Khan decided that national elections would be held in Pakistan based on a universal franchise, and that a new federal government would be established in order to give provincial governments a maximum of power. Elections were held in December 1970, and the Awami League, an East Pakistan-based political party, won a majority: 160 of the 300 seats in the federal parliament. All of its seats were in East Pakistan. The Awami League's competitor in West Pakistan, the Pakistan People's Party, led by Zulfiqar Ali Bhutto, won only 81 seats, and all of these were in West Pakistan. Because of East Pakistan's larger voting population, the West Pakistanis had been outvoted and faced the prospect of having the federal legislature dominated by Bengalis.

Intense negotiations followed in the wake of the elections as Bhutto attempted to gain concessions from Sheikh Mujibur Rahman, the leader of the Awami League, but the talks arrived at an impasse. The military leadership of Pakistan—all West Pakistanis—fearing the results of the negotiations, imposed a military solution to the political impasse by declaring martial law in East Pakistan on 25 March 1971. The army's mission in the East—dubbed "Operation Searchlight"—was to arrest the Awami League's leadership, eliminate the League's political power and organization, disarm and disband Bengali army and police units, con-trol the flow of information in the province, secure the province generally through control of both urban and rural areas, and finally, restore order. Pakistani troops were initially successful, but faced stiffening resistance from Bangladeshi "freedom fighters."

As it had done in Tibet in 1959 and Nepal in 1960, the Indian government in 1971, led by Indira Gandhi, offered a safe haven to political refugees from East Pakistan and most of the Awami League's leadership and large numbers of Bengali soldiers fled to India. What started out in March and April as a small trickle of refugees fleeing the military crackdown in East Pakistan, turned into a torrent by late May, comprising over 3.5 million people. By mid-July, nearly 7 million refugees had poured over the border, placing an enormous economic burden on India, and overloading its ability to deal effectively with the problem. India faced a refugee crisis of mammoth proportions and refused to consider any political settlement of the civil war in East Pakistan that did not provide for the repatriation of these refugees; the Pakistani government viewed the refugees, most of whom were Hindus, as "traitors," and seemed unwilling to accept any settlement that did. While U.N.-sponsored efforts to resolve the issue stalled, both India and Pakistan began to mass troops at the India-East Pakistan border in preparation for war.

By late summer 1971, the Indian government seemed disposed toward war. The refugee problem had worsened. Pakistan remained obstinate, and to India's dismay, had not been condemned by the world community. India feared that if the civil war dragged on much longer and the Bengalis did win, a much more radical government would come into power than was currently predicted—a more radical government that would be a threat to India. Finally, severing Pakistan's eastern wing would weaken its old nemesis and strengthen India's claims to be a major Asian power. When war finally came on 3 December 1971, Indian troops faced the difficult task of dislodging well-trained Pakistani troops in their "liberation" of East Pakistan as well as facing troops on a western front (see Map 38). Both sides fought well, but by 16 December, Dhaka had fallen, Pakistani troops in East Pakistan surrendered, and India ordered a cease-fire. The two-week war was over, and Indira Gandhi proclaimed the birth of a new country in South Asia: the People's Republic of Bangladesh.

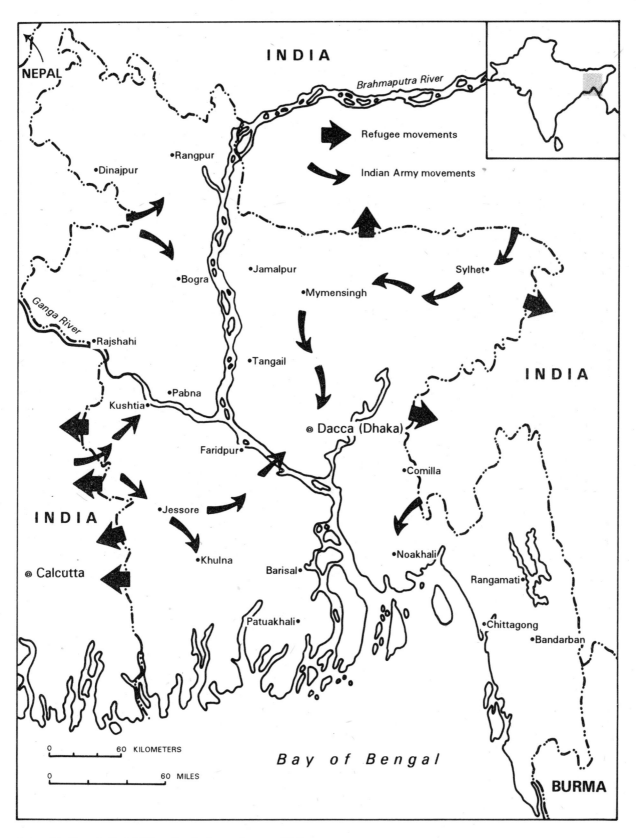

Map 41 Bangladeshi War for Independence, 1971

42   India, Pakistan, and Bangladesh in 1972

By 1972, the face of South Asia had changed. A new country, Bangladesh, was born, while another country, Pakistan, was forced to deal with the results. Given the troubled history of the subcontinent since Independence, it was unusual that in 1972 the leaders of the three largest countries were all in office through popular mandate.

In India, Indira Gandhi was prime minister. In the area of external affairs, 1972 was a good year for Indira Gandhi. At the Simla Summit (June), she met with Zulfikar Ali Bhutto and successfully normalized relations with Pakistan after the break caused by the war the year before. Indira Gandhi was generally recognized as the most prominent and well-respected of the Third World's leaders. Domestically, Mrs. Gandhi remained popular. In March 1972, legislative assembly (Vidhan Sabha) elections were held in sixteen states. Buoyed by the recent victory over Pakistan, Mrs. Gandhi's Congress party won 70 percent of all the seats and thereby gained control of fourteen state legislatures.

But India also faced some difficulties in 1972. Several Cabinet ministers were involved in a bribe-taking scandal which rocked national politics. A terrible drought (affecting some 180 million people) struck the country that year, subjecting many of its already impoverished people to more serious privations and even death. High postwar inflation, labor strikes, and high population growth were all significant problems.

Defeated in the 1971 civil war and stripped of its eastern wing, Pakistan in 1972 sought to recover its national dignity. The loss of East Pakistan affected more than just the size of the country, its economy, and national politics. The loss meant it no longer had a sizable Hindu minority and turned Pakistan into an almost totally Islamic state—a fact which shifted its geopolitical and religious center away from South Asia and more toward Southwest Asia. Pakistan's leadership in 1972 was civilian—the first since 1958. Zulfikar Ali Bhutto, Pakistan's president, moved quickly to lift martial law, and purged the military of troublesome officers. He reintroduced an element of democracy by summoning the National Assembly, and worked to rebuild the country's shattered economy, which in 1972 was burdened with a 25 percent inflation rate.

Early in January 1972, Sheikh Mujibur Rahman (1920-75) arrived in the newly created state of Bangladesh and became Bangladesh's first president (for two days) and then its first prime minister. Mujib had in 1970 won an electoral majority in Pakistan's elections, but the West Pakistanis refused him the right to form a government (see Map 41). Having returned to Dhaka in triumph, Mujib faced governing a country ravaged by civil war. Tens of thousands of people had been killed, raped, tortured, or displaced from their homes. Many of the refugees who had earlier fled to India now returned. In this environment, law and order broke down. Guerrilla forces still controlled much of the countryside and refused to cooperate with the new government. Some even established their own territories. Although Mujib later suspended civil liberties and became a dictator, in 1972 he was still democratically inclined and promulgated a new democratic constitution, modeled on India's, which was adopted in November that year.

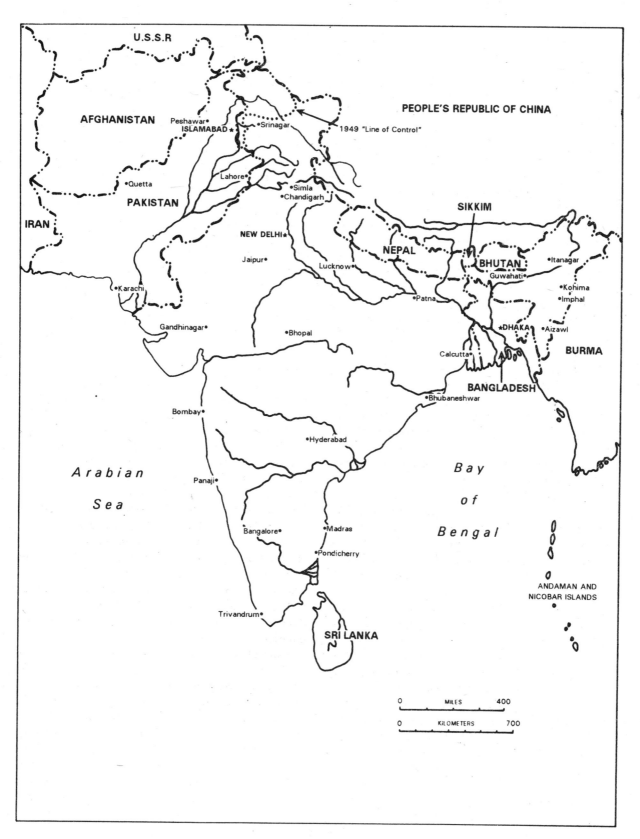

Map 42 India, Pakistan, and Bangladesh in 1972

43 India, Pakistan, and Bangladesh Today

The countries of South Asia face both difficulty and promise as the 1990s progress. As of late 1994, P. V. Narasimha Rao continued as India's prime minister, but he faced increasing discontent with his political leadership, both from the electorate and even from within his own Congress party. Part of the discontent stemmed from changes wrought by his adherence to economic reforms designed to liberalize the Indian economy and make it more efficient. In a labor-intensive economic system like India's, however, increasing efficiency means the loss of many hundreds of thousands, or perhaps millions, of jobs.

Narasimha Rao's political woes were not just limited to labor unrest. Communalism was also a continuing problem. Growing animosities between right-wing Hindus (some of whom advocate the desecularization of India and its conversion into a theocracy based on Hinduism) and Muslim minorities burst into communal violence in early December 1992 over the destruction of a Muslim mosque in Ayodhya, Uttar Pradesh, by Hindu extremists. These Hindus justified their actions by claiming that the mosque had been constructed over a Hindu temple destroyed by Muslims in the fifteenth century. Communal rioting quickly spread throughout India and resulted in over 2,000 deaths before tensions finally subsided in early 1993.

Despite its many political problems, India remains the world's most populous functioning democracy. The Indian economy, though experiencing the pain of readjustment to a more free-market system, shows signs of slow improvement. An interesting feature of India's changing socio-economic scene is the steady growth of a middle class: people who have sufficient disposable income to purchase consumer items like televisions, washing machines, motor scooters, and even automobiles. Though their exact numbers are difficult to assess, it has been estimated that in the early 1990s over 20 percent of the population could be classified as middle class (Gordon and Oldenburg 1992).

India's neighbor, Pakistan, has been experiencing similar difficulties. In early 1994, Benazir Bhutto, the Cambridge-educated daughter of slain Pakistani prime minister, Zulfikar Ali Bhutto, was again in power, but faced continual criticism from the opposition led by Nawaz Sharif.

The performance of the Pakistani economy showed signs of slight improvement and per capita income remained roughly equivalent to that of India. In the area of literacy, however, Pakistan still lags behind India: only about 35 percent of its population is literate, while India's literacy rate stands at 48 percent.

Another difficulty which Pakistan faces is its growing nuclear program. No conclusive evidence yet exists, but intelligence services in the United States have suggested that Pakistan now has the materials need to assemble a nuclear device and perhaps has already done so. This situation has not only added to the already heightened tensions between Pakistan and India, but has also strained the former's relationship with the United States. The U.S. has put pressure on Pakistan by reducing the amount of foreign aid it grants Pakistan and by calling for a nuclear-free zone in South Asia. While both Pakistan and India accept the theoretical premise of such a zone, both are suspicious of each other and a concrete acceptance of the idea remained elusive.

The Kashmir question remains unresolved and is one of the major obstacles to better relations with India. Although both countries claim all of Kashmir, Pakistani and Indian forces face each other across a cease-fire line over 600 kilometers long (over 400 miles long) established in 1972. This line has become the de facto boundary. Violations of the cease-fire continue to be frequent, especially around the strategic Siachen Glacier in the Karakoram Mountain Range in Ladakh.

In late 1994, Abdur Rahman Biswas remained president of Bangladesh, sharing power with Begum Khaleda Zia, leader of the Bangladesh Nationalist party, who won her position after national elections were held in 1991. Begum Zia is the widow of former president Ziaur Rahman and is Bangladesh's first female prime minister.

Bangladesh's economy showed some improvement by 1994, although per capita income was still only slightly over half that of India and Pakistan. Substantial increases in population continued to put pressure on the country's limited resources. With less than half the land area of Pakistan, but with an equivalent population, Bangladeshis crowd onto even the poorest of land, which is often subject to frequent flooding (as occurred in 1993), or in the track of destructive cyclonic storms which all too frequently hit the country's coastal areas.

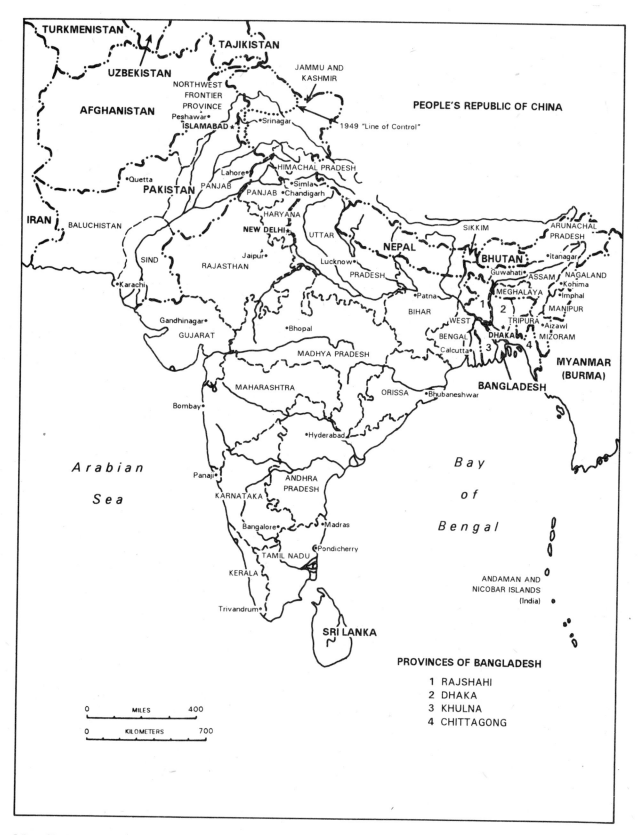

TURKMENISTAN

UZBEKISTAN

TAJIKISTAN

JAMMU AND
KASHMIR

NORTHWEST
FRONTIER
PROVINCE

AFGHANISTAN

Peshawar•

PEOPLE'S REPUBLIC OF CHINA

ISLAMABAD ★   •Srinagar

1949 "Line of Control"

•Quetta

Lahore•   HIMACHAL PRADESH

PAKISTAN   PANJAB

IRAN

BALUCHISTAN

PANJAB   •Simla
          •Chandigarh

HARYANA

NEW DELHI•

SIKKIM

ARUNACHAL
PRADESH

SIND

RAJASTHAN

Jaipur•

UTTAR

Lucknow•

PRADESH

NEPAL

BHUTAN   •itanagar

Guwahati•   ASSAM   NAGALAND
                    •Kohima

•Karachi

•Patna

MEGHALAYA   •Imphal
                MANIPUR

Gandhinagar•

GUJARAT

•Bhopal

BIHAR

WEST
BENGAL

1

DHAKA

2

TRIPURA   •Aizawl
              MIZORAM

3   4

•Calcutta

MADHYA PRADESH

BANGLADESH

MYANMAR
(BURMA)

MAHARASHTRA

ORISSA   •Bhubaneshwar

Bombay•

Arabian

Sea

•Hyderabad

Bay

of

Panaji•

ANDHRA
PRADESH

KARNATAKA

Bengal

Bangalore•   •Madras

TAMIL NADU   •Pondicherry

ANDAMAN AND
NICOBAR ISLANDS
(India)   •

KERALA

Trivandrum•

SRI LANKA

PROVINCES OF BANGLADESH

1 RAJSHAHI
2 DHAKA
3 KHULNA
4 CHITTAGONG

0   MILES   400

0   KILOMETERS   700

Map 43 India, Pakistan, and Bangladesh Today

95

Economic, Social, and Cultural History

Although the beginning of trade with East Asia is difficult to date, South Asia's trading relations with the Western world can be traced back as far as the Harappan Culture, as evidenced by the discovery of Harappan or Harappan-style artifacts in archaeological digs conducted in the ancient cities of Mesopotamia.

Until the fourth century BCE, however, South Asian trade with the West was sporadic and consisted largely of luxury items, such as silks, jewels, ivory, and such live rarities as peacocks and apes. With the establishment of the Mauryan Empire (322-185 BCE), and the accompanying state protection of overland and overseas trade from South Asia, a wide variety and higher volume of goods left Indian towns and cities bound for Western markets via caravan or ship.

Goods were carried along four major trading routes from South Asia to cities and ports in the Western world, either overland or by sea. The northern land route began at the Mauryan capital of Pataliputra. Caravans traveled northward on the Royal Highway, which paralleled the Ganga River to the plains of Panjab and then snaked eastward to the ancient city of Taxila, where goods from China, brought along the Silk Road, could be found. From there, traders journeyed eastward through the Hindu Kush mountains via the Khyber Pass to Kabul, northward to Bactria, and from there skirted the eastern and northern edge of the Kara-Kum Desert to reach the Caspian Sea. Goods were then carried by boat to the western shore of the Caspian, where the land route re-emerged and extended through the Caucasus Mountains. Following mountain passages, traders and their pack animals moved westward along the northern frontier of Asia Minor to the busy market cities of Byzantium.

The central route also began in India, following the same route as the northern, until it reached Bactria, where caravans diverted westward to the city of Merv. From there, they angled to the southwest through the Plateau of Iran to Ecbatana and thence to the Mesopotamian city of Seleucia. If they could not find a suitable market for their goods in Seleucia, traders repacked their goods and left, bound for Antioch, and the larger market opportunities of that Mediterranean port city.

Caravans using the southern land route left India at Taxila, traveled westward to Kapisa, and from there moved southward to Kandahar. From there, traders paralleled the Helmand River, then moved westward again through Kepman to Persepolis and Charax, and thence across the northern edge of the Arabian Peninsula to the city of Petra.

The two major sea routes to the West from South Asia began in the city of Bharukaccha (Broach), the terminus of several domestic South Asian commercial land and sea routes. Ships carrying South Asian cargoes took one of two passages to the West. The first sea route involved following the coastline of Persia through the Gulf and then on to Charax, where goods were off-loaded on caravans and carried overland on the southern route. On the alternate sea route, captains piloted their vessels across the Arabian Sea and skirted the southern coastline of the Arabian Peninsula until they reached the Red Sea. From there, the merchant ships sailed northward to dock at ports such as Arisone on the Gulf of Heroopolite, or Aelana on the Gulf of Aqaba.

The types of goods carried to the West by traders and sea captains varied with the goods' points of origin and whether or not the goods arrived at their final destination after being first transshipped from an entrepôt or other such location. Bactria, for example, was a great crossroads for the international silk trade between China, India, and the West. Beginning with the later Mauryan period, South Asian merchants also exported to Western markets foodstuffs such as rice, wheat, and sugar, and spices including turmeric, pepper, and cinnamon. Live animals such as lions, tigers, and parrots, animal products in the form of hides, furs, and wool, and tropical hardwoods and cotton also found their way to busy Western marketplaces. Goods from China (with whom India had a growing maritime trade beginning in the Later Han period, 25-225 CE) were either consumed domestically or, as was more often the case, transshipped to the West.

From the West, South Asians imported a number of different products, such as flax, linen, frankincense, sweet clover, tin, copper, and glass, but in comparatively smaller volumes. These low volumes were due to the fact that most South Asia merchants demanded gold coin (specie) in return for their exports to the West. By the first century CE, specie flows from the Roman Empire to South Asia were a cause of considerable consternation to Roman commentators like Pliny. Despite this, trade between South Asia and the West (especially Rome) remained vigorous and mutually beneficial throughout the following two centuries.

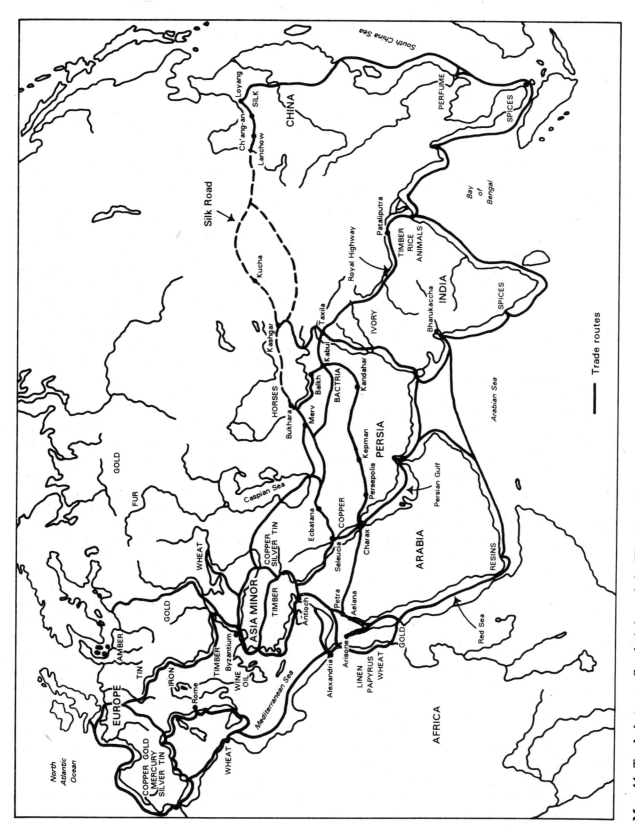

Map 44 Trade between South Asia and the World to 200 CE

99

45 Economy of the Mughal Empire, 1526-1707

For the times, the Mughal economy was large and prosperous, and built upon several pillars, the most important of which was agriculture. Indian peasants during the Mughal period grew a wide variety of crops, including such food crops as wheat, rice, and barley, as well as non-food cash crops like cotton, indigo, and opium. By the middle of the seventeenth century, Indian cultivators had also begun to grow extensively two new crops, maize and tobacco, both introduced from the Western Hemisphere. The Mughal revenue system affected the types of crops produced: cultivators were encouraged to grow higher-value cash crops to meet their tax burdens, while tax incentives created an impetus to clear forests in order to cultivate new lands. Successive Mughal governments also provided funding to build irrigation systems to increase the amount of cultivated land under irrigation—irrigated lands produced much higher crop yields and increased the net revenue base. Overall, agricultural production gradually increased during the Mughal period, despite periodic setbacks like localized crop failures.

The role of urban centers in the Mughal economy is clear. Cities and towns acted as markets for the sale of agricultural products, especially those not destined for purely local consumption like grains. They also provided homes for a variety of merchants, traders, shopkeepers, artisans, moneylenders, weavers, and other craftspeople, as well as retired minor officials, and religious figures. The growth of market cities was most pronounced during the seventeenth century, and reflected the overall growth in the Mughal economy.

The interregional trade within the subcontinent comprised another important element in the economy. Partially processed manufactures like yarns, thread, raw silk; jute-based products; metalware; and food items like sugar, oils, and butter, among many other items, all formed part of the extensive interregional trade, moving overland or via coastal shipping from production areas to markets. Some items, like raw silk (sericulture), were produced in one area (in this case, Bengal) and then transported to another area (Gujarat) for further processing.

Manufacturing was not limited to particular areas or centers within the empire: it was rather widely dispersed, with only some luxury products and minerals out of necessity remaining site-specific. The single largest manufacture of Mughal India was cotton textiles, the production of which encompassed piecegoods, calicos, and muslins, all available either unbleached or in any variety of colors.

Cotton textiles formed a large part of the international trade of Mughal India with Europe in the seventeenth century. Declining Portuguese power in the Indian Ocean paved the way for the growth of trading companies based in other European countries such as the Netherlands, England, and France. In addition to the demand for cotton textiles, early modern Europe also constituted a large and growing market for pepper and other spices, indigo, silks, and saltpeter (used in munitions). In sharp contrast to the enormous European demand for Indian products, the demand for European products in Mughal India was quite small. Because Mughal India was virtually self-sufficient, Europeans had very little to offer in the way of return trade except some woolens, unprocessed metals, and a few luxury items. Like their Roman counterparts centuries before, Europeans of the early modern period were forced to export to Mughal India vast quantities of gold and silver specie to pay for their South Asian imports.

An often overlooked facet of the Mughal economy is the existence of an extensive road network, which formed a vital part of the overall economic infrastructure. The Mughals maintained a public works department to design, construct, and maintain roads linking major cities and towns throughout the empire. Although their main purpose was to facilitate the security and efficient administration of the far-flung empire, as well as travel by the emperor, roads in Mughal South Asia also made trade within the empire easier to conduct (Farooque 1977).

Despite its relatively high economic output, compared to those of Europe the Mughal economy was neither competitive nor innovative. Devoid of the international competition for markets then commonplace in Europe, and unpressured by the need to cut costs by saving labor, the Mughal economy began to lose ground relative to its European counterparts by the beginning of the eighteenth century. A relatively unchanging demand level for products by the masses, a general absence of interest in developing commercial technology, and a lack of socio-economic mobility all led to a growing economic inertia in the Mughal Empire—a condition which had far-reaching consequences for the future.

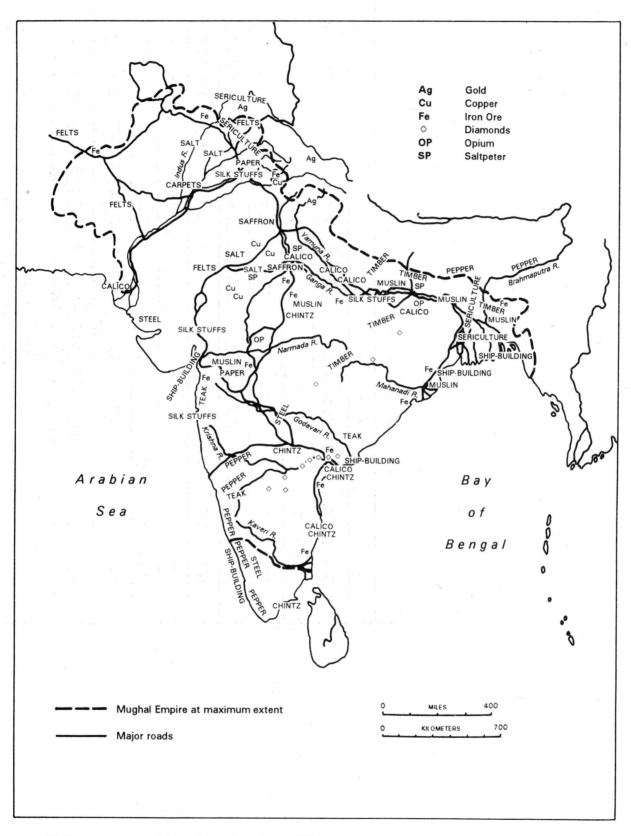

Map 45 Economy of the Mughal Empire, 1526-1707

46 The Indian Economy, 1700-1757

By the beginning of the eighteenth century, the prosperity the Indian subcontinent had known under the Mughals had begun to decline. Imperial disintegration, internal rebellions, and external invasions had all taken their toll. As central authority waned, huge market cities in northwestern India like Delhi began to decay as merchants and artisans relocated to more secure environs (Agra suffered a similar fate until its occupation by the **Jats** and Marathas in the second quarter of the century reversed its decline). One by one, as the number of independent kingdoms increased, so too did the number of customs regulations. Interregional trade in some areas, especially in the west, began to dwindle, and many large centers of manufacturing production and shipping rapidly decayed.

The decline in the Indian economy in the first half of the century—the pre-colonial economy—does not appear to have been as total and ruinous as was once thought. To be sure, decline was evident, but it seems to have been rather unevenly distributed. In contrast to the northwest—which suffered greatly from the competition between the Marathas, Sikhs, and Afghans in the wake of the Mughal collapse—the economy of Bengal, for example, based on cotton textiles, silks, and sugar, continued to thrive despite the often adverse political situation. Powerful Indian bankers in Bengal, like Jaget Seth, rose to prominence in this period and became fabulously wealthy. Some areas in western India, many of which relied on the coastal trade, also remained unaffected. And even as old commercial centers declined, new ones developed. Provincial cities in the east, like Faizabad and Varanasi, grew in prosperity, partly in response to the increasing turmoil in the northwest.

In the early 1700s, agriculture was still the largest producer of wealth on the subcontinent; by midcentury, it had become increasingly commercialized. Market forces led to such changes as the creation of credit systems, advance purchasing of crops by buyers, and the increased production of non-food cash crops like indigo and tobacco. Despite the generally high crop yields per acre found in much of India and the dramatic shift away from purely subsistence agriculture, agricultural productivity stagnated overall. The burden of agricultural taxes was still quite high—often 50 percent or more—and led to less risk-taking and innovation in regard to new cropping techniques or plowing technology. Farmers felt ill-equipped to take chances when the cost of failure was so high.

The lack of innovation in agriculture also extended to manufacturing. Unlike in Europe or even China during the same period, advances in labor-saving technology were met in India largely with apathy. The reasons for this disinterest are still unclear, but seem to be linked to a lack of domestic market-demand stimuli, extreme specialization of labor under the caste system, and fear of unemployment. As a result, manufactures like cotton textiles, their high quality notwithstanding, still tended to be made in largely the same way as they had been for well over a century.

Leaving its other economic difficulties aside, India by the 1720s began to exhibit characteristics of modern economic integration. Interregional trade improved, even as the political situation on the subcontinent worsened. While rural hinterlands continued to supply major cities almost exclusively through local networks, the development of linkages between large coastal markets such as Bengal, Coromandel, and Gujarat was largely a result of the turmoil inland. Roads were poor and travel was fraught with difficulties, but goods from one region could arrive in another by entering the coastal trade, carefully avoiding the political problems on land.

Because of the tremendous economic impact British rule had on India after 1757, historians over the last hundred years have debated whether India was on the verge of an industrial revolution before its occupation by the British. Accurate data on production and other economic factors is scarce and a definitive answer seems, therefore, unlikely. Compared with other countries, however, important qualitative factors of economic development seem to be absent in India prior to the advent of British rule. India had not undergone an agricultural revolution, showed virtually no technological advancement, and relied almost exclusively on animate power. Most of all, India in the early eighteenth century suffered from a lack of scientific and commercial innovation. As historian Tapan Raychaudhuri points out, it seems improbable, given the social, technological, and intellectual condition of India in the pre-colonial period, that it was on the threshold of industrial development (Kumar 1983). But British colonial rule prevented the possibility of Indians later initiating such development, like that which occurred in France, the United States, and Germany in the nineteenth century.

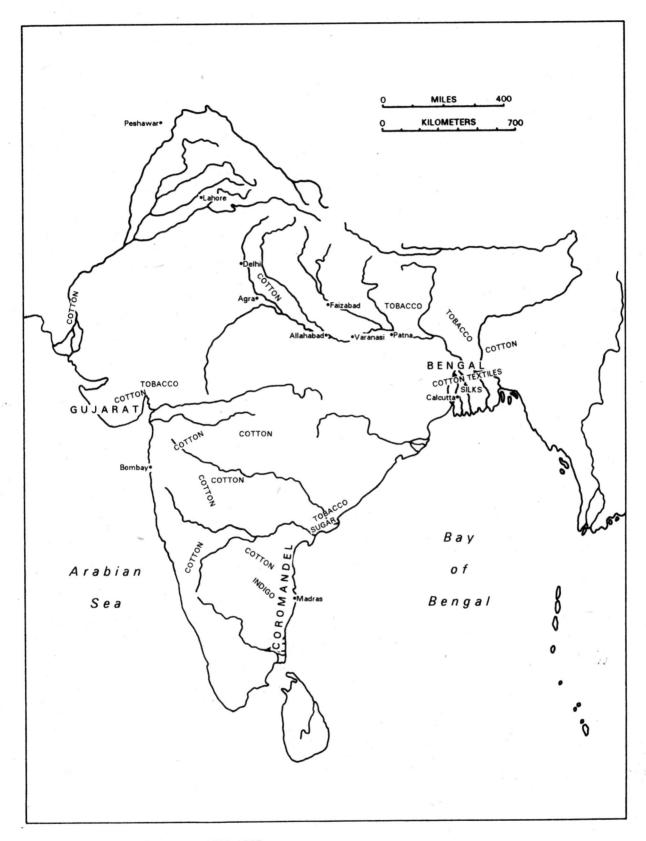

Map 46 The Indian Economy, 1700-1757

47 Import and Export Economy, 1800-1947

From 1757 until 1813, London's mercantilist policies supported the dominance of the English East India Company over India's foreign trade. The Company's monopoly over that trade was more theoretical than real, however, because it was unable to prevent individuals in the Company's employ from engaging in illegal private trade.

Exports during this early period consisted of cotton piecegoods, raw silk, indigo, sugar, rum, opium, and raw cotton, while imports were restricted—because of low Indian demand—to precious metals and specialized manufactured goods. Exports far exceeded imports and resulted in a favorable balance of trade for India, effectively negating the principles of mercantilism. Recognition of this fact finally led the British parliament to pass the Charter Act of 1813, which abolished the Company's monopolistic trading rights and allowed private individuals to invest directly in Indian development.

After the passage of the Charter Act of 1813, India's foreign trade experienced a rapid and dramatic growth. The rise in imports was particularly striking: by 1817-18 imports had risen over 80 percent from their 1813-14 levels. This huge increase can be explained by the changing nature of manufacturing in Britain and, indeed, in Europe. Per-unit costs had declined and Indians were thus able to import large numbers of relatively inexpensive manufactured goods.

As India became increasingly tied to the global economy, it began to experience the same cyclical fluctuations in its trade patterns, although to a lesser degree than its largest trading partners who had more advanced economies. The boom and depression cycles were most pronounced in the latter half of the nineteenth century, a reflection of India's growing economic integration with the outside world.

Adequate foreign trade statistics for India are not available until 1835, but from that date onward, some clear patterns emerge. Until the outbreak of the Second World War, the annual average growth rate in exports was 3.23 percent, while imports grew at 3.68 percent. Because they reflect only averages over a very long period of time, these figures obscure the nature of India's foreign trade in the shorter term. India's exports and imports grew at a much faster annual rate (for example, in 1835-65 they grew at 5.61 percent and 6.01 percent, respectively) than they did in the years that followed. Needs generated by the Crimean War and the development of railways in India account for much of the growth in this period. Until 1914, average import growth rates exceeded those of exports, but still did not match the higher rates of the earlier period. Two factors seem to account for the moderate post-1865 decline: severe famines in the 1870s and in the 1890s, and a slow, but relentless, depreciation of the rupee caused by a decline in the value of silver. The decline of the rupee was finally halted in 1893 through governmental intervention, but that year also marked the beginning of a worldwide recession, and consequently India's foreign trade position did not improve until later in the decade.

The First World War provided a direct economic stimulus to India, mainly in the form of an increase in exports to help the Allied war effort (see Map 34). By war's end, however, the export stimulus was replaced by the onset of a postwar recession in India in 1919-20, made worse by above-normal railway demand, industrial labor strikes, poor agricultural performance, a devastating outbreak of influenza, and the destruction of prewar markets for Indian products in Central Europe. Postwar imports improved, but in 1920 they, too, finally succumbed to the recession.

During the 1920s, rates declined in both sectors and even experienced a negative rate of growth. Conditions in both sectors improved slightly as the decade wore on, but later, both suffered additional shocks with the advent of the global depression in 1929. Growth rates in imports and exports improved again after 1932 and were even higher than in the previous decade, but the overall value of India's foreign trade in the 1930s was much lower because the volume of trade had contracted by over 40 percent from predepression levels.

The outbreak of the Second World War accelerated the recovery of India's foreign trade to some degree. Because of wartime inflationary pressures, commercial restraints, and a reduction of governmental statistical collection activities, however, the actual condition of India's trade during the war is difficult to ascertain.

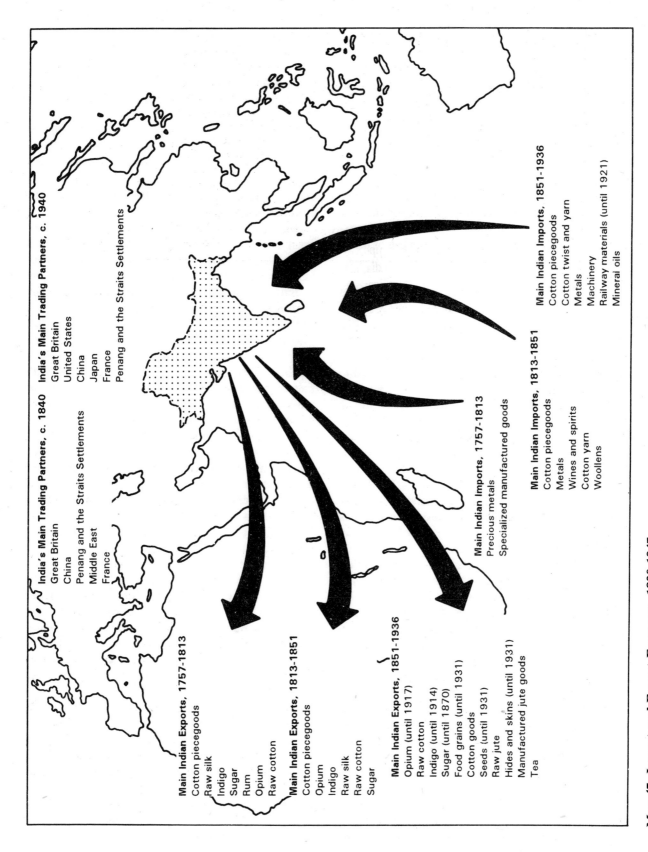

India's Main Trading Partners, c. 1840
Great Britain
China
Penang and the Straits Settlements
Middle East
France

India's Main Trading Partners, c. 1940
Great Britain
United States
China
Japan
France
Penang and the Straits Settlements

Main Indian Imports, 1851-1936
Cotton piecegoods
Cotton twist and yarn
Metals
Machinery
Railway materials (until 1921)
Mineral oils

Main Indian Imports, 1813-1851
Cotton piecegoods
Metals
Wines and spirits
Cotton yarn
Woollens

Main Indian Imports, 1757-1813
Precious metals
Specialized manufactured goods

Main Indian Exports, 1757-1813
Cotton piecegoods
Raw silk
Indigo
Sugar
Rum
Opium
Raw cotton

Main Indian Exports, 1813-1851
Cotton piecegoods
Opium
Indigo
Raw silk
Raw cotton
Sugar

Main Indian Exports, 1851-1936
Opium (until 1917)
Raw cotton
Indigo (until 1914)
Sugar (until 1870)
Food grains (until 1931)
Cotton goods
Seeds (until 1931)
Raw jute
Hides and skins (until 1931)
Manufactured jute goods
Tea

Map 47 Import and Export Economy, 1800-1947

48 Railway Development, 1853-1947

The first railways developed under the encouragement of the governor-general Lord Dalhousie, who, as a former president of the Board of Trade in London, had intimate knowledge of the development of railways in Britain. In 1853, the first line of railway track opened between Bombay and Thana—a distance of only 34 kilometers (21 miles). The success of this experiment was followed by a period of tremendous railway development under the "Guarantee System." Under this system, which lasted until 1869, private British companies received land grants from the Government of India, a guaranteed rate of 5 percent interest on their investment, and 50 percent of the profits.

By 1869, these private railway companies had laid 8,050 km/5,000 miles of track, but as the rate of return was guaranteed by government regardless of results, management tended to be wasteful and inefficient. The Government of India, consequently, assumed the role of railway builder, but the decade of the 1870s proved to be one of financial adversity, and only 3,542 km/2,200 miles of track were laid. Famines also took their toll on scarce resources, and added a renewed sense of urgency to the construction of track; together, these facts resulted in the return to India of private-company development.

Under the "New Guarantee System" (1879-1914), railway companies were again given land grants and a guaranteed rate of return, but the Government of India now offered them an interest rate of only 3.5 percent, and only 40 percent of the profits.

As the twenty-five-year contracts of the original private companies expired, the Government of India purchased their lines. By 1914, therefore, most of the railway lines in India were state-owned. Beginning in 1893, the Government of India encouraged the development of "feeder" or branch lines by offering rebates to companies which built such lines. The system lasted until 1924 and added thousands of additional kilometers of track.

After the First World War, railway construction entered a new phase. The Acworth Committee (1920-21) thoroughly reviewed railway management and policy and urged that the railway budget be separated from the general governmental budget. This recommendation became policy in 1924 and resulted in greater management efficiency and railway growth. Meanwhile, the Government of India undertook much-needed equipment repairs and renewals, and continued its program of construction and state purchase of lines (by 1927, the Government of India owned 72 percent of all railway mileage in India).

The decade of the 1930s and the Second World War both put an intense strain on the railways. A lack of adequate finances due to the Great Depression, later coupled with the cost of the war, led to a neglect of proper railway maintenance. Only after the war was this situation corrected.

The construction of railways had a huge impact on the overall development of the subcontinent. Railway construction took place primarily for economic reasons: routes were laid and rates developed to make the export of Indian foodgrains and other agricultural products cheaper and more efficient, and to provide for the inexpensive delivery of coal to markets. Just as in other countries with railways, rail development in India was not without adverse economic consequences. While efficient railway transportation led to a decrease in the cost of goods and to an increase in the widespread availability of new consumer items by turning India into one large market, the railways also led to dramatic and often destructive changes in the Indian economy. The introduction of the railways, for example, helped complete the undermining of India's small-scale cotton textile industries, created additional unemployment, and converted India into an exporter of raw cotton. And as trade patterns shifted, some traditional trade centers—those which were bypassed by the early rail network—experienced a marked decline.

In addition to generating changes in the Indian economy, the railway also served British strategic interests. Railways in Bengal, for example, helped bring to Calcutta badly needed supplies of raw jute which then were used by Britain during the Crimean War. Later growth allowed the Government of India to quickly transport troops to potential flashpoints throughout the subcontinent, thus enabling them to reduce the number of troops needed overall.

The development of railways in India undoubtably served British imperial interests—both economic and strategic—first. But as with many of the institutions left behind by the British, the railway also had positive aspects. Passenger travel proved quite popular from the very beginning and helped create a sense of unity among the diverse regions of the subcontinent. And at Partition in 1947, India had the best railway system of any non-Western country in the world.

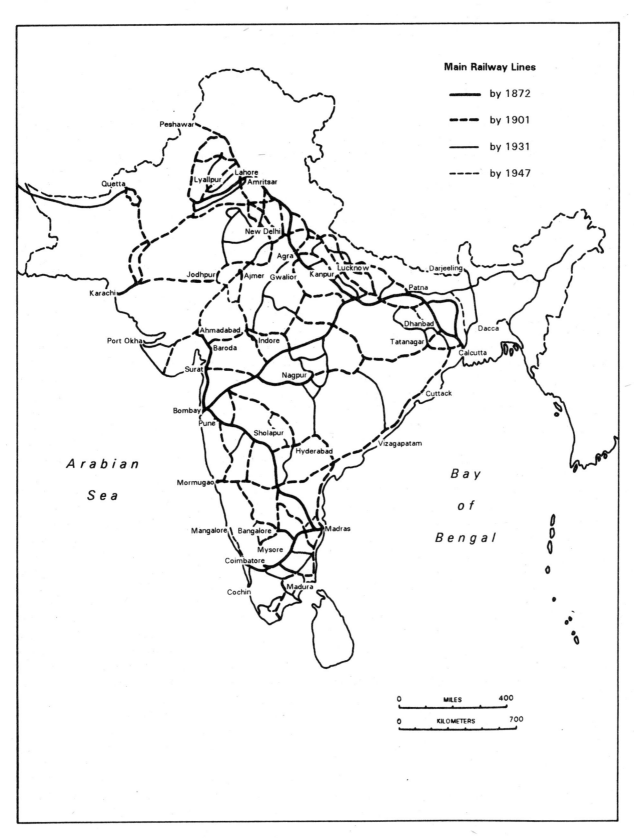

Map 48 Railway Development, 1853-1947

49 Economic Development in Panjab, 1849-1939

After the British had destroyed the power of the independent Sikh kingdom and annexed its lands in 1849, they wasted no time in consolidating their position there. The governor-general, Lord Dalhousie (1848-56), was anxious to convert what he saw as a hostile, warrior population into "industrious subjects." He had very definite plans for the remolding of Panjab, immediately appointed a "Board of Administration for the Affairs of the Punjab," and gave it wide-ranging powers to undertake that task. Once the British had restored peace and secured the defense of Panjab, they turned their attention to developing the province's economic base. Although the British implemented many civil and administrative changes in Panjab, they had their most lasting impact on the development of the region's economic infrastructure.

With sufficient water, the soil of Panjab was extremely productive, but capricious weather often led to a shortage of rainfall in the growing season. This, in turn, often resulted in lower crops yields, crop failures, and, ultimately, famine. With this problem in mind, the board decided that Panjab, with its five major rivers and numerous tributaries, was an ideal area for the construction of a system of irrigation canals. Canal-building was, however, not a new idea in Panjab. Previous rulers had already constructed some canals. The Bari Doab Canal, for example, extended for some 403 kilometers (250 miles) through this important agricultural region. Soon after annexation, the board ordered the canal enlarged to improve its water-carrying capacity, Other existing canals in Derajat and Multan were also improved. Despite the obvious benefits to agriculture, further canal construction was delayed until after 1857 because of disputes over costs. By the 1880s, British canal construction in Panjab had reached a high point, as several canals, including the Western Yamuna, the Lower Chenab, and many smaller ones, were all either built, modified, or extended. Additional new major and minor canals were built through the end of the period until, by 1939, 5.24 million hectares (13.1 million acres) were under canal irrigation.

The Board of Administration, and subsequent British governments in Panjab, also gave considerable attention to road-building, and developed an extensive plan to crisscross Panjab with roads, bridges, and viaducts. Although early road-building activity served primarily British strategic needs in Panjab, linking military outposts, cantonments, and major cities, Panjabis also benefited in the long-term from the improved communications. By the beginning of 1853, some 2,174 kilometers (1,350 miles) of road had actually been built, another 4,025 kilometers (2,500 miles) traced, and some additional 8,533 kilometers (5,300 miles) surveyed. The Grand Trunk Road, which over the years had fallen into disrepair, was reconstructed, and lengthened. Road-building continued throughout the rest of the period, but the construction of "metalled," or paved, roads was always hampered by lack of adequate government financing (in 1901, less than 8 percent of roads in Panjab were paved—this figure rose only to 18 percent in 1939).

In addition to infrastructure, the British also helped develop Panjab's natural resources. Large borax deposits along with iron ore and coal were discovered and exploited. British investors set up refineries to process saltpeter, used in explosives and in leather tanning. Prior to British annexation, Panjab had been largely denuded of forest for fuel. At the prompting of Lord Dalhousie, the board enacted a number of new regulations designed to encourage the conservation of forest lands and the promotion of tree-planting. The board planted trees around public buildings and along canals, and offered incentives to landholders who planted trees. After the passage of the Forest Act of 1878, the Government of India divided forests in Panjab into three classes: "reserved," "protected," and "unclassed." "Reserved" forests were permanently tended and rigidly controlled by government. "Protected" forests were less strictly controlled: local populations were allowed some access. Finally, "unclassed" forests were available for use by the public with almost no restrictions. Under the new Forest Act, the need for conservation was carefully balanced with the need for wood and fuel, and although the number of acres devoted to forest lands gradually decreased prior to 1939, there were still nearly twice as many acres devoted to forests as there were in 1849.

Although British construction of economic infrastructure in Panjab served mainly British interests, it nevertheless had a beneficial impact on the people of the region. Now divided between India and Pakistan, Panjab is still the most prosperous region of each country and, in part, this prosperity can be attributed to British development.

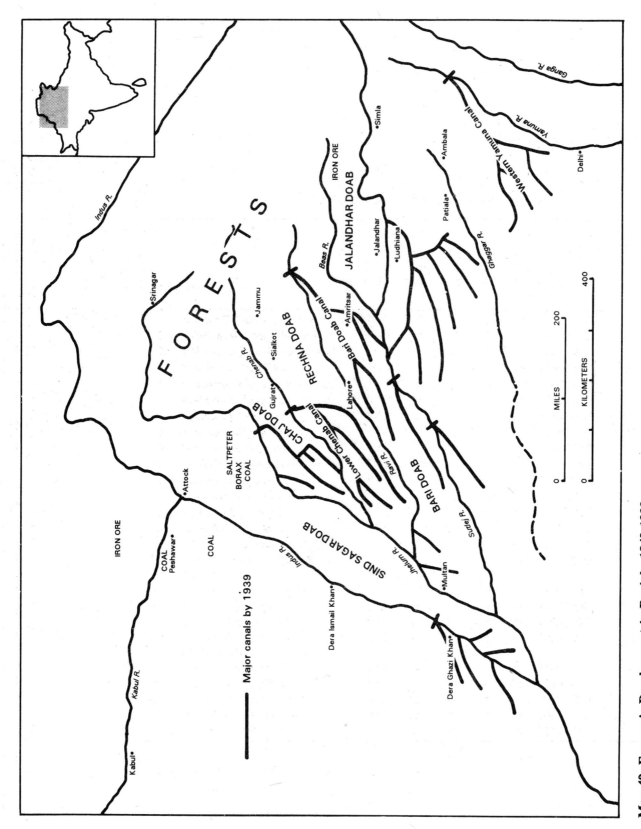

Map 49 Economic Development in Panjab, 1849-1939

109

50   Growth of the Cotton Textile Industry, 1854-1947

Although India has produced cotton garments and cloth for centuries, the factory-based cotton textile industry began only in 1854, with the establishment of the first modern cotton mill in Bombay. By 1861, twelve mills had been established in the Bombay Presidency, most on Bombay Island. The outbreak of the U.S. Civil War that year drove Indian raw cotton prices higher as supplies from the southern United States to Great Britain all but dried up. Speculation in cotton was rampant: many of the speculators, such as Jamshedji Tata (1839-1904), were Indian businessmen who made vast fortunes by exporting raw cotton to British mills. The huge increase in raw cotton exports curtailed the expansion of the cotton industry in India—only eight new mills were built between 1861 and 1872. After 1872, the industry recovered from the postwar depression. Thirty-six new mills—including J. N. Tata's Empress Cotton Mill founded at Nagpur in 1877—were built by the end of the decade, employing some 43,000 workers. By 1879, almost 75 percent of all mills were located in Bombay Presidency, with over 50 percent on Bombay Island alone. Spinning was the dominant product during this period, with some yarn produced for export to Japan and China. Woven products were coarse, and supplied the bulk of the domestic market; finer goods came from the mills of Lancashire in Britain.

The final two decades marked a period of substantial overall growth in the cotton industry. By 1895, there were 144 mills in operation (most owned by Indians), employing over 140,000 workers. The industry experienced some spatial dispersal as more mills were built in the so-called "cotton tracts" of Ahmadabad, Nagpur, and Sholapur. The percentage of mills concentrated in Bombay Presidency thus dropped to 70, with only 45 percent located on Bombay Island. As with the earlier period, spinning was still the dominant product, but improvements in machinery had edged out hand spinning of coarse yarns, allowing factory-produced yarns to capture the Indian home market. Other areas of progress included the development of finer yarns, the production of a greater variety of yarns, and the opening of new markets. Exports of cotton yarn to both China and Japan grew at a rapid rate until 1890, when the opening of the first cotton mills in Japan reduced demand. Japan thereafter began purchasing primarily raw cotton from India. Growth slowed between 1895

and 1900 due to two major famines (which affected most of the cotton tracts as well as Bombay), as well as to the outbreak of plague in Bombay in 1896.

Growth in the textile industry continued to be slow even after 1900. In 1902, U.S. speculation in Indian raw cotton led to higher prices. After the turn of the century, China, India's largest yarn market, sank into economic depression, and demand for Indian yarn dropped. After 1907, conditions in the industry improved and there was slow but steady progress until the outbreak of the First World War. By 1914, weaving was experiencing rapid growth and had even surpassed spinning as the primary product. Further mechanical improvements led to even finer quality products as new markets for woven garments and cloth opened in Persia, Arabia, East Africa, the Straits Settlements, and Ceylon. The percentage of cloth produced for export climbed from 9 to 15 percent. By the beginning of the war, India had 271 mills in operation, employing over a quarter of a million workers.

From 1914 to 1923, the Indian textile industry prospered. A number of factors accounted for this strong growth: a wartime shortage of shipping led to higher freighting charges for Lancashire's products; high revenue duties and a decline in competition gave India a greater competitive market advantage; wages remained low during the war; prices rose dramatically in 1918-20 to three times their prewar level and resulted in greater profits. By 1923, the postwar depression caught up with the overheated industry, prices fell, and growth stalled through the rest of the decade.

With the advent of the Great Depression in 1929, India's cotton textile industry suffered an even greater shock as prices fell dramatically, and overseas competition, particularly from Japan, cut into the Indian market. Although market conditions for textiles remained poor through the rest of the 1930s, per-capita consumption of cotton cloth actually increased, due, in part, to the **swadeshi** movement and by the Government of India's imposition of higher duties on non-British cotton imports.

The outbreak of the Second World War gave a much-needed boost to India's sagging textile industry. Demand for domestic products increased as the supply from Britain fell and, after 1941, when Japanese sources were stopped. Export demand increased as well. The growth trend continued through 1947.

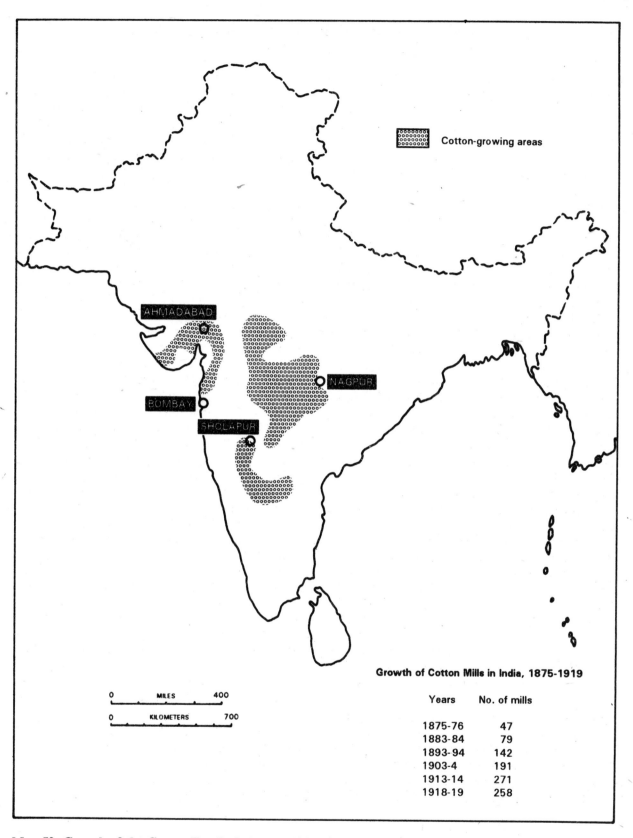

| Cotton-growing areas |

AHMADABAD

NAGPUR

BOMBAY

SHOLAPUR

0 — MILES — 400

0 — KILOMETERS — 700

Growth of Cotton Mills in India, 1875-1919

Years	No. of mills
1875-76	47
1883-84	79
1893-94	142
1903-4	191
1913-14	271
1918-19	258

Map 50 Growth of the Cotton Textile Industry, 1854-1947

111

51   Economic Development in India since 1947

In 1947, independent India inherited an economy from the British that was essentially colonial. The bulk of the population was engaged in agriculture and related activities, and industrial development was low; overall, the British had left behind a stagnating economic structure.

Jawaharlal Nehru, India's first prime minister (1947-64), an avowed socialist, had great plans for the revitalization and development of India, based on centralized economic planning, with a strong focus on industrialization. Under Nehru's guidance, India adopted a course of development under Five-Year Plans, similar to those then in use in communist countries like the Soviet Union and China, but with the continued presence of a large private sector.

The First Five-Year Plan (1951-56) called for an 11 percent increase in national income by 1956. The Indian government spent US$3.7 billion during the First Five-Year Plan, but over US$3 billion was used just to restore pre-war production capabilities, communications, and agriculture. Agricultural yields did increase by 25 percent, but because of population increases and weather-related famines, India still had to import grain from overseas and remained an importer of grain for the next twenty years. Because of the need to rebuild, less than 19 percent of the funds went toward new industrial, mining, and power generation development.

India's Second Five-Year Plan (1956-61) was at once more costly and more effective than the first plan. By 1961, food-grain production increased by another 23 percent, iron ore production almost trebled, coal production climbed over 42 percent, and power-generation capacity doubled. Despite emphasis on heavy industry, steel production did not meet the plan's targets. Cotton textiles remained the country's largest industry.

Building on earlier successes, the Third Five-Year Plan (1961-66) provided for the construction of new steel mills which helped produce a nearly 200 percent increase in steel output and an over 200 percent increase in iron production over the Second Plan. Coal production increased by nearly 40 percent and power capacity more than doubled over 1961 levels. By 1966, India ranked seventh among industrialized countries.

While India's achievements in industrial development were laudable, its agricultural sector lagged behind. Pro-ductivity had steadily increased since 1947, but food-grain production in 1966 had risen only 75 percent over 1951 levels. With India's population growing by 13 million per year, what was needed was scientific innovation to produce higher agricultural yields. The breakthrough came with the introduction of genetically superior wheat and rice into India's farmlands in the late 1960s; the so-called Green Revolution had begun and agricultural yields rapidly improved under the Fourth Five-Year Plan (1966-71).

Economic disturbances and structural upheavals in the Indian economy caused the Fourth Plan to be revised in 1970; the Bangladesh War, the global oil crisis of 1973, and a major drought delayed the initiation of the Fifth Five-Year Plan until 1974. By then, it seemed clear to the Indian leadership that while government-sponsored development had been successful in many ways, it had also created major structural inefficiencies which were acting as a drag on further development. Despite slightly improved economic performance in some sectors under Indira Gandhi's emergency rule (1975-77), the bulk of India's millions still lived in grinding poverty. Further economic growth seemed to depend on liberalization of the economy.

Some structural changes came after 1984, when Rajiv Gandhi, the son of Indira, became prime minister. Gandhi surrounded himself with young technocrats and embarked on a modified version of Reaganomics in order to propel India's lagging economy forward; he was moderately successful. In the 1980s, gross domestic product (GDP) increased an average of 5.3 percent annually, compared with 3.3 percent and 3.5 percent in the 1960s and 1970s, respectively. Per-capita income rose by 40 percent and the export sector grew by slightly over 17 percent by the end of the decade.

While the Indian government's policies spurred growth in the private sector, the large, inefficient, state-owned public sector continued to consume valuable financial resources. Public sector losses were offset by governmental deficit-spending, but this activity put pressure on the credit markets, and fueled inflation.

In 1991, India's new Prime Minister, P. V. Narasimha Rao, began instituting a number of free-market reforms as a corrective, but by late 1994 it was still too early to tell if they would have the desired long-term impact on India's ailing economy.

112

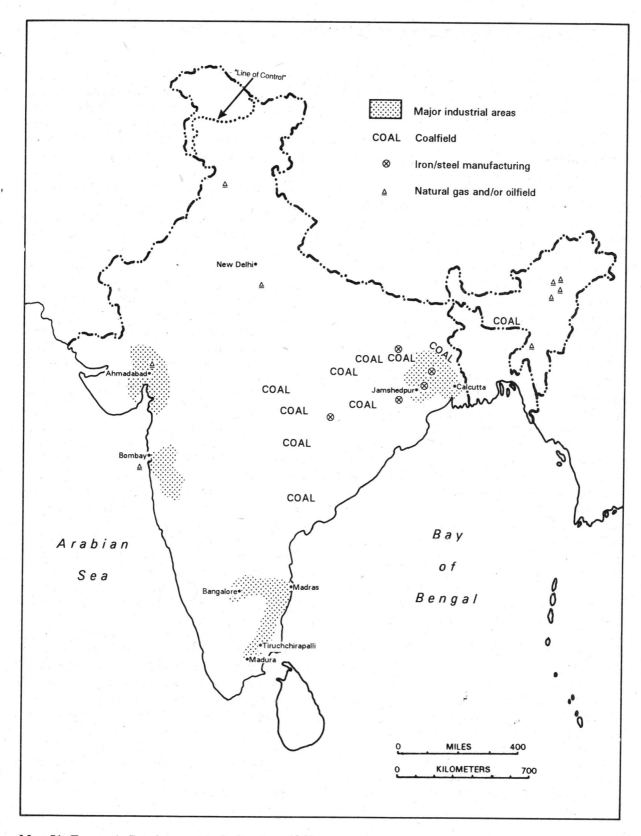

Map 51 Economic Development in India since 1947

113

52 Economic Development in Pakistan since 1947

Like India, Pakistan inherited a weak colonial economy from the British after Independence. And like those of India, Pakistan's leaders sought to convert Pakistan from an agricultural state into an industrial one. In developing Pakistan's economy, however, its leaders faced a number of difficult tasks. Partition had weakened the traditional links between the area and the rest of India. What became West Pakistan had, prior to Partition, produced primarily grain and other agricultural products—cotton, sugarcane, hides, and skins—which were then supplied to India for further processing. After 1947, Pakistan lost its established markets in India. Pakistan also lost most of its business class which, comprising mainly Hindus, fled to India. The majority of indigenous Muslims, and most of those migrating to Pakistan from India, were agriculturalists. Few had business experience. The virtual lack of a business class consequently hindered Pakistan's early development.

Despite its troubled birth, Pakistan's economy performed well overall in the first three decades after Independence. Whereas independent India opted for heavy investment in the public sector through socialistic Five-Year Plans, Pakistan's government used its Five-Year Plans to encourage more private sector development, reserving for the public sector only defense, hydroelectric power, and basic infrastructure like telephone, telegraph, and radio. The government also implemented a number of restrictions and controls on foreign trade and exchange, all designed to encourage private sector development, and to quickly generate an entrepreneurial class.

Governmental policies helped spur the construction of factories and mills by transferring wealth from agriculture to industrial development, often to the detriment of agriculture. In the 1960s—a decade of considerable growth—Pakistan's gross domestic product grew at an average of 6.7 percent annually, up from 3.1 percent per year in the 1950s. In the 1950s, while the industrial sector grew, albeit slowly, the agricultural sector stagnated. By the end of the 1960s, this condition improved as both sectors rapidly expanded.

Government's attempts to encourage the development of a commercial class met with mixed results. The size of the class increased over time, but by 1968, the government determined that twenty industrial "families" controlled 66 percent of Pakistan's industries, as well as 80 percent of all banking and insurance assets. Consequently, the country's wealth was highly concentrated in the hands of a few. The government made some efforts at reform, but because those same families dominated the political life of the country, real reform stalled.

The Pakistani civil war and the subsequent severance of East Pakistan dealt a considerable shock to Pakistan's economy. Since Independence, West Pakistan had treated East Pakistan like a virtual colony, a captive market for goods produced in the country's West wing. East Pakistan supplied the West with tea and foreign exchange through the export of raw materials like jute, while governmental policies, formulated in the West, favored industrial development in that wing, allowing the East's manufacturing potential to languish. After the civil war and Bangladeshi independence, the West wing, the inheritor of the name "Pakistan," was forced to recover from the cost of the war itself, as well as the loss of the economic output and markets of its eastern wing.

Beginning in 1972, Pakistan's new president, Zulfikar Ali Bhutto, attempted to restimulate Pakistan's shaken economy by devaluing the rupee by 57 percent, and by nationalizing over thirty large factories throughout Pakistan's major industries. Bhutto also intervened in agriculture by lowering ceilings on landholdings, and by increasing mechanization. Instead of boosting economic growth, however, Bhutto's reforms further stalled Pakistan's economy in the 1970s. And although Bhutto's reform efforts were geared ostensibly toward altering the serious imbalance in national income distribution, there seems to be little evidence that he was successful.

In 1977, Bhutto was ousted in a military coup d'etat and most of his policies reversed. The new government, headed by Mohammad Zia ul Haq, favored Islamizing the economy, i.e., using Quranic principles in developing economic policy, but for the most part did not actively pursue that policy. Pakistan's economic performance did improve during the Zia years, its growth rate reaching over 6 percent annually by the mid-1980s. Since then, Pakistan's economy has again declined, partly in response to the global recession and new changes in governmental policy.

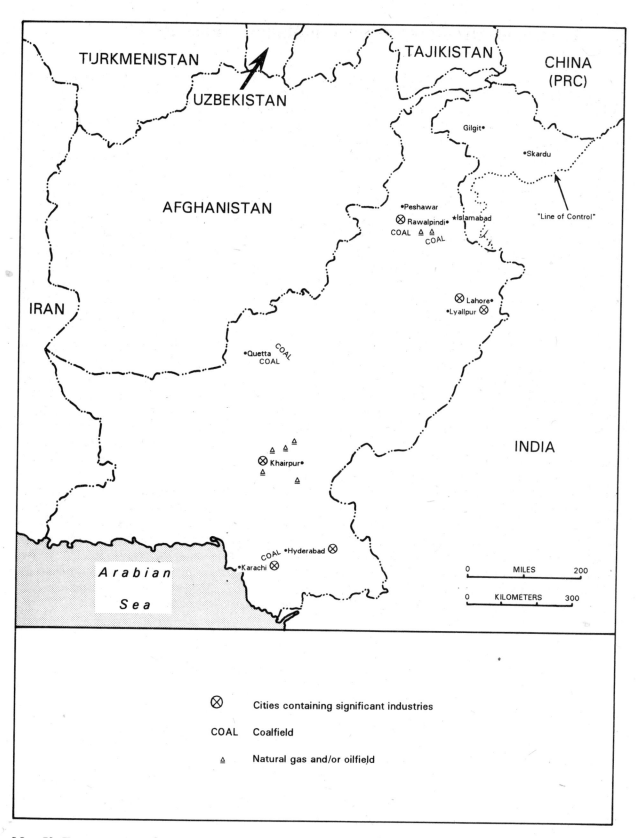

Map 52 Economic Development in Pakistan since 1947

115

53 Economic Development in Bangladesh since 1972

East Pakistan formally emerged as the new state of Bangladesh in 1972 after its war for independence (see Maps 41 and 42). But its poor condition in 1947, twenty-four years of economic subordination to West Pakistan, and the recent war had all taken their toll. In 1972, Bangladesh ranked first in rural population density in the world; its population, the majority of which suffered chronic malnutrition, was growing between 2.5 and 3 percent annually; and it had to cope with the relocation of some 10 million refugees who had temporarily fled to India during the war.

In addition to its many social problems, the independent Bangladeshi economy was in ruin. Bangladesh had only a tiny business class, and few scientific, engineering, and technical personnel. The remainder of its work force, though large, was undertrained and mostly illiterate. Due to wartime disruptions, food supplies were in short supply, and overseas markets for jute products had been lost. The country had few industries, and even fewer developable resources. Its transportation infrastructure, not well developed prior to 1972, had been heavily damaged by the war. To add to its misery, Bangladesh was still recovering from a 1970 cyclonic storm which caused massive property damage and a quarter of a million deaths.

Borrowing from the Indian model, Bangladeshi leaders implemented the Five-Year Plan system as the best vehicle for rebuilding and developing the economy of the new country. The government of Bangladesh, under its revolutionary leader and first president, Sheikh Mujibur Rahman (popularly known as "Mujib"), nationalized industrial plants abandoned by their West Pakistani owners, the banking and insurance industries, and the export trade in jute. Mujib's government, how-ever, proved corrupt, and his economic policies failed to produce expected growth. By 1975, when Mujib was assassinated in a military coup d'etat, Bangladesh's overall economic development had been seriously retarded.

In 1977, under a continuing, but considerably less corrupt, military dictatorship, the Bangladeshi economy began slowly to improve. President Zia (Maj. Gen. Ziaur Rahman) concentrated on the need to increase economic output, especially in foodstuffs, and to stimulate rural development, including population planning. Zia cooperated with foreign countries and international aid programs to receive much-needed foreign assistance, including capital, foodgrains, and technical advice. Under Zia, agricultural productivity increased. Industry also improved. Although low when compared to India and Pakistan, Bangladesh's percentage of gross domestic product due to industry rose nearly 4 percent between 1970 and 1980, from 8.4 percent to 12.2 percent. The bulk of this increase took place after 1977. Within two years after Zia's takeover, real GDP had grown to 6.1 percent per year. Despite high economic growth figures in the late 1970s and early 1980s, Bangladesh's increasing population outstripped any gains, and the country remained a foodgrain importer.

In the late 1980s, continuing political turmoil and poor weather had an adverse effect on the country's growth. By the early 1990s, despite the return to constitutional government, the annual economic growth rate was holding steady at only 4 percent, a level insufficient to raise the bulk of the Bangladeshi people out of poverty. Bangladesh today remains the most populous poor country in the world.

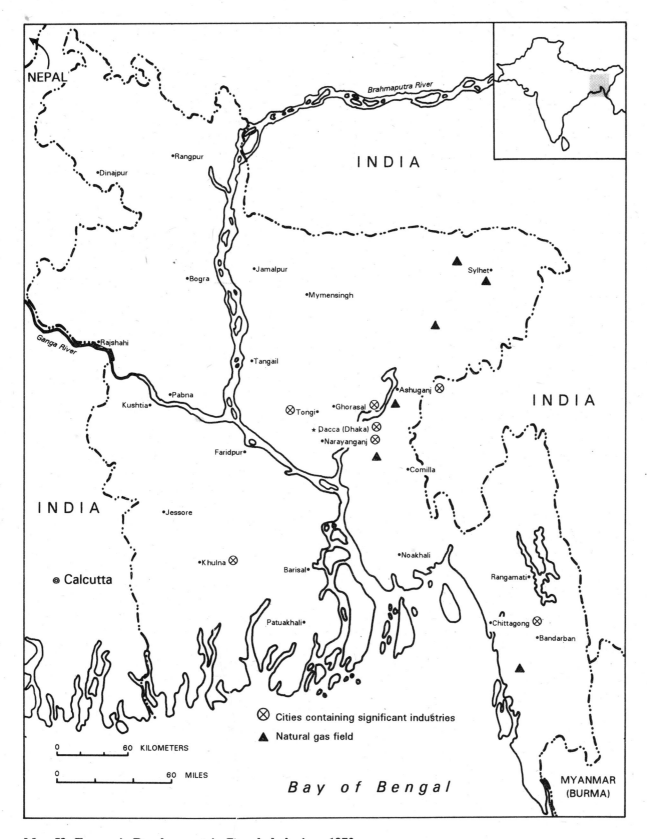

Map 53 Economic Development in Bangladesh since 1972

117

The ethical protests which gave rise in the sixth century BCE to both Jainism and Buddhism were precipitated by changes and stresses of crisis proportions in South Asian politics and society. During the various wars of conquest among the mahajanapadas which had taken place in the preceding century, political and military power concentrated in the few states able to muster the necessary resources. The successful waging of war and defense of one's territorial holdings was dependent on the quality of one's troops—high-quality troops required better training and more advanced equipment. Stimulated by these needs, Indian kings invested heavily in new military technologies such as river-borne war fleets and catapults, and in more conventional elements such as chariots and elephants. Almost continuous warfare throughout the sixth century BCE produced in northern India a drastically altered map as well as a more authoritarian political climate.

In addition to changes in politics, this period saw sharp changes in the economic and social landscape. Trade became more complex as large cities developed as centers of economic production and as the waterways of the Ganga and its tributaries were used by merchants to circulate goods. As trade increased and became more profitable, it spawned the development of a sizable urban merchant class, which gained in status at the expense of the small agriculturalist.

Societal pressures followed the structural changes taking place in the political economy of the Gangetic plains. As the monarchies grew in power, their rulers obtained greater status. No longer chieftains subject to the will of the clan, these new rulers became absolutist, hereditary monarchs. The kings of northern India were supported by the Brahmans who, as intermediaries between the gods and the rulers, proclaimed the divinity of the monarchs, and assisted them in securing their power through sacrificial rituals. Monarchs soon became dependent on Brahman priests who served to enhance their legitimacy and status. To protect their orthodoxy and power, the Brahmans gave sanction to the new state of affairs through an increase in ritualism and the codification of laws governing the social order, thereby undercutting any increase in social mobility brought about by economic changes. With the establishment of the doctrine of monarchical divinity, and the accompanying increase in power of both rulers and Brahmans, society became increasingly stratified between those who represented orthodoxy and the governing elite—Brahmans and rulers—and the merchants and artisans in the cities. These latter two groups had gained considerable material wealth and desired a greater share of the state's political power, but they were largely alienated from it by the growing rigidity of the system.

It was in this environment of crisis, a ferment of political, economic, and social change, that several heterodox belief systems arose, the most important of which were Jainism and Buddhism. Among the many groups adversely affected by the political and military upheavals of the preceding century, the **kshatriyas** and the republics were in many ways the ones who lost the most during the transition from less complex lineage-based governments and societies to more complex state-based systems. Not surprisingly, perhaps, the founder of Jainism, Mahavira (c. 540-468 BCE), and Buddha (c. 563-483 BCE), were both kshatriyas and both founded their respective systems of thought not in monarchies, but in republics, where Brahmanical supremacy had not taken hold. In contrast to *Brahmanical orthodoxy*, Jainism and Buddhism were philosophies which emphasized the role played by individuals in their own salvation. For Jains and Buddhists, salvation was not dependent on one's social standing at birth, but rather on the quality of one's actions during a lifetime.

Both Jains and Buddhists pointed out that the pursuit of selfish desires led the individual away from salvation; of the two systems, however, Buddhism was the more moderate in this regard and thus engendered a greater lay following, especially among the **vaishyas**, who comprised the bulk of the urban merchant class. Jainism and Buddhism offered a viable alternative to Brahmanical orthodoxy for those who were dissatisfied with that system, or for those who, like the **shudras**, were excluded from Brahmanism altogether. During their lifetimes, both Mahavira and Buddha traveled extensively, spreading their views of enlightenment and salvation to any who would listen. The early dispersion of Jainism and Buddhism was limited to parts of northern India by c. 450 BCE. In the centuries that followed, however, facilitated by royal patronage, both philosophies spread throughout the subcontinent and, in the case of Buddhism, even into the rest of Asia.

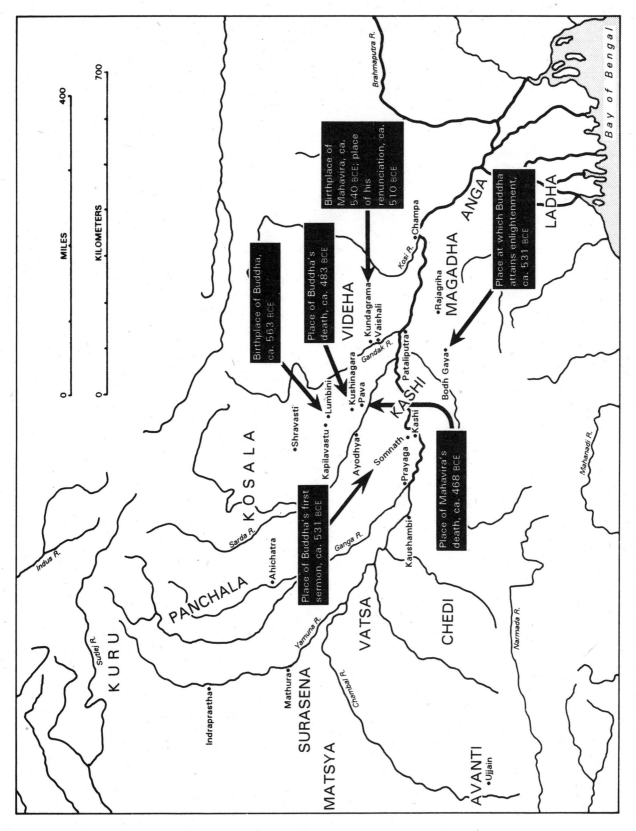

Map 54 Origins of Jainism and Buddhism in South Asia, c. 500 BCE

119

The period 400 BCE-320 CE witnessed an upsurge in the growth of adherents to both Jainism and Buddhism, and although Brahmanism also remained popular, it underwent some dramatic changes during this time.

At the death of Mahavira, Jainism had spread to many areas in the eastern Gangetic plain, but centered on Bihar. By c. 200 BCE, Jainism had spread as far west as Panjab, Rajasthan, and Gujarat, and as far south as Orissa. Unfortunately, many of the North Indian Jaina temples of the ancient period did not survive the destruction of the Muslim invasions after c. 1100, but Jain literary evidence mentions the most prominent sites. Inscriptional evidence shows that a Jain temple was built at Shaketa (Ayodhya) sometime in the first century BCE. Another of the earliest centers of Jainism was Mathura, where a temple was built in the second century BCE. Other great Jain centers included Kaushambi, dating to c. 100 BCE, where the famous Pabhosa cave contained Jain images and sculpture; Shravasti, which contained the temple of Sambhavanatha; Ahicchatra, a town sacred to Parshvanatha; and Bharukachccha, a port city frequented by many Jain monks. By c. 150 CE, the Jains experienced a schism which resulted in the division of the religion's followers into two distinct sects, the Shvetambaras and the Digambaras. Geographically, the Shvetambaras are located in Gujarat and western Rajasthan, while the Digambaras can be found in eastern Rajasthan, Uttar Pradesh, and South India; the schism had an effect on religious iconography and on structures created subsequently in these different geographic areas.

After the death of the Buddha, several of the major states of northern India laid claim to the holy relics left behind. The eight claimants divided the relics among themselves and subsequently constructed stupas in which to house them. These eight stupas, run by lay people, not by monks, marked the beginning of the establishment of Buddhist religious sites throughout South Asia. Under Ashoka Maurya, the great ancient patron of Buddhism, the original eight stupas were reopened, and the relics were reallocated among other stupas which he had ordered built throughout the empire. According to Buddhist sources, Asoka had nearly one thousand stupas built during his reign. These stupas, and others built during the centuries that followed, like the ones at Bharhut and Sanchi (although the core of the Sanchi stupa seems to date to Ashoka's time), became centers of lay Buddhism where teachers met students and passed on Buddhist doctrine. Several pilgrimage sites also became quite important for lay worshippers, including the Buddha's place of birth, and the pipal tree under which he obtained enlightenment (Akira 1990).

Although monastic Buddhism had existed for over two centuries, it came to full fruition in the post-Maurya period when it was called Nikaya Buddhism. Characterized by the growth of monasteries throughout South Asia, Nikaya Buddhism owed its existence largely to royal and merchant patronage. Patrons donated money, land, and even cave-temples to the Buddhist orders, enabling them to live a life of quiet study and contemplation.

A later schism among Buddhists in South Asia led to the development of a well-defined lay Buddhism, called Mahayana. The most important royal patrons of Mahayana Buddhism were the Kushanas, especially Kanishka, who convened the Fourth Buddhist Council in Kashmir, at which the schism between Nikaya (or Hinayana, as it was subsequently called) Buddhism and Mahayana Buddhism was officially recognized. Kanishka also built an enormous stupa at Peshawar, the base of which was nearly 90 meters (300 feet) in diameter.

Adherents to Brahmanism in this period, located in the Gangetic plain, Rajasthan, and eastern and southern India, gradually revived Vedic sacrificial rituals. Sects which had originally formed in reaction against orthodox Brahmanism, such as **Vaishnavists** and **Shaivists**, were subsequently incorporated into Brahmanism which, because of its transformation, could now be more properly called Hinduism. Early Brahmanical religious and cultural sites, especially along the Ganga River, continued to be important, while newer Vaishnavist and Shaivist sites, such as Mathura and Ujjain, grew in importance.

Of the many cultural sites of this period, one deserves special mention: Taxila (in Sanskrit: Takshashila). In addition to being a center of religion for Buddhists, as well as Hindus, Taxila was a thriving center for art, culture, and learning. At the crossroads of cultural and economic exchange between South Asia, China, and the West, Taxila was also home to a great university.

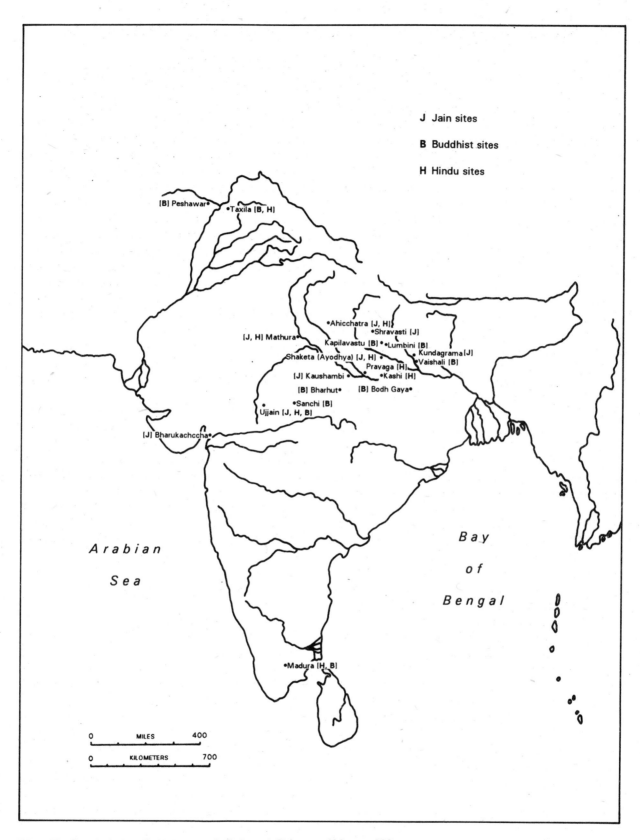

J Jain sites

B Buddhist sites

H Hindu sites

[B] Peshawar• •Taxila [B, H]

•Ahicchatra [J, H]
  •Shravasti [J]
[J, H] Mathura•
  Kapilavastu [B] •Lumbini [B]
  • •Kundagrama [J]
Shaketa (Ayodhya) [J, H] • •Vaishali [B]
  Pravaga [H]
[J] Kaushambi • •Kashi [H]
  [B] Bharhut• [B] Bodh Gaya•
  •Sanchi [B]
Ujjain [J, H, B]

[J] Bharukachccha•

Arabian

Sea

Bay

of

Bengal

•Madura [H, B]

0   MILES   400

0   KILOMETERS   700

Map 55 South Asian Religious and Cultural Sites, c. 400 BCE-320 CE

121

56   Spread of Hindu and Buddhist Culture to Southeast Asia

Beginning sometime during the first century CE, prolonged and constant interaction developed between South Asians and Southeast Asians. This interaction had a significant impact on the early development of Southeast Asia: elements of Indian culture—first Hindu, later Buddhist—began to take root in the region, and several political entities arose which, although ruled by indigenous sovereigns, shared many of the same cultural and political characteristics of states in South Asia. The causes of the contact between the two regions are still debated by historians, as are its consequences, but several explanations have emerged from recent research.

Extended Indian relations with Southeast Asia seem to have been informed initially by the desire of Indian merchants to increase commercial contacts with that region. Several events made the gradual increase in maritime trade possible. First, during the first century CE the Asian world apparently experienced a critical shortage of gold. Indian merchants, like other merchants involved in the maritime trade, depended on gold as the primary medium of exchange for commercial transactions; the shortage prompted attempts to secure other sources, including the legendary gold deposits of Southeast Asia. Second, new sailing techniques and innovations in ship design led to the ability to carry much larger cargoes, thus stimulating a much higher volume of trade. Third, religion also aided the increase in trade. In contrast to many of their South Asian Hindu counterparts, Buddhists readily accepted the business of commerce and many Buddhists were actively engaged in the maritime trade. Buddhism was introduced in China in the first century, and by the sixth century had became firmly entrenched. Buddhist monks traveling between India and China during this period often stopped at newly established Buddhist centers in Southeast Asia, making the region an important geographic link between India and China. The spread of Buddhism throughout South, Southeast, and East Asia provided a common intellectual underpinning among these regions—one that facilitated commercial relations. Finally, the increase in maritime trade was also the product of changing political conditions in China. The collapse of the Later Han dynasty (25-220 CE) in the late second century led to incessant conflict between its successor states, the Three Kingdoms (220-c. 280 CE). This turmoil, coupled with the obstruction of the northern overland trade route with the West due to the depreda-

tions of northern "barbarians," led Chinese merchants to seek a safer, overseas alternative to the south (Hall 1985).

Economic interaction between Indians and Southeast Asians led naturally also to political and cultural interaction. One of the earliest examples of the impact of Indian ideas and institutions on Southeast Asia was the development of that region's first state: a land described in Chinese sources as "Funan." According to legend, Funan rose to prominence in the early third century after a local princess married an Indian Brahman who had traveled to Southeast Asia. Historians have suggested that the legend, even if unverifiable, may be taken to symbolize the melding of Sanskritic Hindu socio-political elements with existing indigenous institutions, the antecedents of which can be found in South India.

As trade with South Asia increased, Funan's rulers acted as the intermediaries between their own populations and foreign traders. Exposed to an ever-increasing realm of experiences based on their involvement in foreign trade, Funan chieftains doubtless saw the benefits to be derived also from selectively adapting Sanskritic Hindu, and to some extent Buddhist, elements of South Asian politics and culture to their own circumstances. Embracing South Asian political organization, for example, led to a greater concentration of power in the hands of Funan's ruling elite, thus giving them an advantage over rivals who still adhered to more traditional, less autocratic, and weaker systems of government. Funan's rulers also adapted elements of South Asian culture, including art, religion, and ceremonies, which served to enhance and legitimize the increasing level of differentiation between the ruling elite and the common people.

Funan declined in the sixth century due to internal dissension and shifting patterns of international trade. Its experiences, however, remained valid and were shared, albeit to differing extents, by many other Southeast Asian states, among them Shrivijaya and the kingdoms of Java. Shrivijaya rose to prominence by occupying a central role in international maritime commerce through the Strait of Malacca between 670 and 1025. In the kingdoms of Java, during approximately the same period, power was diffused within the island, and was derived not from participation in the maritime trade, but from the propagation of religion and the construction of temples.

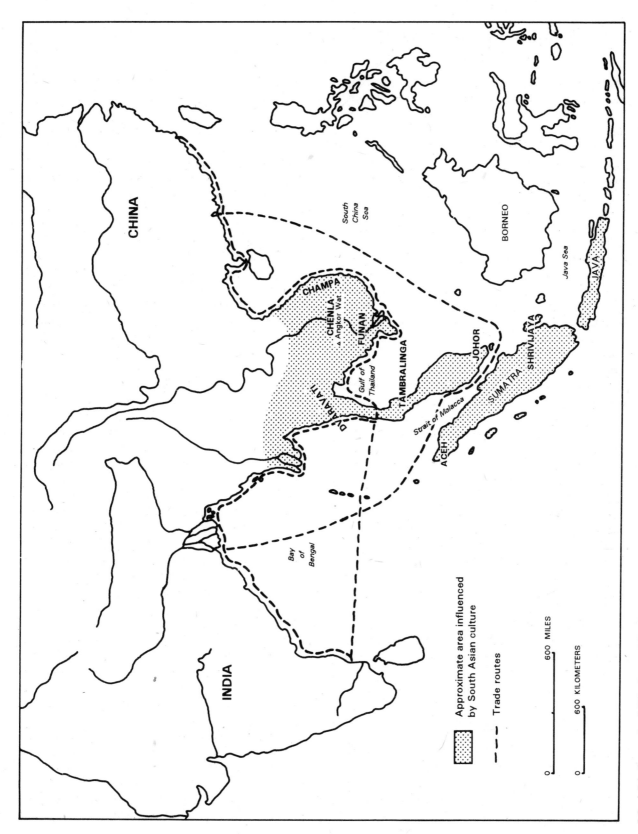

Map 56 Spread of Hindu and Buddhist Culture to Southeast Asia

CHINA

South
China
Sea

BORNEO

Java Sea

JAVA

CHAMPA

CHENLA

△ Angkor Wat

FUNAN

Gulf of
Thailand

DVARAVATI

TAMBRALINGA

JOHOR

SHRIVIJAYA

SUMATRA

Strait of Malacca

ACEH

INDIA

Bay
of
Bengal

Approximate area influenced
by South Asian culture

Trade routes

600 MILES

600 KILOMETERS

0

0

123

57   Famine in South Asia, 1769-1943

Although famine has been an endemic problem throughout much of the history of South Asia, clear information regarding famine conditions were not available until after 1757. During the period of British rule in South Asia, the subcontinent experienced a total of twenty-three famines, and numerous severe shortages of food between 1770 and 1943 (Ghosh 1987).

The historical causes of famine in India varied according to location and time period, but some common factors are discernible. In most cases, extremes of either unseasonal rains or drought, brought about by variations in monsoonal weather patterns, led to the failure of the kharif (summer) harvest of such crops as rice and millet, upon which the majority of the population was dependent. Failure of the kharif harvest constricted the overall food supply and put abnormal pressure for success on rabi (winter) crops, such as wheat. If this crop was successful, a severe scarcity might still result, but most would have at least something to eat, if in small quantities. If the rabi harvest also failed, the scarcity of food led rapidly to famine, and large numbers of people would quickly starve.

During the period of Company rule, 1765-1858, the subcontinent experienced a dozen famines and four severe shortages. Over the next fifty years, either a famine or a severe shortage occurred in South Asia at an average of every two and one-half years. After 1908, no major famines occurred in South Asia until the Bengal famine of 1943.

While the primary causal factor in all of these famines was the failure of crops, a linkage can be found between the upsurge in the frequency of famines and severe food scarcities in the nineteenth century, and changes in South Asian economic conditions and development under the British. For example, before the development of railroads in India, grain shortages and famine in one area affected only that particular locale. After the widespread construction of railroads in India, however, famine conditions in one area often spread to others due to the transportation of grain to the affected area. This activity left shortages of grain in otherwise unaffected areas, putting them, in turn, at risk. This chain reaction continued as grain shortages in high-production areas—whose grain had been diverted elsewhere—drove prices higher, out of the purchasing range of already impoverished rural and urban laborers, thus creating artificial food scarcities and famines. To make matters worse, during the latter half of the nineteenth century, India was a major exporter of grain; this trade not only diminished the overall availability of grain within the subcontinent, but drove prices higher as well. Even during extreme famine conditions, the export of India's grain to Britain and the rest of Europe, for which there was a much more profitable market, continued unabated. Although the British were largely responsible for many of the changes in the subcontinent's economic structure, many grain exporters and merchants were Indians who, like other entrepreneurs, sought higher profits for their grains.

The first major famine to take place after the establishment of Company rule in Bengal occurred in 1769-70. The famine spread over a wide area, encompassing Bengal and parts of Bihar. By the end of the famine, an estimated 10 million people—approximately one-third of the total population in the affected area—had died. Another major famine took place in 1837-38, which cost the lives of 800,000 in northwestern India.

In 1860-61, just two years after the British government took possession of India, a second major famine occurred in northwestern India, centered on Delhi and Agra. A drought that year left a relatively small area affected by famine conditions. Nearby areas were unaffected and produced sufficient food to compensate for the isolated deficiency. Soon, however, grain prices soared, ranging between 60 and 180 percent, and many thousands died of starvation. The Government of India made no attempt to control prices, and their relief efforts were limited to providing work to those who were able and food to those who were not (Bhatia 1991).

Not until 1880 was any attempt made by the Government of India to deal with famines in any systematic way. In that year, Lord Lytton, the viceroy, appointed a Famine Commission to make recommendations; the result was the Famine Code of 1883 which laid out a policy of transporting grain to affected areas, and providing food and work relief to those in need. The code was subsequently strengthened in 1897 and again in 1900.

Improved governmental policies as well as advances in irrigated agriculture after c. 1910 helped prevent the loss of life due to famine until the disastrous Bengal famine of 1943. A combination of war, a shortage of foodgrains, profiteering by grain merchants, and gross government inaction and incompetence left between 1.5 and 3 million dead.

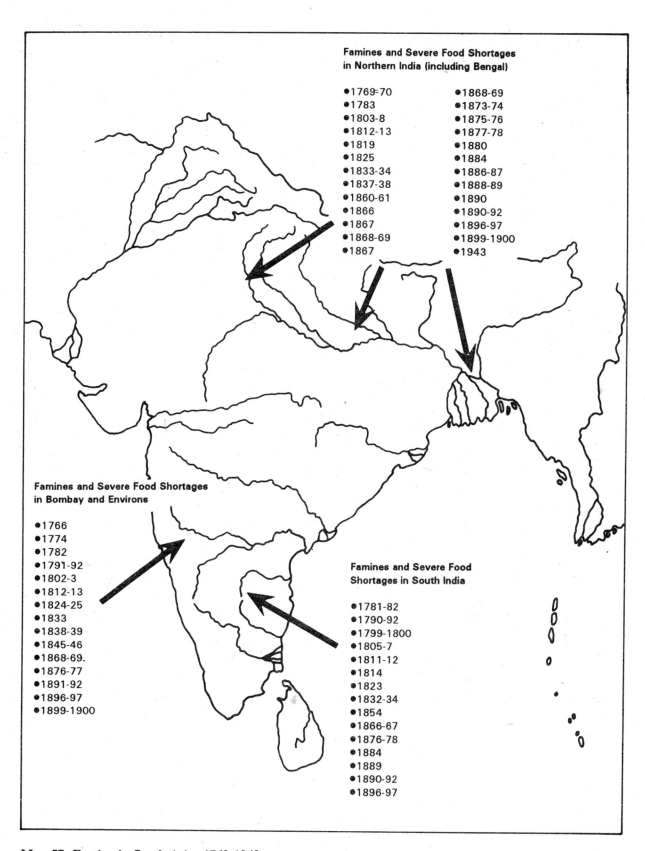

**Famines and Severe Food Shortages
in Northern India (including Bengal)**

- 1769-70
- 1783
- 1803-8
- 1812-13
- 1819
- 1825
- 1833-34
- 1837-38
- 1860-61
- 1866
- 1867
- 1868-69
- 1867

- 1868-69
- 1873-74
- 1875-76
- 1877-78
- 1880
- 1884
- 1886-87
- 1888-89
- 1890
- 1890-92
- 1896-97
- 1899-1900
- 1943

**Famines and Severe Food Shortages
in Bombay and Environs**

- 1766
- 1774
- 1782
- 1791-92
- 1802-3
- 1812-13
- 1824-25
- 1833
- 1838-39
- 1845-46
- 1868-69.
- 1876-77
- 1891-92
- 1896-97
- 1899-1900

**Famines and Severe Food
Shortages in South India**

- 1781-82
- 1790-92
- 1799-1800
- 1805-7
- 1811-12
- 1814
- 1823
- 1832-34
- 1854
- 1866-67
- 1876-78
- 1884
- 1889
- 1890-92
- 1896-97

Map 57 Famine in South Asia, 1769-1943

58   Higher Education in India, 1857-1947

In 1857, the British Government of India established the first three Indian universities at Bombay, Calcutta, and Madras. Both vernacular and English education were available to students at various schools and "colleges" in British India, but prior to the establishment of the three universities, no system of higher education on par with universities in Britain existed to produce degree-holders.

The decision to establish the three universities marked the culmination of several decades of debate over the question of whether the East India Company should, with Company funds, support vernacular or English education in British India. In February 1835, Lord Thomas Macaulay, Lord William Bentinck's legal advisor and president of the General Committee of Public Instruction, issued his famous Minute on Education in which he advocated spending Company funds on English education only; Lord Bentinck concurred. For the British in India, English education had a great many practical reasons to recommend it. Imparting education through the "superior" medium of English would aid Britons in their "civilizing" mission in India. English education would also help increase the ties between rulers and ruled through a common language. And since one of the goals of the Company was to have a large pool of English-speaking civil servants to draw upon, English education also made sense in this respect (Basu 1982).

Initially, the Universities of Bombay, Calcutta, and Madras were modeled on the University of London, and functioned only to examine aspiring degree candidates. They were not teaching universities—no course work was offered. Students attended any number of university-affiliated colleges, and fulfilled required course work there, before presenting themselves for university examinations.

Despite the enormous political changes wrought by the War of 1857, and the subsequent steady growth in degrees granted, British higher educational policy in India remained virtually unexamined until the Government of India appointed an Education Commission in 1882 to report on the status of higher education in India. The commission was limited to report on collegiate rather than university conditions, but nonetheless found a number of defects: poor instructional methods; curricula geared primarily toward the arts, with the almost total exclusion of technical education; and the existence of far too many "feeder colleges" affiliated to the universities, a condition which sacrificed overall student and instructional quality. Among the various recommendations the commission offered to correct deficiencies, only one, a grants-in-aid program to colleges, was adopted by the Government of India. It ultimately backfired by encouraging quantitative rather than qualitative growth within the collegiate system. As a result, Indian higher education suffered and stagnated. Later reforms, under the Indian Universities Act of 1904 implemented by Lord Curzon, corrected some of the glaring defects described by the Education Commission twenty-two years earlier. In addition, under the 1904 Act the original three universities joined the ranks of Panjab University (founded 1882) and Allahabad University (founded 1887) by creating some academic departments and adding teaching to their duties. The vast majority of candidates for university examinations at Bombay, Calcutta, and Madras, however, still received their instruction from the over two hundred university-affiliated colleges. Additional universities were founded during the First World War at Benares and Mysore (1916), Patna (1917), and Osmania (1918). Expanding postwar demand for higher education spurred the creation of new universities. During the 1920s, universities were founded at Aligarh, Dacca, and Lucknow in 1921, as well as at Delhi (1922), Nagpur (1923), Waltair (Andhra University, 1926), Agra (1927), and Annamalai (1929).

The advent of the Great Depression exacerbated already difficult problems inherent in Indian higher education. By 1930, the majority of university graduates were still schooled in the arts, and because of limited private employment opportunities, large numbers took jobs as clerks and civil servants with the Government of India. Only a very few entered the professions. Many were unemployable. Despite worsening economic conditions, the demand for university education continued unabated, although the creation of new universities did slow dramatically for the rest of the decade; only one new university was founded—at Travancore in 1937.

Three additional universities were founded prior to Partition: Utkal (1943), Sagar (1946), and Rajputana (1947). After Partition, India had a total of nineteen universities capable of providing higher education to its people, while Pakistan had only two.

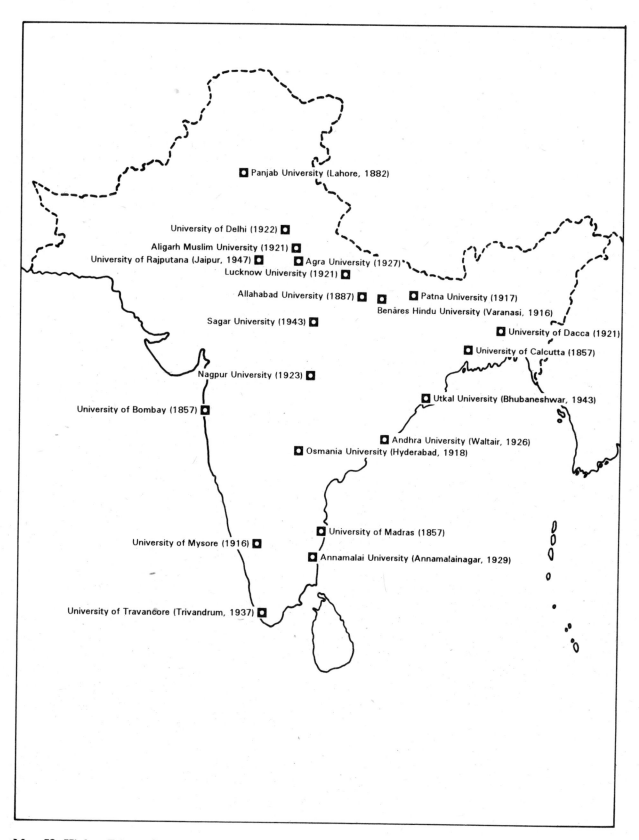

Map 58 Higher Education in India, 1857-1947

59   South Asians Overseas, 1830-1994

Patterns of South Asian overseas emigration can be divided broadly into three chronological periods: 1830-1920, 1920-50, and 1950-94. Each has its own distinct characteristics. The first period was characterized by the migration of Indian laborers to Ceylon (now Sri Lanka), Southeast Asia, East and South Africa, and Latin America. Initially, these Indians filled a growing labor vacuum left by the abolition of the slave trade within the British colonies after 1808, and later by the abolition of slavery itself in 1833.

As the nineteenth century progressed, the demand for tropical products such as sugar, coffee, tea, and, later, rubber, grew. These products were all grown on plantations and their cultivation was highly labor-intensive. European agents annually recruited thousands of Indian laborers, or "coolies," as they were then known, from overpopulated agricultural districts in South Asia and delivered them to emigration agents at ports like Calcutta or Madras. The Indians then were booked for passage on ships which would carry them overseas to their ultimate destination. Once they arrived at their new homes, Indian laborers faced the grinding and dehumanizing lifestyle of indentured servitude. Over time, the migration of Indian laborers became in essence a "new system of slavery." Contract labor had replaced the blatant injustice of slave labor, but working conditions and terms improved little for those who toiled in the fields of those same tropical plantations (Tinker 1974).

Although critics of the new labor system appeared at its very inception, they remained ineffective in spurring any changes. Not until the 1870s was any action taken by the British government either at home or in India, and even this action was largely confined to parliamentary studies and reports of the problem. Finally, under pressure from anti-indenture activists, the Government of India in 1916 decided to take the necessary steps to abolish Indian indentured servitude; this task was finally completed in 1920 when the last procurer of Indian indentured labor, Fiji, ordered all indenture contracts canceled.

Between 1920 and 1950, the migration of Indians overseas entered a new phase. During this period, overseas Indians faced a new menace: racial discrimination. In 1921, approximately 2.5 million Indians lived and worked overseas within the British Commonwealth;

the vast majority lived in predominantly non-white colonies, entry into which, even for permanent domicile, was fairly easy to obtain. Indians who wanted to emigrate to the white dominions, however, faced hardships. Temporary domicile for study or travel was readily obtainable, but permanent immigration was severely restricted and was designed specifically to exclude Indians. Indians who already lived in the dominions were subject to increasingly discriminatory laws.

Under Secretary of State Edwin Montagu (1917-22), the Government of India made some earnest effort to obtain racial equality for Indians within the Commonwealth, but it failed to achieve its objectives in the face of stiff resistance. A succession of Conservative-dominated British cabinets after 1922 (interrupted briefly twice by Labour governments, 1924 and 1929-31), declined to take effective action in the colonies under their direct control, or to pressure the white dominions for any agreement on Indian immigration. As a result, conditions for overseas Indians worsened dramatically, most especially in South Africa. Conditions did finally improve, but only after 1947, when Indians achieved some measure of equality through political independence.

The history of South Asians overseas since 1950 (when India became a republic) is complex. Traditional emigration—by those seeking better employment opportunities—continued to take place. Indians and Pakistanis traveled to the United Kingdom and elsewhere, both within and outside the Commonwealth, in search of work. Skilled laborers frequently migrated to Southwest Asia to work in the petroleum fields or on construction projects. Middle-class South Asians, many of whom were trained as technicians, engineers, and physicians, migrated in search of the higher pay that the West had to offer. That same middle class, in the three decades after 1950, sent their children to receive higher educations in the universities of the United Kingdom. By the 1980s, South Asians saw the United States as a viable alternative to the United Kingdom: thousands migrated there every year, seeking either employment or a higher education. With the world's third largest pool of technical skill, but without the ability to absorb them all, South Asia continues to be a major source of the world's emigrants.

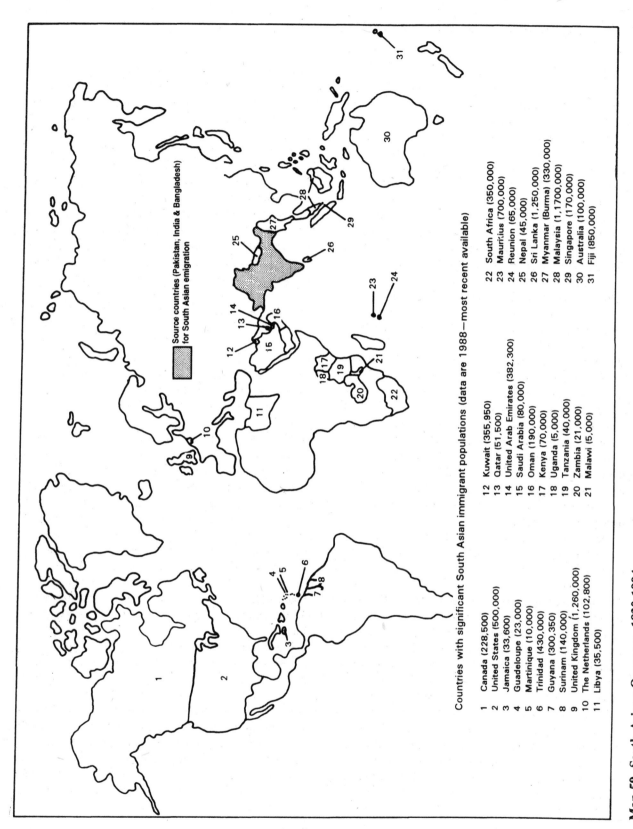

Countries with significant South Asian immigrant populations (data are 1988—most recent available)

1	Canada (228,500)	12	Kuwait (355,950)	22	South Africa (350,000)
2	United States (500,000)	13	Qatar (51,500)	23	Mauritius (700,000)
3	Jamaica (33,600)	14	United Arab Emirates (382,300)	24	Reunion (65,000)
4	Guadeloupe (23,000)	15	Saudi Arabia (80,000)	25	Nepal (45,000)
5	Martinique (10,000)	16	Oman (190,000)	26	Sri Lanka (1,250,000)
6	Trinidad (430,000)	17	Kenya (70,000)	27	Myanmar (Burma) (330,000)
7	Guyana (300,350)	18	Uganda (5,000)	28	Malaysia (1,1700,000)
8	Surinam (140,000)	19	Tanzania (40,000)	29	Singapore (170,000)
9	United Kingdom (1,260,000)	20	Zambia (21,000)	30	Australia (100,000)
10	The Netherlands (102,800)	21	Malawi (5,000)	31	Fiji (850,000)
11	Libya (35,500)				

Source countries (Pakistan, India & Bangladesh) for South Asian emigration

Map 59 South Asians Overseas, 1830-1994

60　Population Growth since 1871

South Asia today contains the second largest regional concentration of human beings in the world (East Asia ranks first). According to the most recent national censuses (1990-91) and estimates, the six countries of South Asia—India, Pakistan, Bangladesh, Nepal, Sri Lanka, Bhutan—have a combined population of nearly 1.2 billion or approximately 22 percent of the world's current total of 5.3 billion.

Since the early nineteenth century, historians and demographers have attempted to determine South Asia's population, but relatively accurate population statistics date from only 1871, when British authorities took the first censuses in India and Ceylon (Sri Lanka). At that time, India (including what are now Pakistan and Bangladesh) had a population totaling approximately 255 million and Ceylon 2.8 million. Because the 1871 census figures for India reflect the averaging of population data gathered over a five-year period (1867-72), they cannot be regarded as entirely accurate. Censuses were taken every decade from 1871 onward, and while it can be reasonably assumed that underenumeration occurred with each census, census-taking methods improved demonstrably each time with ever-increasing accuracy. In light of these improvements, census data from 1901 onward can be considered accurate, but these older censuses are available only for India, Pakistan, Bangladesh, and Sri Lanka. Nepal only recently began conducting official censuses; Bhutan has never held a census.

Although the region's population has steadily increased over time, the great bulk of South Asia's population growth has occurred since the Second World War. And of the six South Asian countries, India, Pakistan, and Bangladesh have experienced the largest increases in population. India leads the three in absolute numbers, but Pakistan ranks first in percentage increase. India's population in 1951 (the first census year after Independence) was 361.1 million. Given current census figures, therefore, India's population has increased by over 145 percent in the last forty-two years. Pakistan's population in 1951 was 33.8 million (West Pakistan only) and grew over 260 percent by 1992, while Bangladesh (as East Pakistan), with 42.1 million in 1951, increased by almost 185 percent during the same period. Given Bangladesh's small size and large population, it had by 1990 the highest population density of any country in the world: 830 persons per square kilometer (2,148 persons per square mile).

Historically, population increases have occurred in South Asia for a number of reasons, including migration, but the chief reason for the increase is that birth rates have far exceeded death rates. Infant mortality in South Asia, while still high by U.S. or Western European standards, has shown a marked decline since 1951, while during the same period life expectancy has risen dramatically. Human intervention to reduce the death rate—improvements in nutrition, the protection of water supplies, better sanitation, vaccinations, and the eradication of deadly diseases like smallpox—has been extremely effective, but measures to reduce the number of births through family planning and birth control have not met with similar success. Many South Asians, especially the poor (who make up the majority of the population), still see children as an economic asset rather than a liability. In their view, a large number children are able to generate extra income, and if they survive into the parents' old age, they become a source of financial security to the parents.

Education is also a factor in South Asia's population growth. There is some correlation between literacy levels and the percentage of population growth in each country. Sri Lanka and India, with annual population growth rates of 1.2 percent and 1.9 percent, respectively, have literacy rates of 87 percent and 48 percent, respectively. Pakistan and Bangladesh, on the other hand, have annual growth rates of 2.9 percent and 2.4 percent, respectively, and literacy rates of 35 percent and 36 percent, respectively. Other factors accounting for high growth rates in South Asia include the percentage of urban versus rural dwellers (urbanites have fewer children on average than their rural counterparts), and the amount of resources devoted to family planning.

The crucial problem with South Asia's high population growth lies in the fact that an ever-increasing amount of resources is devoted to simply sustaining a growing population, while those resources could probably best be used to develop each country more fully and thereby increase the average person's standard of living. Continuing high population growth patterns in the three large, mainland countries, coupled with a slowdown in economic growth rates, means that for most South Asians an improved standard of living may be a long time in coming.

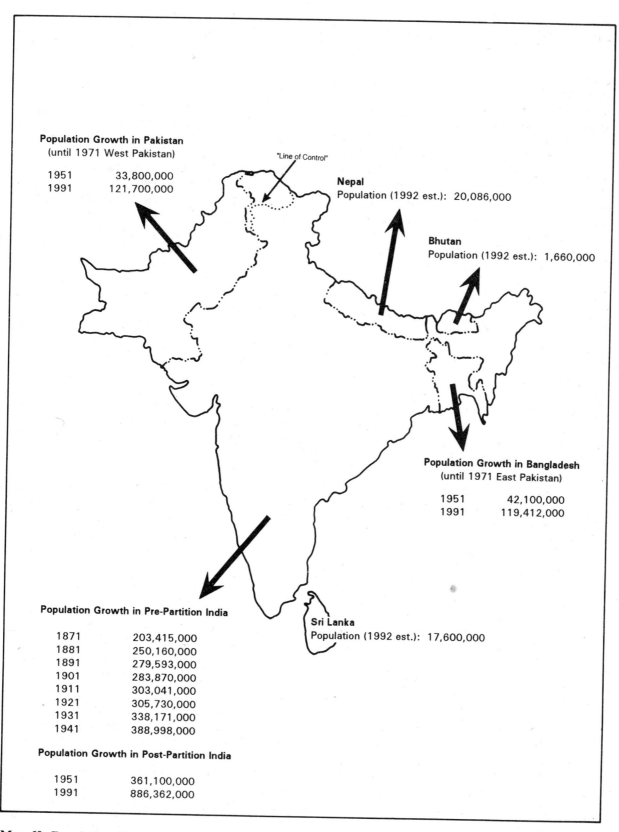

Population Growth in Pakistan
(until 1971 West Pakistan)

| 1951 | 33,800,000 |
| 1991 | 121,700,000 |

"Line of Control"

Nepal
Population (1992 est.): 20,086,000

Bhutan
Population (1992 est.): 1,660,000

Population Growth in Bangladesh
(until 1971 East Pakistan)

| 1951 | 42,100,000 |
| 1991 | 119,412,000 |

Population Growth in Pre-Partition India

1871	203,415,000
1881	250,160,000
1891	279,593,000
1901	283,870,000
1911	303,041,000
1921	305,730,000
1931	338,171,000
1941	388,998,000

Population Growth in Post-Partition India

| 1951 | 361,100,000 |
| 1991 | 886,362,000 |

Sri Lanka
Population (1992 est.): 17,600,000

Map 60 Population Growth since 1871

61   Popular Unrest in India, 1900-1947

Expressions of popular unrest during this period had many causes and took many forms. Virtually every section of the Indian population was affected, either as individuals involved in expressing their dissatisfaction with the status quo, or as targets of that dissatisfaction. Types of dissatisfaction can be broadly classified as tribal, peasant, labor, communal, and political. While most popular unrest had political underpinnings and could, therefore, legitimately be classified as "political," differentiating between a peasant anti-landlord movement and civil disobedience against the British Raj is important in order not to obscure the wide variations in motivation among the various groups.

British rule brought with it a number of changes which often affected the way of life of India's tribal groups. In 1900, for example, the Mundas of southern Bihar rose in rebellion to protest continued penetration of their lands by moneylenders and missionaries, and the imposition of forced labor. Although the civil authorities crushed the rebellion, the Mundas did get some recognition of their plight. One of the major causes of tribal rebellions in this period was anger over increasing British restrictions on forest use. British efforts at forest conservation often conflicted with tribal needs and sometimes led to bloodshed as in Jagdalpur (1910) and Kumaon (1921). Occasionally, tribal groups sought independence as a means of redressing their grievances. The Bhils of southern Rajasthan twice tried to gain independence (1913 and 1922), but were unsuccessful.

Peasant movements and uprisings in this period often reflected growing dissatisfaction over excessive landlord demands, increases in taxation, or low wages. In 1907, peasants in Panjab protested governmental increases in water rates in the canal colonies of Chenab and the Bari doab. Rather than face continued turmoil in one of their traditionally loyal provinces, the British conceded to the peasants' demands. Other peasants were less fortunate. In 1925, 156 peasants in Alwar, a princely state, were killed and over 600 wounded during an uprising against higher taxes. By the 1930s, peasants' concerns became increasingly intertwined with the freedom struggle.

Labor was extremely active prior to independence, especially in the 1920s and 1930s. Working conditions in the first two decades of the century were exceedingly poor, and laborers found the strike an effective protest. In 1905, workers in Bombay successfully struck to pro-test an attempt by mill owners to increase the workday to between 15 and 16 hours. Labor unrest reached a new high after the First World War. Declining economic conditions put pressures on owners to curtail costs, which they often directed against labor. In 1919-20, widespread and massive strikes rocked the country, affecting Calcutta, Madras, Bombay, and many other cities. Although Bombay and Calcutta were the main centers of labor unrest, other cities also experienced major strikes in the 1920s, like Ahmedabad, Lahore, Jamshedpur, and Sholapur. As the nationalist movement gained strength in the 1930s, labor protest took on an increasingly politicized tone.

Hindu-Muslim **communalism** gradually became more intense after 1900, especially in the wake of the partition of Bengal (1905). Large communal riots broke out in many of the western districts of East Bengal in 1906 and 1907. The First World War brought additional social pressures which led to outbreaks of communal violence in Bihar in 1917 and in Calcutta in 1918. During the Khilafat movement (1919-22), large-scale communal violence died down due to improved Hindu-Muslim relations, but the death of the movement in 1922 led to renewed outbreaks. Riots took place in many cities throughout India, but were especially pronounced in the United Provinces (now Uttar Pradesh) where over 90 communal outbreaks took place between 1923 and 1927. The worst communal violence, however, came with Partition in 1947 (see Map 37).

Political unrest prior to Independence manifested itself in a variety of ways, ranging from peaceful demonstrations of civil disobedience to acts of terrorism. Protests led or inspired by Gandhi, a devoted believer in non-violence, included numerous satyagrahas and salt marches in the 1920s and 1930s to signal popular dissent from British rule. Far more often, however, political protests turned violent, e.g., after the Amritsar massacre (1919), during the civil disobedience movement (1930-34), and in the 1940s. Acts of extreme violence also gained in popularity among some groups who felt that only terrorism would drive the British out of India. The first terrorist organizations formed in Bengal soon after 1900. Sporadic acts of terrorism followed until 1930, when a wave of terrorism spread throughout India, reaching a height of 104 reported incidents in 1932 alone. Police repression led to a decline in terrorism by the end of the decade.

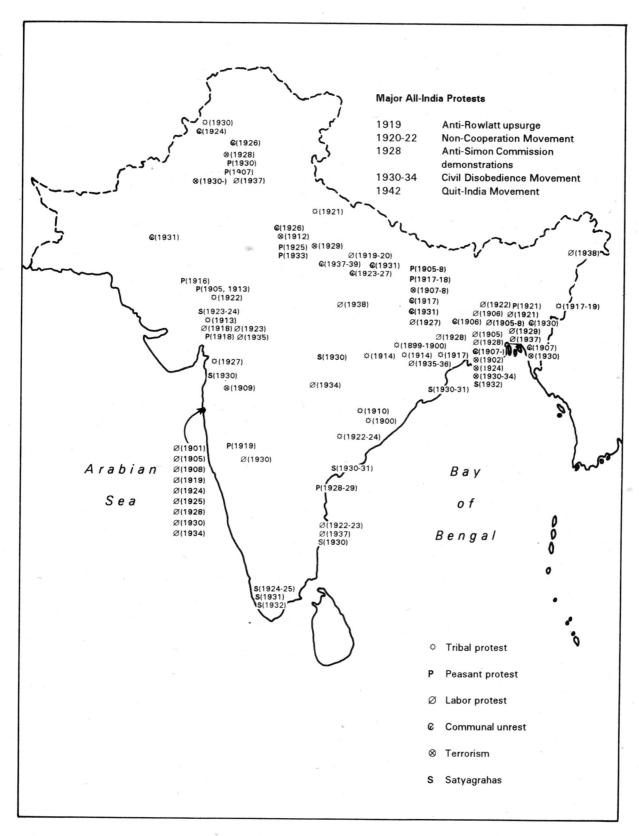

Major All-India Protests

1919	Anti-Rowlatt upsurge
1920-22	Non-Cooperation Movement
1928	Anti-Simon Commission demonstrations
1930-34	Civil Disobedience Movement
1942	Quit-India Movement

✿(1930)
ℭ(1924)
ℭ(1926)
⊗(1928)
P(1930)
P(1907)
⊗(1930-) ∅(1937)

ℭ(1931)

✿(1921)

∅(1938)

ℭ(1926)
⊗(1912)
P(1925) ⊗(1929)
P(1933) ∅(1919-20)
ℭ(1937-39) ℭ(1931)
ℭ(1923-27) P(1905-8)
P(1917-18)
⊗(1907-8)
ℭ(1917)
ℭ(1931)
∅(1927)

P(1916)
P(1905, 1913)
✿(1922)
S(1923-24)
✿(1913)
∅(1918) ∅(1923)
P(1918) ∅(1935)

∅(1938)

∅(1922) P(1921) ✿(1917-19)
∅(1906) ∅(1921)
ℭ(1906) ∅(1905-8) ℭ(1930)
∅(1905) ℭ(1929)
∅(1928) ∅(1937)
✿(1899-1900) ℭ(1907-) ℭ(1907)
S(1930) ✿(1914) ✿(1914) ✿(1917) ⊗(1902) ⊗(1930)
∅(1935-36) ⊗(1924)
⊗(1930-34)
S(1932)

✿(1927)

S(1930)

⊗(1909)

∅(1934)

S(1930-31)

✿(1910)
✿(1900)

✿(1922-24)

∅(1901)
∅(1905)
∅(1908)
∅(1919)
∅(1924)
∅(1925)
∅(1928)
∅(1930)
∅(1934)

P(1919)

∅(1930)

S(1930-31)

P(1928-29)

∅(1922-23)
∅(1937)
S(1930)

Arabian

Sea

Bay

of

Bengal

S(1924-25)
S(1931)
S(1932)

✿	Tribal protest
P	Peasant protest
∅	Labor protest
ℭ	Communal unrest
⊗	Terrorism
S	Satyagrahas

Map 61 Popular Unrest in India, 1900-1947

62   Urbanization and Urban Growth in South Asia to 1994

Although a majority of its people still live in rural areas, South Asia has long had cities, dating as far back as the Harappan Civilization. In both the premodern and modern periods, cities in South Asia have served as administrative centers for a plethora of governments; have performed vital economic functions as centers of commerce and manufacturing; and have served as wellsprings of intellectual and religious activity.

In discussing the history of the city in South Asia, an important distinction must be drawn between "urban growth" (an increase in the size of cities and towns) and "urbanization" (an increase in the percentage of the total population living in cities and towns). Urban growth is a phenomenon which can be seen throughout the history of South Asia, but urbanization is a decidedly recent phenomenon, restricted largely to the last two centuries and most especially to the post-Independence period.

Information on urban growth in the premodern period is sketchy due to the lack of census data. Any information that is available is based on estimates by both modern scholars and contemporary observers. Archaeologists have estimated Harappa's population, for example, based on its size and location, to have been approximately 35,000. Delhi during the Sultanate period (1206-1526) may have had as many as 100,000 people. In 1585, a British merchant named Ralph Fitch estimated that the population of both Agra and Fatehpur Sikri stood at roughly 200,000 each. These estimates and observations, along with many others, while useful, do not tell us much about either urban growth or urbanization in South Asia. Only with the advent of accurate census-taking in the late nineteenth century does South Asia's urban picture become clearer.

Beginning with the 1881 Census of India, the Government of India defined an urban area as one with 5,000 people or more. In 1881, India's urban population stood at 9.3 percent of the total population, with Sri Lanka's slightly higher (reliable data is not available for Nepal until 1952-54 and for Bhutan until after 1981). By 1951, urbanization had increased to 17.3 percent in India, and 15.3 percent in Sri Lanka. West and East Pakistan, now separated from India, had urbanization figures of 17.6 percent and 4.4 percent, respectively. By 1991, 28 percent of Pakistan's population was urban, followed by 26 percent of India's, 24 percent of Bangladesh's, and 22 percent of Sri Lanka's. Nepal and Bhutan trailed the four main South Asian countries with 7 and 5 percent of their respective populations living in urban areas.

In the last century, therefore, urbanization in South Asia has shown a steady, but slow, increase; each country, however, is still clearly dominated by its rural sector. In looking only at the figures for urbanization, and not at those of urban growth, one can easily overlook half of the total urban picture. While the urbanized percentage of India's population has increased only roughly 17 percent in the last century, the rate of urban growth has increased more dramatically. In the last century, for example, Bombay has increased in population from 821,764 in 1891 to 9,901,547 in 1991—an increase of over 1,100 percent. Calcutta and other large metropolitan cities have seen similar increases.

Urban growth over the last century has been skewed in favor of cities of 100,000 people or more. Cities in the 50,000 to 99,999 range have increased only slightly in size, and cities and towns of less than 50,000 have all declined measurably in the last one hundred years, with the most dramatic decline in towns of 5,000 people or less. This trend is highly indicative of the causes of both urban growth and urban decay. Larger cities have grown ever larger due to rural-urban migration, caused by dislocation on the village level such as drought; war (as in 1971); famine; and the prospect of better employment opportunities. Natural increase has also been a factor in urban growth in the past century, especially since Independence.

City planning in South Asia has not been effective. Under the British, provincial legislative councils established improvement trusts for some major cities such as Bombay, Calcutta, Delhi, Kanpur, Lucknow, and Allahabad. Improvement trusts helped correct urban water supply and sanitation problems, but were unable to improve the most serious urban problem: overcrowding. After Independence, mechanisms for urban planning in India, Pakistan, and Bangladesh have attempted to improve the lot of urban dwellers, but the enormous increase in urban population has overwhelmed all such efforts. Slums and squatter settlements are on the rise in all major cities, especially in Bombay, Calcutta, Delhi, Karachi, and Dhaka.

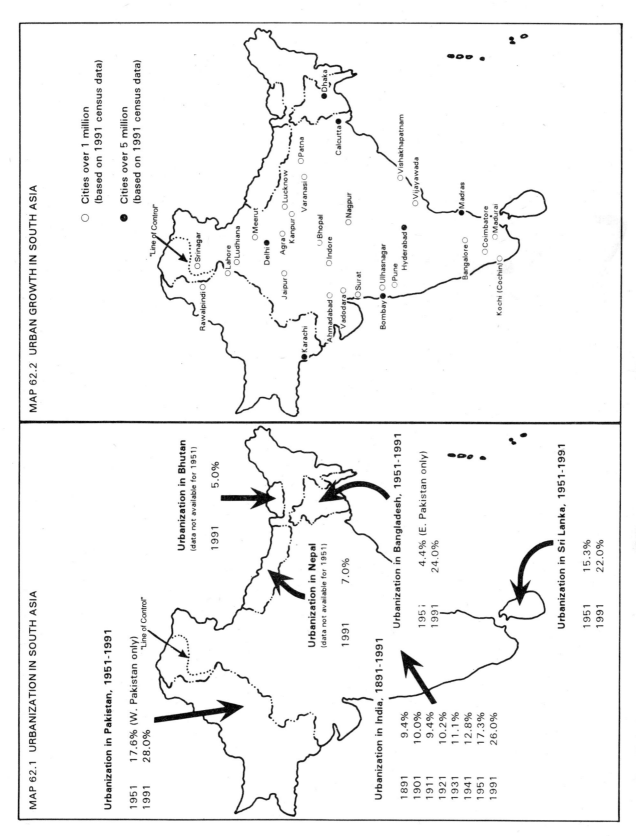

MAP 62.2 URBAN GROWTH IN SOUTH ASIA

○ Cities over 1 million
(based on 1991 census data)

● Cities over 5 million
(based on 1991 census data)

"Line of Control"

●Dhaka

●Calcutta

○Srinagar

○Vishakhapatnam

○Lahore
○Ludhiana

○Meerut

○Lucknow

○Vijayawada

○Madras

●Delhi ○Agra ○Kanpur
○Varanasi

○Coimbatore

○Patna

○Bhopal

○Nagpur

○Madurai

○Jaipur

○Indore

○Pune ●Hyderabad

○Bangalore

○Rawalpindi

○Surat ○Ulhasnagar

○Ahmadabad ○
○Vadodara

Bombay●

Kochi (Cochin)○

●Karachi

MAP 62.1 URBANIZATION IN SOUTH ASIA

Urbanization in Pakistan, 1951-1991

1951   17.6% (W. Pakistan only)
1991   28.0%

"Line of Control"

Urbanization in Bhutan
(data not available for 1951)

1991   5.0%

Urbanization in Nepal
(data not available for 1951)

1991   7.0%

Urbanization in Bangladesh, 1951-1991

195¡   4.4% (E. Pakistan only)
1991   24.0%

Urbanization in India, 1891-1991

1891	9.4%
1901	10.0%
1911	9.4%
1921	10.2%
1931	11.1%
1941	12.8%
1951	17.3%
1991	26.0%

Urbanization in Sri Lanka, 1951-1991

1951   15.3%
1991   22.0%

Maps 62.1-62.2 Urbanization and Urban Growth in South Asia to 1994

Nepal, Sri Lanka, and Bhutan

63   Nepal to 1814

Nepal's history can be dated archaeologically to before the common era, but not until the fifth century CE, when the Lichchavi dynasty arose, is there a coherent historical record. The Hindu Lichchavis, likely the first Nepali kings of Indian origin, ruled over the Nepal valley between 500 and 700 CE. Their neighbor to the north was a strong, unified Tibetan kingdom which held sway over large parts of Central Asia. Increasing interaction between India, Nepal, and Tibet during this period converted Nepal from an isolated kingdom into the leading cultural and economic crossroads between Central and South Asia. Buddhist culture, for example, spread to Tibet through Nepal.

Between the eleventh and eighteenth centuries, the Malla dynasty ruled the Nepal valley. Although the historical record is unclear, the Mallas seem to have been high-caste Indian Hindus who, for most of their long reign, ruled with tolerance over predominantly Buddhist subjects. In the early fifteenth century, however, King Jaya Sthiti Malla imposed a new Hindu social and legal code which gradually **Sanskritized** the people of the Nepal valley and in other principalities throughout the surrounding Nepali hill country.

During the Muslim invasions of India which began in the eleventh century, Nepal remained largely unaffected. Only one Muslim attack in the thirteenth century involved the Mallas and they, along with the other Nepali rulers, were able to maintain their full independence. During the early period of Muslim rule in India, a large number of high-caste Hindus—Brahmans and kshatriyas—fled India and resettled in Nepal. In time, this Hindu elite, of Rajput origin, supplanted most of the indigenous rulers of Nepal and established their own kingdoms.

Political forms and structures continued to evolve in Nepal after the Rajput influx until by the sixteenth century two loose political associations emerged in Nepal: the Baisi Confederation and the Chaubisi Confederation. Both confederations were of roughly the same size, comprising a little over twenty Hindu principalities each. Some small indigenous tribal states still survived in Nepal, but the twin confederations dominated Nepal's political life. The Hindu ruling elites in Nepal commonly intermarried, which led to strong familial connections between the ruling families of different states.

Such close connections between the many states of Nepal could have led to Nepal's early unification under a Nepali Rajput dynasty, but because the perceived cultural and political center of Nepal, the Nepal valley, was still ruled by a non-Rajput Hindu dynasty, the Mallas, unification was delayed until the eighteenth century (Rose and Scholz 1980).

The founder of modern Nepal was Prithvi Narayan Shah (r. 1742-75), the Rajput king of Gorkha, a state sixty-five kilometers (forty miles) west of Kathmandu. After ascending the throne, Prithvi Narayan Shah devised plans for unifying Nepal under his rule. He first reorganized his troops according to British military methods in use at the time, and then acquired control over the northern and southern trade routes leading into the Nepal valley. Both the British in India and the Tibetans, who shared an interest in expanding trade between them, grew concerned by Prithvi Narayan Shah's conquests. In 1767, the British sent troops into Nepal to reopen the trade routes, but neglected to take account of the monsoon, and the mission failed. Meanwhile, Prithvi Narayan Shah's economic stranglehold seriously weakened Malla rule, and in 1769, when Gorkha troops entered the Malla kingdom, it quickly disintegrated.

Following the collapse of the Malla kingdom, Prithvi Narayan Shah moved quickly to consolidate and improve his position in Nepal, a task which still lay incomplete in 1775, when he died. Prithvi Narayan Shah's successors shared his vision of a unified state, and within fifteen years Gorkha troops had conquered other areas in Nepal, bringing the whole country, from Sikkim to Karnali, under Gorkha rule. Nepal's unification was complete.

The new state of Nepal was, however, founded upon an essential weakness at the center. The traditional Hindu principle of kingship that the ruler must delegate authority, coupled with divisions after 1775 within the royal family, led to increasing factionalism at court, and resultant political instability. It was precisely these unstable conditions that led to the increasing influence at court of Bahadur Shah, the regent of the Nepali king Rana Bahadur. The regent attempted to silence his opposition and strengthen his position at court by drawing Kathmandu into wars of aggrandizement with Tibet in 1788-89, and with China in 1791-93. Both attempts failed and Bahadur Shah was dismissed, but the stage was set for another—and this time disastrous—confrontation with another of Nepal's neighbors: the British in India.

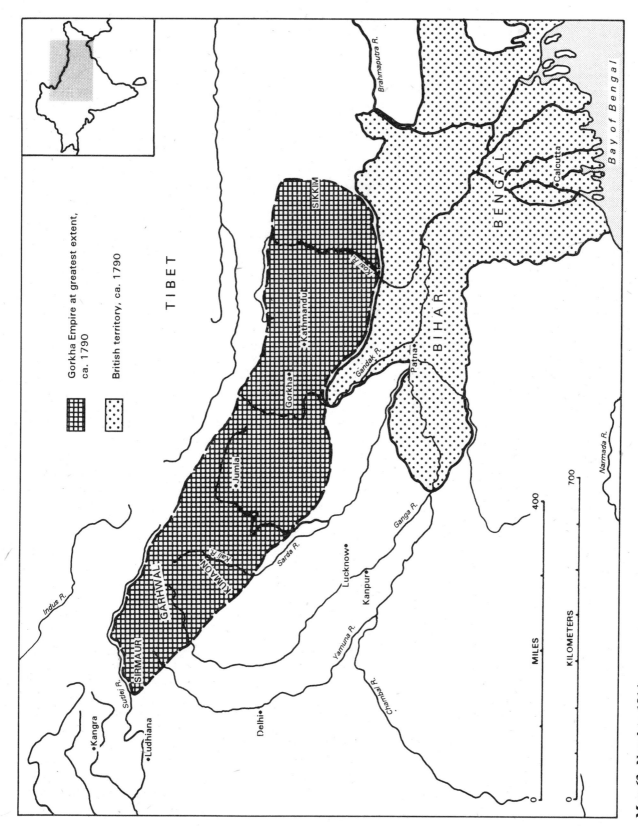

Map 63 Nepal to 1814

64   Anglo-Nepali War of 1814-16

Antagonisms between the Nepali government and the British Government of India had been growing for many years prior to the outbreak of war between them in 1814. In 1794, a new faction had come to power in the Kathmandu Darbar; it guarded the country's independence jealously, and opposed any further growth of British influence in Nepal. The Darbar, for example, discontinued a 1792 commercial treaty with British India, ignored further economic and diplomatic overtures in 1795-96, and, in 1804, Nepali hostility to an 1801 Anglo-Nepali treaty forced Governor-General Wellesley to terminate it unilaterally.

Wellesley was tempted to resolve the growing disagreement with Nepal by force, but the intervening outbreak of the Napoleonic Wars in Europe in 1803, coupled with the ongoing conflict with the Marathas in India, prevented any further commitment of military resources. From 1805 to 1814, the British in India could ill afford a war with Nepal and sought, therefore, to maintain the status quo. Nepal's government, meanwhile, spent those ten years bolstering its army in preparation for what it predicted would be a future armed conflict with the British.

By 1814, circumstances in India had changed. Napoleon was in exile on Elba Island and British forces were suddenly available for use in India. In addition, the Sikhs offered no threat—Ranjit Singh had signed a treaty of friendship with the British in 1809 (that same year, the Nepalis had rejected Sikh overtures of alliance)—and the Marathas could not form an alliance with Nepal without Sikh help. Finally, the British were convinced that if they attacked Nepal, China would not intervene.

With these considerations in mind, the governor-general, Lord Hastings (1813-23), felt confident enough to press Nepal for the settlement of an ongoing border dispute. In March 1814, Hastings issued an ultimatum to the Nepalis stating that unless they recognized British jurisdiction over the two border districts of Sheoraj and Butwal, the British would take them by force. When the deadline for a reply to the ultimatum lapsed, British troops seized both districts. By May, the bulk of British forces had been withdrawn due to the imminence of the malarial season; the Nepalis took advantage of the withdrawal and reoccupied the two districts. The British took this action as an act of war, and prepared for a full-scale conflict to begin at the end of the rainy sea-son. The Nepalis made use of the summer lull to try to secure allies in the expected autumnal conflict. They were unsuccessful. The Chinese rejected Nepal's appeals; the Sikhs, Marathas, and Bhutanis, although interested, declined as well.

In September 1814, after the retreat of the monsoon, the British sent 16,000 troops into Nepal. After initial British success in conquering parts of the **Terai**, Nepali resistance increased, and the British suffered a number of setbacks in their four-pronged attack. The only other success during the winter campaign of 1814-15 was Gen. Ochterlony's capture of territory between the Kali and Sutlej rivers. By early 1815, it became clear that any further attacks would have to wait until after the monsoon. Meanwhile, the Nepalis stalled for time in the hope that an outside country would come to their aid.

After a failed attempt at peace over the early winter months of 1815-16, the British resumed their campaign against Nepal that February. Criticism from the East India Company's board of directors, however, forced Calcutta to alter its strategy: British forces would now concentrate on capturing Kathmandu. After outflanking Nepali forces at Makwanpur, Ochterlony and his troops prepared to march on the Nepali capital. With their defenses crumbling, the Nepali Darbar accepted peace based on the abortive 1815 treaty. Ochterlony was hesitant; he doubted the sincerity of the Nepalis. The war was proving expensive, however, and with the likely possibility of another Maratha conflict erupting, Calcutta was eager to end the war in Nepal. In March 1816, therefore, Ochterlony accepted Nepal's surrender based on the Sagauli treaty.

The Treaty of Sagauli, although not as harsh a settlement as Lord Hastings had originally suggested, nonetheless imposed significant penalties on Nepal and had important consequences for the future. Nepal was forced to accept the stationing of a British Resident at Kathmandu, the surrender of all claims to Garhwal and Kumaon district hill territories west of the Kali River, the surrender of disputed Terai territories, and the surrender of territories in the east between the Tista River and the Singalila mountain range. The loss of these areas deprived Nepal of substantial revenue, common frontiers with other Indian states, i.e., possible Indian allies, and marked the end of all future Nepali resistance to the British in India.

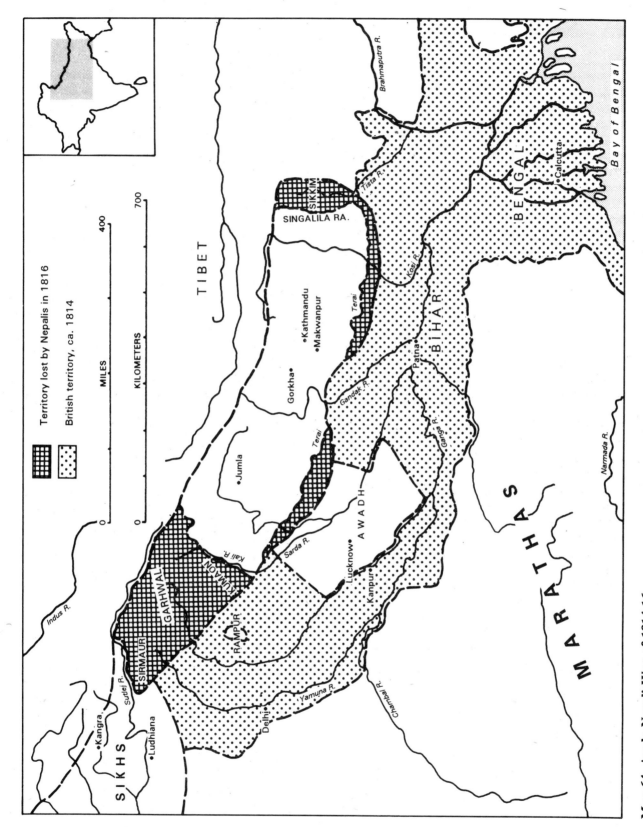

Map 64 Anglo-Nepali War of 1814-16

Territory lost by Nepalis in 1816

British territory, ca. 1814

MILES

KILOMETERS

0   400   700

TIBET

SIKKIM

SINGALILA RA.

Brahmaputra R.

Tista R.

BENGAL

Bay of Bengal

Calcutta

•Kathmandu
•Makwanpur

Gorkha•

Kosi R.

Terai

BIHĀR

Patna•

Jumla•

Gandak R.

Ganga R.

Terai

Narmada R.

AWADH

Kali R.

Sarda R.

Lucknow•

M A R A T H A S

KUMAON

GARHWAL

Kanpur•

Indus R.

SIRMAUR

RAMPUR

Sutlej R.

•Kangra

Delhi•

Yamuna R.

Chambal R.

•Ludhiana

S I K H S

141

65　Nepal since 1816

The end of the Anglo-Nepali War of 1814-16 brought many lessons for the Nepalis and the British alike. For the Nepalis, the war marked the end of their expansionist period; no longer could territorial aggrandizement work in their favor. For their part, the British learned about the difficulty of fighting the well-trained Nepalis on their own land, and the near-impossibility of making Nepal a part of British India. From 1816 onward, therefore, the British in India accepted Nepal as a buffer state between themselves and the Chinese. Meanwhile, the Nepalis and the British continued their respectful relationship, with each wary of the other.

With the outbreak of the War of 1857-58, the Anglo-Nepali relationship changed dramatically. Despite strong pressure from his restless army and some nobles at court, the Nepali king, Jang Bahadur, opted to aid the British rather than fight against them. Although Lord Canning, the Indian governor-general (1856-62), was initially reluctant to accept Nepal's assistance, in the end some six thousand Nepali troops fought to restore British control over India. At war's end, the British, who had long eyed Nepal with suspicion, rewarded their northern neighbor for its help by restoring to it the Terai lands taken in 1816. In addition, the two sides also entered into an entente. The British agreed henceforth to respect Nepal's internal autonomy and isolationism. In return, Nepal agreed to be guided by British advice in external affairs and allowed the British to recruit Gurkhas for the army in India. Despite restrictions on British movements in Nepal and the nominal subordination of Nepal's foreign policy to the British, the entente proved mutually beneficial. Although Nepal became essentially a British protectorate, Britain later recognized Nepal's loyal services by granting it complete independence in 1924.

Unlike its external politics, Nepal's domestic politics after the 1814-16 war hardly changed at all. The instability of the prewar years (see Map 63) remained constant as interfamilial struggles at court led to conspiracy and assassination among the country's leading officials. In 1846, after the infamous Kot Massacre in which one prominent family faction killed off its opposition, the structure of Nepal's government changed. Jang Bahadur Kunwar, head of the winning faction (the Ranas), usurped the real power of the king of Nepal, and installed himself as maharaja and prime minister, a position which he made hereditary. Soon, Jang Bahadur entrenched himself and used his newly-won power to construct the Rana system, characterized by the reorganization, modernization, and centralization of government, while at the same time securing the Ranas' present and future power. Jang Bahadur and his heirs were so successful in designing and constructing the Rana system that it kept their opposition at bay until 1951, when India intervened.

The Indian government interceded in the politics of Nepal in 1950 in order to resolve the growing political conflict between the Ranas and their opposition. Its goal was to replace the Rana system entirely, to restore Tribhuvan, the king of Nepal, to his throne as a constitutional monarch, and to encourage the growth of democratic institutions in Nepal. Continued conflicts within the government of Nepal, however, diminished its effectiveness and led King Tribhuvan to assume more direct control over the decision-making process. After assuming the throne on his father's death in 1955, King Mahendra sought to strengthen the powers of the monarchy and moved decisively to eliminate the democratic element in his government. Nepal's first elections were held in 1959, but in the following year the king assumed direct personal control, quickly dissolved the parliament, and banned political parties.

From 1962 until 1980, Nepal's kings ruled the country directly and largely by fiat, while giving nominal support to a panchayat system—something they considered to be "grass roots" democracy. In 1979, King Birendra announced that a national referendum would be held the following year to decide whether to modify the panchayat system and to share power. The referendum passed and direct parliamentary elections were held in Nepal in 1981.

A border dispute with India in 1989-90 caused India to close its border crossings with Nepal. This action led to an economic crisis, months of politically motivated violence, and a resultant call for further political reform. King Birendra reacted by dissolving parliament in early 1990. Meanwhile, opposition groups formed an interim government and drafted a new constitution which reestablished Nepal's constitutional monarchy. In May 1991, the moderate Nepali Congress won nationwide elections and formed the first government under Nepal's new constitution.

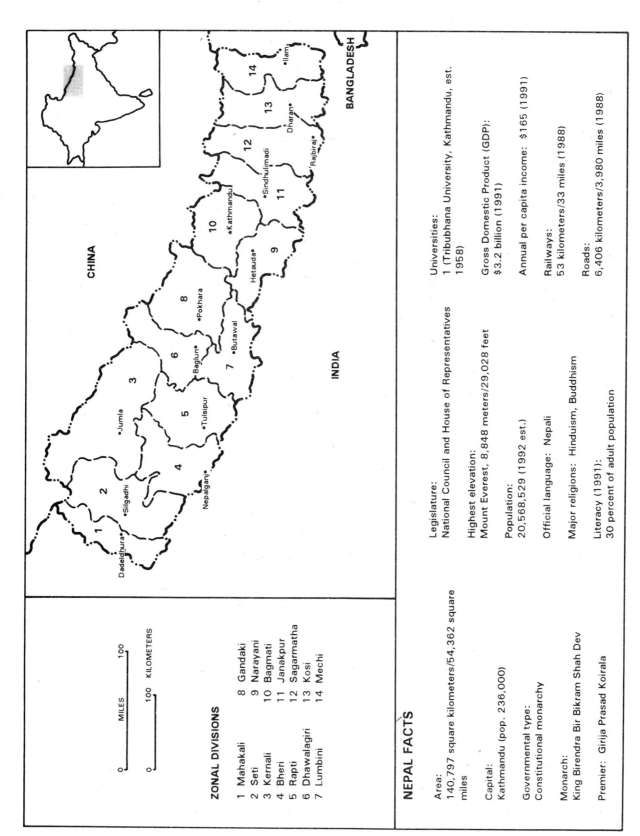

ZONAL DIVISIONS

1 Mahakali	8 Gandaki
2 Seti	9 Narayani
3 Kernali	10 Bagmati
4 Bheri	11 Janakpur
5 Rapti	12 Sagarmatha
6 Dhawalagiri	13 Kosi
7 Lumbini	14 Mechi

NEPAL FACTS

Area:
140,797 square kilometers/54,362 square miles

Capital:
Kathmandu (pop. 236,000)

Governmental type:
Constitutional monarchy

Monarch:
King Birendra Bir Bikram Shah Dev

Premier: Girija Prasad Koirala

Legislature:
National Council and House of Representatives

Highest elevation:
Mount Everest, 8,848 meters/29,028 feet

Population:
20,568,529 (1992 est.)

Official language: Nepali

Major religions: Hinduism, Buddhism

Literacy (1991):
30 percent of adult population

Universities:
1 (Tribubhana University, Kathmandu, est. 1958)

Gross Domestic Product (GDP):
$3.2 billion (1991)

Annual per capita income: $165 (1991)

Railways:
53 kilometers/33 miles (1988)

Roads:
6,406 kilometers/3,980 miles (1988)

Map 65 Nepal since 1816

66   Sri Lanka to 1815

The early history of Sri Lanka (until 1972, Ceylon) is shrouded in legend. Although archaeological evidence suggests the existence of far older indigenous cultures on the island, the first historical figure to arise in Sri Lanka is Vijaya who, along with a band of seven hundred followers, arrived on the island in the fifth century BCE from northern India. The arrival of Vijaya forms part of the Sinhalese creation myth and is anachronistically intertwined with the advent of Buddhism on the island. Buddhism was only one of many influences in the early development of Sri Lanka (along with cultural and commercial interaction with South and Southeast Asia); in time, it became the dominating influence, but not apparently until the first century BCE.

By 137 BCE, after years of intergroup warfare, the island was unified under one ruler, Dutthagamani (161-137 BCE), whose brother and heir, Saddhatissa (137-119 BCE), began the ten-century-long dominance of the Sinhalese Anuradhapura kingdom, famous not only for its cultural accomplishments, but also for its development of a huge and efficient irrigation system. Over the centuries, the politically-unifying influence of Anuradhapura waxed and waned, depending on the power and ability of individual rulers to combat centrifugal forces on the island. In addition, by 600 CE Sinhalese rulers faced growing political opposition from minority Tamils, descendants of Dravidians who had migrated to northern Sri Lanka from South India and had become firmly settled on the island by the third century BCE. The rise of the militant South Indian Hindu kingdoms of the Pandyas, Pallavas, and Cholas, in the fifth and sixth centuries, foreshadowed the end of the Anuradhapura kingdom, which was drawn into the quickly changing politico-military calculus of the region. The kingdom finally collapsed after the Chola invasion in the tenth century.

The Chola occupation of Sri Lanka did not last long, and by 1070, the Sinhalese had regained control of the island, but they soon plunged into civil war. After a nearly a century of internecine conflict, a Sinhalese ruler, Parakramabahu I (1153-86), restored order on the island, and founded the Polonnaruva kingdom. He and his successor, Nishshanka Malla (1187-96), attempted too quickly to regain past glories. While they accomplished much in a short period of time, their foreign policy and public works ambitions, coupled with administrative overcentralization, overwhelmed the king-dom and led to its decline. As a result, after c. 1250, the Sinhalese retreated from the island's "dry zone" to the "wet zone" in the southwest, while the Tamil Jaffna kingdom to the north gained power.

In 1415, Parakramabahu VI (1411-66) founded the Kotte kingdom, and reversed the long decline of Sinhalese power. He successfully repelled forces from Vijayanagara on the Indian mainland, and subdued both the Vanni principalities and the Jaffna kingdom (which had earlier become a Vijayanagara client state). Despite great political achievements, the administrative machinery Parakramabahu put into place to run the newly-unified island kingdom was ineffective and within a decade of his death that unity had collapsed. Kotte controlled only the southwest and a small portion of the northwest, the Jaffna kingdom was once again independent, and the Kandyans in central Sri Lanka were asserting their independence.

Its precipitant decline notwithstanding, the Kotte kingdom was still the most important of the Sri Lankan kingdoms when, in 1505, the Portuguese first arrived, beginning a new phase in Sri Lankan history. In 1521, a partitioned Kotte willingly became a Portuguese client state, and the Portuguese, interested in dominating the spice trade in the Indian Ocean (see Map 19), began to expand their influence on the island. By the end of the sixteenth century, only the Kandyan kingdom remained outside the Portuguese orbit, and for the next fifty years it continued to apply pressure on the Portuguese to abandon their hold over the rest of Sri Lanka. In 1652, Kandyan ruler, Rajasimha II (1635-87), joined forces with the Dutch to attack the Portuguese; together, they expelled the Portuguese from Sri Lanka in 1658.

The Dutch, however, quickly betrayed Rajasimha, taking possession of nearly one-half of the former Portuguese colony in Sri Lanka in exchange for their share of the cost of the war. By 1670, the Dutch extended their control to the entire coast of the island and, Rajasimha, despite early resistance, now seemed resigned to their presence. The Dutch remained in control over much of Sri Lanka until 1796, when the British, fearful of further French influence in the Indian Ocean, forced the Dutch to surrender their Sri Lankan possessions, which became a British **Crown Colony** in 1802. In 1815, the British overthrew the last Kandyan ruler, Sri Vikrama Rajasimha (r. 1798-1815), and took possession of the entire island.

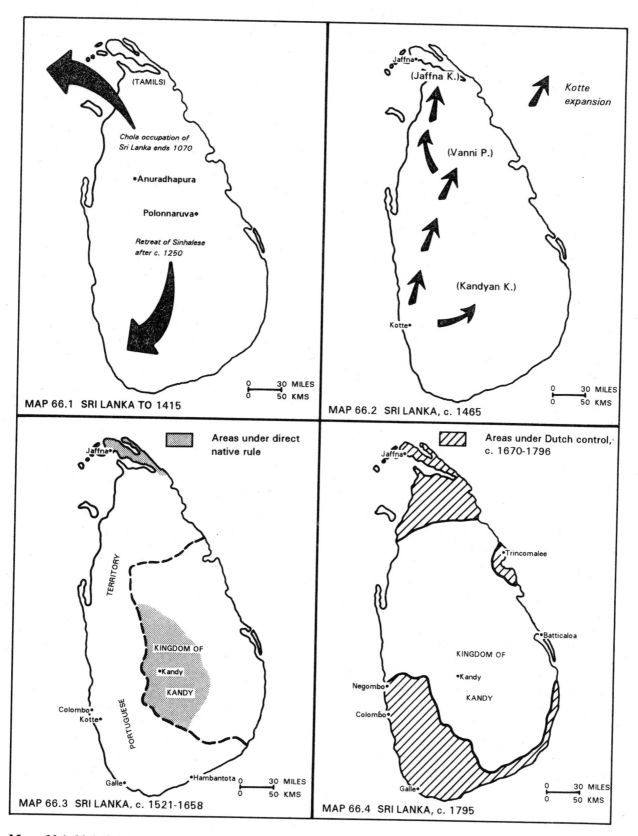

MAP 66.1 SRI LANKA TO 1415

(TAMILS)

Chola occupation of
Sri Lanka ends 1070

•Anuradhapura

Polonnaruva•

Retreat of Sinhalese
after c. 1250

0   30 MILES
0   50 KMS

MAP 66.2 SRI LANKA, c. 1465

Jaffna•
(Jaffna K.)

Kotte
expansion

(Vanni P.)

(Kandyan K.)

Kotte•

0   30 MILES
0   50 KMS

MAP 66.3 SRI LANKA, c. 1521-1658

Areas under direct
native rule

Jaffna•

TERRITORY

KINGDOM OF
•Kandy
KANDY

PORTUGUESE

Colombo•
Kotte•

Galle•   •Hambantota   0   30 MILES
                              0   50 KMS

MAP 66.4 SRI LANKA, c. 1795

Areas under Dutch control,
c. 1670-1796

Jaffna•

•Trincomalee

•Batticaloa

KINGDOM OF
•Kandy
KANDY

Negombo•

Colombo•

Galle•   0   30 MILES
                              0   50 KMS

Maps 66.1-66.4 Sri Lanka to 1815

145

67　Economic Development in Sri Lanka, 1815-1948

Dominated by the British East India Company and a British colonial government, the Sri Lankan economy was very rigidly structured and controlled. The Company maintained its grip on Sri Lanka's economic life through its monopoly on the cinnamon trade. Until 1830, cinnamon was the main product of the colonial economy, an item exported in large quantities to Europe where it had a reputation for being the finest in the world. Other export products included **arrack**, coconut oil, and coffee. Coffee, one of the very few export products in the hands of independent merchants, faced discriminatory tariffs in Britain due to the influence of the Company at Whitehall. With the exception of food, the colony imported almost everything else, especially luxury items for use by Europeans. Imports were expensive because they did not arrive at Sri Lankan ports directly, but rather were first transshipped through South Asian entrepôts such as Madras and Calcutta, allowing re-exporters in India to glean high profits at the expense of importers in Sri Lanka.

By 1850, Sri Lanka's commodity-based, export-oriented plantation economy had become firmly entrenched and experienced even greater growth as the century progressed. Despite a depression in 1846-47, coffee cultivation continued to expand and soon became the premier industry on the island. After 1855, coffee planters forced a change in what had been previously a rather cautious governmental fiscal policy: the colonial government now began to devote resources to the development of communications infrastructure such as roads, and later, a railway. Government also encouraged greater Indian immigration, mainly in an effort to recruit cheap labor to work on the plantations, but many laborers also found work in railway construction.

Coffee's seemingly unstoppable growth—from 20,000 hectares/50,000 acres planted in 1847 to 102,400 hectares/256,000 acres planted in 1881—was cut short by a fatal leaf disease, which first appeared in 1869 and which by the early 1890s had swept through the island, destroying every coffee plantation in its wake. Despite such a crushing blow, the island's plantation economy recovered, but coffee was supplanted as a cash crop by tea, rubber, and coconut. Coffee planters had begun growing tea as early as the 1860s in an attempt to diversify crops at low cost, but because coffee remained a profitable enterprise, large-scale tea

cultivation did not take place until after the coffee industry's demise. Tea was easier to grow than coffee: it had a greater cultivation altitude range, and it thrived in Sri Lanka's copious tropical rains. Increasing British demand for tea and a declining Chinese market share enabled Sri Lankan planters to expand tea cultivation. By 1900, tea was, by acreage, the single largest crop grown on the island, and accounted for over one half of the colony's total export earnings. The vast increase in tea cultivation also had a profound effect on the island's ethnic make-up. Unlike coffee, tea required year-round care; consequently, year-round labor quickly replaced seasonal labor. Because the Sinhalese lacked interest in working the tea plantations, Indian labor immigration to the island increased dramatically. In time, these Indian workers, drawn to the plantations and other opportunities for work, became permanent residents, forever altering the ethnic composition of Sri Lanka.

During the period 1910-28, Sri Lanka suffered under general economic stagnation. Exports of tea and coconut products continued to rise until the outbreak of war in 1914; thereafter, both tea and coconut experienced setbacks, due initially to oversupply. Rubber exports fared well during the war because of increased military demand, but experienced a postwar slump due to declining demand as well as oversupply. Tea, rubber, and, to a lesser extent, coconut, all made strides toward recovery near the end of the 1920s, but were again jolted by declining commodity prices with the advent of the Great Depression. As in the early 1920s, plantation owners voluntarily cut back on production, but ultimately only international agreements, restricting world output of tea and rubber, helped those industries survive. In the absence of similar production agreements, the coconut industry—owned almost entirely by indigenous Sri Lankans—nearly collapsed, and recovered only after global demand and prices rose later in the decade.

The outbreak of the Second World War increased demand for rubber and tea, providing a much-needed stimulus to those industries, and to the Sri Lankan economy overall. Upon gaining its independence in 1948, however, Sri Lanka inherited an economy which was still dependent on the same three price-volatile export crops: tea, rubber, and coconut—all mainstays of the colonial economy.

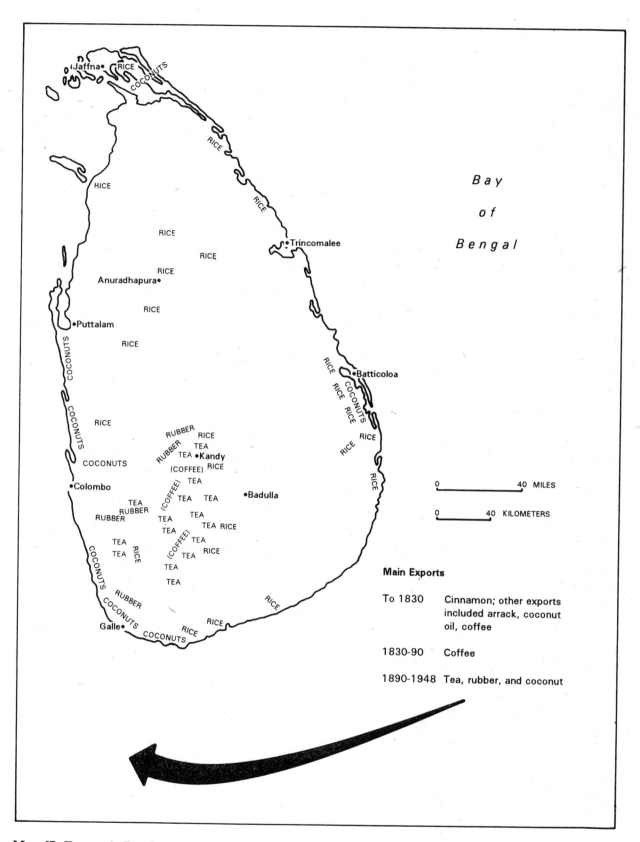

Map 67 Economic Development in Sri Lanka, 1815-1948

147

68   Sri Lanka since 1948

Unlike in the rest of South Asia, where independence was accompanied by the violence of Partition in India and civil war in Burma, the transfer of power from the British to the people of Sri Lanka was peaceful. Sri Lanka's first prime minister, D. S. Senanayake, was critically aware, however, of the tenuousness of that peace and how dependent it was on maintaining a secular state which protected the rights of minorities, particularly those of the indigenous Tamils. But ethnic tensions would not so easily disappear. The 1948 Citizenship Act drew distinctions between "Ceylon Tamils," whom the government considered indigenous, and "Indian Tamils," who, as plantation workers or descendants of plantation workers, were more recent arrivals. The government of Sri Lanka continued to discriminate against Indian Tamils, a group whom it saw as unassimilable, and consequently denied them citizenship.

In 1956, the government of Sri Lanka, led by Prime Minister S. W. R. D. Bandaranaike, passed legislation, directed at the Tamils, which made Sinhala the country's only official language. Non-Sinhala speakers in government employ, i.e., Tamils, were given three years to learn the language or face dismissal. Tamils responded by staging civil disobedience actions throughout the country, especially in the Northern Province where concentrations of Tamils were heaviest. In the spring of 1961, the government declared a state of emergency and used force to put down the disturbances. The crackdown lasted until that fall when Tamil protests tapered off. Meanwhile, the new prime minster, Sirima-vo Bandaranaike, the modern world's first female elected head of state, used her first five years in office (1960-65) to force Tamils out of the armed forces and government service. After five years out of office, she served again during 1970-75. Despite continued Tamil unrest, her main opposition, however, came not from the Tamils, but from radical, left-wing political groups such as the Janatha Vimukht Peramuna (JVP, or People's Liberation Front), which was formed in 1967, and which was determined to overthrow the government of Sri Lanka by force. In April 1971, after the government declared another state of emergency, JVP insurgents launched attacks at police stations and government offices, and disrupted power and communications in several cities. The insurrection lasted only a week as government security forces quickly restored order. Over 10,000 were arrested in connection with the JVP uprising, and some three thousand were tried, with most receiving suspended sentences. Trials lasted until December 1974, but the state of emergency remained in effect until 1977, when it was lifted in anticipation of general elections.

Sri Lankans learned important—though not always constructive—lessons in the aftermath of the JVP insurrection: the government learned about counter-insurgency and increased its security forces, and many young Tamils saw that violence against the state might be a weapon they could use to force the creation of a separate Tamil homeland in Sri Lanka.

In the mid-1970s, Tamils continued to agitate for political reforms. Some formed radical resistance groups designed to pursue—through violent means—the goal of an independent Tamil state in Sri Lanka. The largest and most visible of the five active groups throughout the 1970s and 1980s was the Liberation Tigers of Tamil Eelam (LTTE), a group which used guerrilla tactics and assassination with great effect. From 1983 until 1987, Tamil resistance erupted into open warfare. The LTTE and other Tamil forces repeatedly attacked Sri Lankan army forces, police stations, banks, government offices, and other targets throughout the country—the government of Sri Lanka seemed powerless to stop them. The Indian government tried to mediate between the Tamils and the Sri Lankan government, but was unsuccessful until 1987, when a peace accord was signed between India and Sri Lanka. Tamil and English became official languages in Sri Lanka, Tamil areas were given autonomy, and Indian troops were invited to enforce the treaty.

Maintaining the peace proved difficult. Many Tamils favored the peace treaty, and four of the five Tamil resistance groups accepted it. The LTTE leadership, however, opposed the peace accord because it did not give the Tamils complete independence, and felt that Indian forces were there simply to shore up a failed Sri Lankan policy. A resurgent JVP also opposed the treaty and in 1987-89 attempted again to overthrow the Sri Lankan government. Amidst continued unrest, but with the protection of Indian troops, the Tamils gained provincial autonomy, but after Indian forces withdrew in June 1990, the still-dissatisfied LTTE stepped up its attacks. The situation in Sri Lanka in late 1994 remained unresolved.

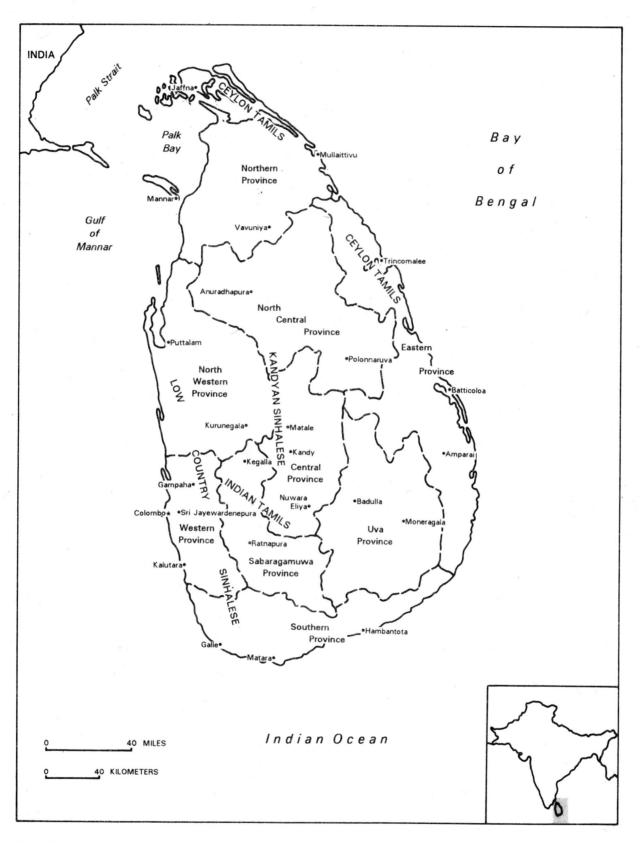

Map 68 Sri Lanka since 1948

69 Bhutan

Because of the paucity of historical materials, very little is known about the history of Bhutan prior to the early seventeenth century. Bhutan did have ties to Tibet from at least the seventh century, when two Buddhist temples were built in Bhutan under the orders of the Tibetan king, Srong-btsan sGampo (r. c. 627-49). Subsequently, Bhutan became a Tibetan satellite.

Bhutan regained its independence from Tibet c. 1630 under Shabdrung Namgyal (1594?-1651), who became the first dharma raja, or spiritual ruler, of Bhutan. Namgyal soon divided the Bhutanese rulership into two parts by creating another position, that of deb raja, or civil administrator. Initially, the dharma raja was the more powerful of the two, but by the eighteenth century the two were roughly co-equal in power, a condition which led to power struggles and a weakening of the state.

British involvement in Bhutanese affairs dates from 1772, when the hereditary commander-in-chief of the neighboring state of Cooch Behar, Nazir Dev Rudra Narayan, applied to the English East India Company for assistance in a succession struggle. After his murder of the infant Raja Debendra Narayan in 1766, Nazir Dev sought to install his own nephew as raja of Cooch Behar. The Bhutanese, with whom Cooch Behar had had a less than cordial relationship, objected and supported the installation of the stepbrother of the murdered raja. When this attempt failed, Shidar, the Bhutanese deb raja, abducted the raja of Cooch Behar; this action prompted Nazir Dev's appeal and British intervention.

After Nazir Dev paid 50,000 rupees to the Company, British forces drove the Bhutanese out of Cooch Behar, and occupied several forts in Bhutan. Fearing the total occupation of their country, the Bhutanese asked Tibet to intercede, and the British ended their advance. The treaty of peace concluded in 1774 favored the British and gave them a number of rights in Bhutan, including the extradition of wrongdoers who had fled to Bhutan, and access to Bhutan's valuable timber resources.

Relations between Bhutan and the British in India remained uneventful until 1826, when disputes erupted over the payment of Bhutanese tribute which the British had inherited from the Burmese Ahoms after the first Anglo-Burmese War (see Map 30). When the British accused the Bhutanese of falling behind in their payments, the latter responded by attacking British settlements along the frontier. Many years of attack and counterattack followed and the issue of Bhutanese incursions into British India remained unresolved. Much of the difficulty lay in the fact that the deb raja was unable to control the actions of his nominal subordinates, Bhutanese officials along the frontier.

During the War of 1857-58, Bhutan was openly sympathetic to the Indian cause, and continued its attacks along the frontier. These raids continued—and even escalated—after the war. In 1864, in response to the poor treatment its envoy had received at the hands of the Bhutanese and that country's refusal to acknowledge a British demand for territory, the British annexed the Bengal Duars (then part of Bhutan), thus beginning the Anglo-Bhutanese War. After initial victories against the British along the frontier, the Bhutanese were forced to sue for peace rather than face an invasion of Bhutan itself. The treaty signed in 1865 stipulated that, in exchange for British financial support, the government of Bhutan promised to prevent further frontier incidents by its subjects.

In 1907, the Bhutan chiefs and principal lamas marked a change in the government of the country by electing the foremost provincial **penslop**, Sir Ugyen Wangchuk, as hereditary maharaja of Bhutan, and thus unified the country. Wangchuk maintained his country's good relations with the British and even signed the Treaty of Punakha in 1910. The treaty increased the annual stipend from the British, and guaranteed British noninterference in Bhutan's domestic affairs in exchange for accepting British guidance in the realm of foreign affairs.

When India became free in 1947, it inherited, among other items, treaty obligations with Bhutan. The Indian government soon opened negotiations with Bhutan regarding the latter's status via-à-vis India. These negotiations resulted in the 1949 Indo-Bhutan Treaty, in which India recognized the full independence of Bhutan, but the Bhutanese government chose to continue to accept foreign policy advice from India.

After sponsoring Bhutan's admission to the **Colombo Plan** in 1962, India continued to support its small neighbor when, in 1971, it applied for membership in the United Nations. Since then, Bhutan has become a full participant in the councils of nations. In 1994, Bhutan was ruled by its fourth hereditary monarch, King Jigme Singye Wangchuk, who ascended to the throne in 1972, after the death of his father.

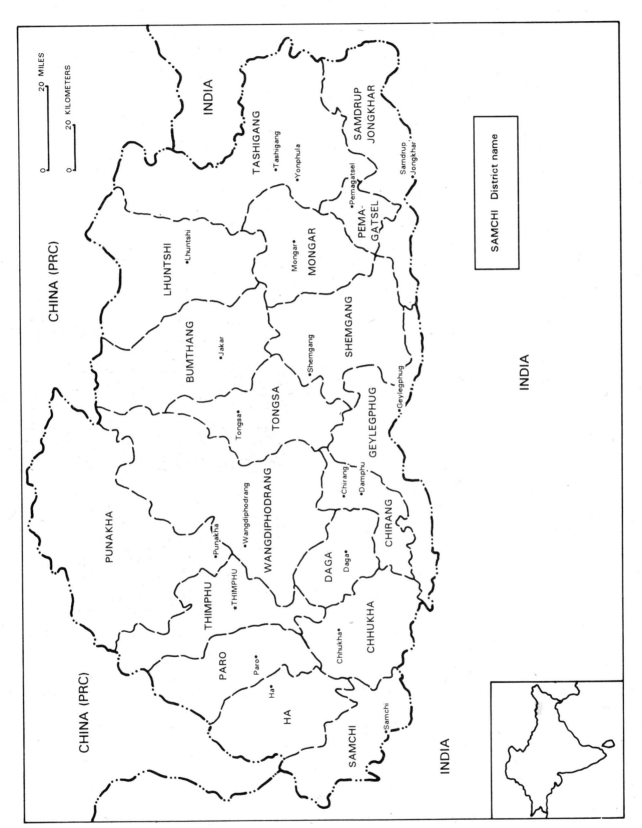

Map 69 Bhutan

151

GLOSSARY

Allahabad pillar inscription contains the first six Pillar Edicts of Ashoka (268-232 BCE) and an inscription commemorating the conquests of Gupta emperor Samudra Gupta (330-75 CE)

Arrack an alcoholic beverage distilled from the juice of the coconut palm or a mash of molasses and rice

Ashvamedha Vedic ritual in which a horse was set loose to wander for a year, and followed by a king's royal guards who staked a claim to all of the territory through which the horse wandered; the horse was ritually killed to commemorate the event

Brahmanical Hinduism phrase used to describe pre-sixth-century BCE Hinduism

Brahmanical orthodoxy see *Brahmanical Hinduism*

Brahmans traditional Hindu priestly class

Caste system social institution which divides all Hindus into four main classes or varna, i.e., Brahmans, Kshatriyas, Vaishyas, and Shudras

Chauth a levy, usually one-fourth of the revenue assessment of a given area

Colombo Plan in full, Colombo Plan for Co-operative Economic and Social Development in Asia and the Pacific; established 1951 in Colombo, Ceylon (Sri Lanka); exists to discuss development plans and problems among member states

Communal see *Communalism*

Communalism belief in, and allegiance to, one's religious group over one's country

Crown Colony in the British imperial system, a possession administered under the direct control of the British monarch

Dhamma lit., "duty"; refers to a philosophical system of Mauryan emperor Ashoka in which duty was paramount

Diwani powers of revenue collection, traditionally granted by the Mughal emperor

Doab lit., "two rivers"; fertile farmland between two rivers

Doctrine of lapse policy pursued by Governor-General Dalhousie (1848-56) in which indigenous rulers forfeited their lands to the East India Company if they had no direct male heir

Dogra a Hindu clan located in the hills of Jammu

Forward School a mode of thought which advocated taking an activist approach to the politics of India's northwestern frontier

India Act of 1784 established a joint government of the East India Company and the British Crown to oversee British possessions in India

Indo-Parthians Persian people inhabiting the Iranian Plateau and Afghanistan

Jagir a tax-free grant of land, usually as a reward for services rendered

Jagirdar one who holds a *jagir*

Jats a Hindu people living in northern India

Kaliph religious head of orthodox Islam

Khalsa Sikh army

Kshatriyas Hindu warrior class

Lichchavi a royal family which lived in northern India from c. fifth century BCE to fourth century CE

Lineage a group of interrelated individuals who trace their descent through one line of parentage

Mahajanapadas group of sixteen major states in India, c. 700-500 BCE

Maharashtra dharma lit., "duty to Maharashtra"; ideological concept promoted by Maratha leader, Sambhaji (1657-89)

153

Mansab Mughal bureaucratic office

Mansabdar one who holds a *mansab*

Nawab Mughal provincial governor

Nizam king; term used exclusively in connection with the nizam of Hyderabad

Non-aligned foreign policy doctrine applied by Jawaharlal Nehru during the Cold War in which India refused to join either the Western Bloc led by the United States, or the Eastern Bloc, led by the Soviet Union

Outcastes those without caste designation, e.g., foreigners, or "untouchables"

Panchayat village ruling council of five

Parthians see *Indo-Parthians*

Penslop governor

Peshwa Maratha hereditary prime minister

Pitt's Act of 1784 see *India Act of 1784*

Rani princess

Rann marshy swamp

Resident British official stationed in the capital of a princely state

Rig Veda oldest of the Hindu scriptures

Sanskritized influenced by Hindu language and culture

Sardeshmukhi type of tax collected in the Maratha homelands

Satyagraha lit., "truth force"; Gandhian concept of nonviolent noncooperation

Shaivists those who worship the Hindu god Shiva

Shaka, Shakas (Scythian, Scythians) ancient people originally inhabiting southern Russia

Shudras menial workers; bottommost of the Hindu varna

Sipahis (sepoys) Indian soldiers in the employ of the East India Company

Subsidiary alliances system in which the British offered protection to Indian princes in exchange for forfeiting all rights to foreign relations

Sultan king

Swadeshi Indian-made products

Swaraj lit., "self-rule"

Terai foothill areas of southern Nepal

Unitary state a state which is centrally administered

Vaishnavists those who worship the Hindu god Vishnu

Vaishyas merchants and landholders; penultimate of the Hindu varna

Varna Hindu class

Vedas collective name for Hindu holy scriptures

Vikramaditya lit., "Son of the Prowess"; title assumed by various Indian rulers in antiquity

Zamorin petty Hindu title of nobility

BIBLIOGRAPHY

Agrawal, Ashvini. 1989. *Rise and Fall of the Imperial Guptas*. New Delhi: Motilal Banarsidass.

Agrawal, D. P., and Sood, R. K. 1982. "Ecological Factors and the Harappan Civilization." In Possehl, ed., *Harappan Civilization*, 223-31.

Akira, Hirakawa. 1990. *A History of Indian Buddhism*. Honolulu: University of Hawaii Press.

Alahakoon, Hector. 1980. *The Later Mauryas*. New Delhi: Munshiram Manoharlal.

Ali, B. Sheik. 1982. *Tipu Sultan: A Study in Diplomacy and Confrontation*. Mysore: Geetha Book House.

Allchin, Bridget and Raymond. 1982. *The Rise of Civilization in India and Pakistan*. Cambridge: Cambridge University Press.

Aris, Michael. 1979. *Bhutan: The Early History of a Himalayan Kingdom*. Warminster, England: Aris and Phillips.

Asthana, Shashi. 1982. "Harappan Trade in Metals and Minerals: A Regional Approach." In Possehl, ed., *Harappan Civilization*, 271-85.

Bajpai, U. S., ed. 1986. *India and Its Neighborhood*. New Delhi: Lancer International.

Ballhatchet, Kenneth, and Harrison, John, eds. 1980. *The City in South Asia*. Collected Papers on South Asia, no. 3. London: Curzon Press.

Banerjee, Gauranga Nath. 1961. *Hellenism in Ancient India*. Delhi: Munshiram Manoharlal.

Banerjee, N. R. 1965. *The Iron Age in India*. New Delhi: Munshiram Manoharlal.

Banerjee, R. D. 1980. *History of Orissa: From the Earliest Times to the British Period*. 2 vols. Delhi: Bharatiya Publishing House.

Banerji, R. D. 1930; reprinted 1981. *The Age of the Imperial Guptas*. New Delhi: Ramanand Vidya Bhawan.

Barua, Kanak Lal. 1973. *Studies in the Early History of Assam*. (Maheswar Neog, comp. and ed.) Jorhat-Gauhati, Assam: Asam Sahitya Sabha.

Basu, Aparna. 1974. *The Growth of Education and Political Development in India, 1898-1920*. Delhi: Oxford University Press.

Basu, Aparna. 1982. *Essays in the History of Indian Education*. New Delhi: Concept.

Bayly, C. A. *Indian Society and the Making of the British Empire*. Vol. 1 of Part II of The New Cambridge History of India. Cambridge: Cambridge University Press.

Becker, Charles, et al. 1992. *Indian Urbanization and Economic Growth since 1960*. Baltimore: Johns Hopkins University Press.

Bhargava, P. L. 1971. *India in the Vedic Age*. Lucknow: Upper India Publishing House.

Bhatia, B. M. 1991. *Famines in India*. Delhi: Konark.

Bhatia, H. S., ed. 1977. *Military History of British India*. New Delhi: Deep and Deep.

Bhatia, Pratipal. 1970. *The Paramaras*. New Delhi: Munshiram Manoharlal.

Bhattacharjee, Arun. 1988. *A History of Ancient India*. 2nd ed. Liverpool: Lucas.

Bouton, Marshall M., and Oldenburg, Philip, eds. 1988. *India Briefing, 1988*. Boulder, Colo.: Westview.

Bruce, George. 1969. *Six Battles for India: The Anglo-Sikh Wars, 1845-6, 1848-9*. London: Arthur Baker.

Bruce, George. 1973. *The Burma Wars, 1824-1886*. London: Hart-Davis, MacGibbon.

Callahan, Raymond. 1972. *The East India Company and Army Reform, 1783-1798*. Cambridge: Harvard University Press.

Cassen, R. H. 1978. *India: Population, Economy, Society*. New York: Holmes and Meier.

Chandra, Satish. 1986. *The Eighteenth Century in India: Its Economy and the Role of the Marathas, the Jatas, the Sikhs, and the Afghans*. Calcutta: Centre for Studies in Social Sciences.

Chapekar, Nalinee M. 1977. *Ancient India and Greece: A Study of their Cultural Contacts*. Delhi: Ajanta.

Charlesworth, Neil. 1982. *British Rule and the Indian Economy, 1800-1914*. London: Macmillan.

Chatterjee, Asim Kumar. 1978. *A Comprehensive History of Jainism*. Vol. I. Calcutta: Firma K.L.M.

Chattopadhyayay, Sudhakar. 1968. *Early History of North India*. 2nd ed. Calcutta: Academic.

Chhabra, B. Ch., and Agrawala, P. K., et al., eds. 1992. *Reappraising Gupta History for S. R. Goyal*. New Delhi: Aditya Prakashan.

Chhabra, G. S. 1962. *Social and Economic History of the Panjab, 1849-1901*. New Delhi: Sterling.

Choudhury, G. W. 1975. *India, Pakistan, Bangladesh, and the Major Powers*. New York: Free Press.

Clarke, Colin, et. al., eds. 1990. *South Asians Overseas: Migration and Ethnicity*. Cambridge: Cambridge University Press.

Coedès, George. 1968. *The Indianized States of South-*

east Asia. Honolulu: East-West Center Press.

Cook, Hugh C. B. 1975. *The Sikh Wars: The British Army in the Punjab, 1845-1849*. London: L. Cooper.

Das, Manmath Nath. 1982. *Partition and Independence of India*. New Delhi: Vision Books.

Das, S. T. 1969. *Indian Military: Its History and Development*. New Delhi: Sagar.

Davies, C. Collin 1959. *An Historical Atlas of the Indian Peninsula*. 2nd ed. London: Oxford University Press.

Davis, Kingsley. 1951. *The Population of India and Pakistan*. Princeton: Princeton University Press.

de Gila-Kochanowski, Vania. 1990. "Aryan and Indo-Aryan Migrations." *Diogenes* 149 (spring): 122-45.

de Silva, K. M. 1981. *A History of Sri Lanka*. London: C. Hurst.

Desai, T. B. 1968. *Economic History of India under the British*. Bombay: Vora.

Devahuti, D. 1970. *Harsha: A Political Study*. London: Oxford University Press.

Dikshit, Durga Prasad. 1980. *Political History of the Chalukyas of Badami*. New Delhi: Abhinav.

Dyson, Robert H., Jr. 1982. "Paradigm Changes in the Study of the Indus Civilization." In Possehl, ed., *Harappan Civilization*, 417-27.

Edwardes, Michael. 1969. *Plassey: The Founding of an Empire*. London: Hamish Hamilton.

Eggermont, P. H. L. 1975. *Alexander's Campaigns in Sind and Baluchistan and the Siege of the Brahman Town of Harmatelia*. Belgium: Leuven University Press.

Ellinwood, DeWitt C. 1978. "The Indian Soldier, the Indian Army, and Change, 1914-18." In *India and World War I*, eds. DeWitt C. Ellinwood and S. D. Pradhan, 177-212. Columbia, Mo.: South Asia Books.

Embree, Ainslie T., ed. 1987. *India in 1857: The Revolt against Foreign Rule*. Reprint. Delhi: Chanakya.

Farooque, Abul Khair Muhammad. 1977. *Roads and Communications in Mughal India*. Delhi: Idarah-i Adabiyat-i Delhi.

Farwell, Byron. 1989. *Armies of the Raj: From Mutiny to Independence, 1858-1947*. New York: W. W. Norton.

Featherstone, Donald. 1968. *At Them with the Bayonet! The First Sikh War*. London: Jarrolds.

Ganguly, Shivaji. 1990. *U.S. Policy Toward South Asia*. Boulder, Colo.: Westview.

Ghosh, Kali Charan. 1987. *Famines in Bengal, 1770-1943*. Calcutta: National Council of Education, Bengal.

Goel, Bhim Sain. 1969. *Development of Education in British India, 1905-1929*. New Delhi: Central Institute of Education.

Gordon, Leonard A., and Oldenburg, Philip, eds. 1992. *India Briefing, 1992*. Boulder, Colo.: Westview.

Gordon, Stewart. 1993. *The Marathas, 1600-1818*. Vol. 4 of Part II of The New Cambridge History of India. New York: Cambridge University Press.

Goyal, S. R. 1967. *A History of the Imperial Guptas*. Allahabad: Central Book Depot.

Grewal, J. S. 1990. *The Sikhs of the Punjab*. Cambridge: Cambridge University Press.

Grewal, J. S., and Banga, Indu, eds. 1980. *Maharaja Ranjit Singh and His Times*. Amritsar: Guru Nanak Dev University Press.

Habib, Irfan. 1982. *An Atlas of the Mughal Empire*. New Delhi: Oxford University Press.

Habib, Mohammad, and Nizami, Khaliq Ahmad, eds. 1970. *A Comprehensive History of India*. Vol. 5 (The Delhi Sultanat, 1206-1526). Delhi: People's Publishing House.

Habibullah, A. B. M. 1961. *The Foundation of Muslim Rule in India*. 2nd rev. ed. Allahabad: Central Book Depot.

Halim, Abdul. 1974. *History of the Lodi Sultans of Delhi and Agra*. Delhi: Idarah-i Adabiyat-i Delhi.

Hall, Kenneth R. 1980. *Trade and Statecraft in the Age of the Colas*. New Delhi: Abhinav.

Hall, Kenneth R. 1985. *Maritime Trade and State Development in Early Southeast Asia*. Honolulu: University of Hawaii Press.

Hasan, Mohibbul. 1971. *History of Tipu Sultan*. 2nd ed. Calcutta: World.

Heitzman, James, and Worden, Robert L., eds. 1989. *Bangladesh: A Country Study*. Washington: GPO.

Hirakawa, Akira. 1990. *A History of Indian Buddhism: From Sakymuni to Mahayana*. Honolulu: University of Hawaii Press.

Indian Railways. 1978. New Delhi: Ministry of Railways.

Jalal, Ayesha. 1985. *The Sole Spokesman: Jinnah, the Muslim League and the Demand for Pakistan*. Cambridge: Cambridge University Press.

Johnson, B. L. C. 1979. *Pakistan*. London: Heinemann.

Johnson, B. L. C. 1982. *Bangladesh*. London: Heinemann.

Johnson, B. L. C. 1983. *Development in South Asia*.

New York: Penguin.

Joshi, Rekha. 1979. *Sultan Iltutmish*. Delhi: Bharatiya Publishing House.

Joshi, Rekha. 1982. *The Reign of Sultan Balban*. Delhi: Ravi.

Kapur, Rajiv A. 1986. *Sikh Separatism: The Politics of Faith*. London: Allen and Unwin.

Kareem, C. K. 1973. *Kerala under Haider Ali and Tipu Sultan*. Cochin: Paico Publishing House.

Ker, James Campbell. 1917; reprinted 1973. *Political Trouble in India, 1907-1917*. Delhi: Oriental Publishers.

Khan, Azizur Rahman, and Hossain, Mahabub. 1989. *The Strategy of Development in Bangladesh*. London: Macmillan.

Kingsbury, Robert C. 1969. *South Asia in Maps*. Chicago: Denoyer-Geppert.

Kulkarni, G. T. 1983. *Mughal-Maratha Relations: Twenty-Five Fateful Years, 1682-1707*. Pune: Dept. of History, Deccan College Post-Graduate Research Institute.

Kumar, Baldev. 1973. *The Early Kusanas*. New Delhi: Sterling.

Kumar, Dharma, ed. 1983; reprinted 1989. *The Cambridge Economic History of India*. Vol. II (1750-1970). Cambridge: Cambridge University Press.

Lal, K. S. 1963. *Twilight of the Sultanate*. New York: Asia Publishing House.

Lal, K. S. 1967. *History of the Khaljis*. London: Asia Publishing House.

Lawford, James P. 1978. *Britain's Army in India*. London: George Allen and Unwin.

Lebra-Chapman, Joyce. 1986. *The Rani of Jhansi: A Study in Female Heroism in India*. Honolulu: University of Hawaii Press.

Mabbett, I. W. 1977. "The 'Indianization' of Southeast Asia: Reflections on the Historical Sources." *Journal of Southeast Asian Studies* VIII, 2 (Sept.), 143-161.

Mahajan, T. T. 1990. *Maratha Administration in the 18th Century*. New Delhi: Commonwealth.

Mahajan, Vidya Dhar. 1965. *Early History of India*. Delhi: S. Chand.

Maity, Sachindra Kumar. 1975. *The Imperial Guptas and their Times*. New Delhi: Munshiram Manoharlal.

Majumdar, R. C., and Altekar, A. S. 1946. *The Gupta-Vakataka Age*. Lahore: Bharatiya Itihasa Parishad.

Majumdar, R. C. 1963. *Hindu Colonies in the Far East*. Calcutta: Firma K.L.M.

Majumdar, R. C. 1963. *The Sepoy Mutiny and the Revolt of 1857*. 2nd ed. Calcutta: Firma K.L.M.

Majumdar, R. C. 1971. *Ancient India*. 6th rev. ed. Delhi: Motilal Banarsidass.

Majumdar, R. C. 1979. *India and South East Asia*. Delhi: B.R. Publishing.

Majumdar, R. C., ed. 1981. *A Comprehensive History of India*. Vol. III, Part 1 (A.D. 300-985). New Delhi: People's Publishing House.

Marr, David G., and Milner, A. C., eds. 1986. *Southeast Asia in the Ninth to Fourteenth Centuries*. Singapore: Institute of Southeast Asian Studies.

Mason, Philip. 1974. *A Matter of Honour: An Account of the Indian Army, Its Officers and Men*. London: Jonathan Cape.

Metcalf, Thomas R. 1964. *The Aftermath of Revolt: India, 1857-1870*. Princeton: Princeton University Press.

Mishra, Vibhuti Bhushan. 1966. *The Gurjara-Pratiharas and their Times*. Delhi: S. Chand.

Misra, R. P., ed. 1978. *Million Cities of India*. New Delhi: Vikas.

Mojumdar, Kanchanmoy. 1973. *Anglo-Nepalese Relations in the Nineteenth Century*. Calcutta: K.L.M.

Mookerji, R. K. 1966. *Chandragupta Maurya and His Times*. Delhi: Motilal Banarsidass.

Mookerji, Radha Kumud. 1965. *Harsha*. 3rd ed. Delhi: Motilal Banarsidass.

Moon, Penderel. 1989. *The British Conquest and Dominion of India*. London: Duckworth.

Moosvi, Shireen. 1987. *The Economy of the Mughal Empire, c. 1595*. Delhi: Oxford University Press.

Mukherjee, B. N. 1970. *The Economic Factors in Kushana History*. Calcutta: Pilgrim.

Narain, A. K. 1967. *From Alexander to Kaniska*. Varanasi: Banaras Hindu University.

Narain, A. K. 1957. *The Indo-Greeks*. Oxford: Clarendon Press.

Narayana, G., and Kantner, John F. 1992. *Doing the Needful: The Dilemma of India's Population Policy*. Boulder, Colo.: Westview.

Nilakanta Sastri, K. A., ed. 1957. *A Comprehensive History of India*. Vol. 2 (The Mauryas and Satavahanas). Bombay: Orient Longman.

Nilakanta Sastri, K. A. 1966. *A History of South India*. 3rd ed. Madras: Oxford University Press.

Nilakanta Sastri, K. A. 1978. *South India and South-East Asia*. Mysore, India: Geetha Book House.

Nyrop, Richard F., ed. 1983. *Pakistan: A Country Study*. American University Foreign Area Studies Series. Washington: GPO.

Nyrop, Richard F., ed. 1985. *India: A Country Study*. American University Foreign Area Studies Series.

Washington, DC: G.P.O.

O'Ballance, Edgar. 1989. *The Cyanide War: Tamil Insurrection in Sri Lanka, 1973-88*. London: Brassey's.

Ojha, K. C. 1968. *The History of Foreign Rule in Ancient India*. Allahabad: Gyan Prakashan.

Panikkar, K. M. 1922. *Sri Harsha of Kanauj*. Bombay: D. B. Taraporevala Sons.

Paranavitana, Senarat. 1971. *The Greeks and the Mauryas*. Colombo, Sri Lanka: Lake House Investments.

Pearson, Michael N. 1987. *The Portuguese in India*. Vol. 1 of Part I of The New Cambridge History of India. Cambridge: Cambridge University Press.

Philips, C. H., and Wainwright, Mary Doreen, eds. 1970. *The Partition of India: Policies and Perspectives, 1935-1947*. London: George Allen and Unwin.

Pitre, K. G. 1990. *The Second Anglo-Maratha War, 1802-1805*. Poona: Dastane Ramchandra.

Possehl, Gregory L., ed. 1982. *Harappan Civilization: A Contemporary Perspective*. New Delhi: Oxford and IBH.

Possehl, Gregory L. 1982. "The Harappan Civilization: A Contemporary Perspective." In Possehl, ed., *Harappan Civilization*, 15-30.

Pradhan, S. D. 1978. "Indian Army and the First World War." In *India and World War I*, eds. DeWitt C. Ellinwood and S. D. Pradhan, 49-68. Columbia, Mo.: South Asia Books.

Prasad, Bisheshwar, ed. 1956. *Expansion of the Armed Forces and Defence Organisation, 1939-45*. Series 3, Vol. III of the Official History of the Indian Armed Forces in the Second World War, 1939-45. New Delhi: Combined Inter-Services Historical Section, India and Pakistan.

Prasad, Bisheshwar, ed. 1962. *Indian War Economy*. Series 3, Vol. IV of the Official History of the Indian Armed Forces in the Second World War, 1939-45. New Delhi: Combined Inter-Services Historical Section, India and Pakistan.

Prasad, Kameshwar. 1984. *Cities, Crafts and Commerce under the Kusanas*. Delhi: Agam Kala Prakashan.

Puri, B. N. 1965. *India under the Kushanas*. Bombay: Bharatiya Vidya Bhavan.

Puri, B. N. 1975. *The History of the Gurjara-Pratiharas*. Delhi: Oriental.

Ramakant, ed. 1988. *China and South Asia*. South Asian Studies Series, no. 18. New Delhi: South Asian Publishers.

Rao, M. A. 1975. *Indian Railways*. New Delhi: National Book Trust.

Rao, S. R. 1982. "New Light on the Post-Urban (Late Harappan) Phase of the Indus Civilization in India." In Possehl, ed., *Harappan Civilization*, 353-59.

Ratnagar, Shereen. 1982. "The Location of Harappa." In Possehl, ed., *Harappan Civilization*, 261-64.

Rawat, P. L. 1970. *History of Indian Education*. Agra: Ram Prasad.

Ray, Niharranjan. 1927. "Harsa Siladitya: A Revised Study." *Indian Historical Quarterly* 3 (December): 769-93.

Raychaudhuri, Tapan, and Habib, Irfan, eds. 1982. *The Cambridge Economic History of India*. Vol. I (c. 1200-1750). Cambridge: Cambridge University Press.

Regmi, D. R. 1975. *Modern Nepal: Rise and Growth in the Eighteenth Century*. Vol. I. Calcutta: K.L.M.

Report of the States Reorganisation Commission. 1955. New Delhi: Government of India.

Richards, John F. 1993. *The Mughal Empire*. Vol. 5 of Part I of The New Cambridge History of India. Cambridge: Cambridge University Press.

Rose, Leo E. 1971. *Nepal: Strategy for Survival*. Berkeley: University of California Press.

Rose, Leo E., and Scholz, John T. 1980. *Nepal: Profile of a Himalayan Kingdom*. Boulder, Colo.: Westview.

Rothermund, Dietmar. 1983. *The Indian Economy under British Rule and other Essays*. New Delhi: Manohar.

Roy, Ashim Kumar. 1984. *A History of the Jainas*. New Delhi: Gitanjali Publishing House.

Roy, S. B. 1989. *Early Aryans of India: 3100-1400 B.C.* New Delhi: Navrang.

Saini, B. S. 1975. *Social and Economic History of the Punjab, 1901-1939*. Delhi: Ess Ess.

Saini, Krishan G. 1978. "The Economic Aspects of India's Participation in the First World War." In *India and World War I*, eds. DeWitt C. Ellinwood and S. D. Pradhan, 141-76. Columbia, Mo.: South Asia Books.

Saini, Shiv Kumar. 1980. *Development of Education in India: Socio-Economic and Political Perspectives*. New Delhi: Cosmo.

Sardesai, Govind Sakharam. 1986. *New History of the Marathas*. 2nd ed., 3 vols. New Delhi: Munshiram Manoharlal.

Sarkar, H. B. 1985. *Cultural Relations between India and Southeast Asian Countries*. New Delhi: Indian Council for Cultural Relations.

Sarkar, Jagadish Narayan. 1976. *A Study of Eighteenth*

Century India. Vol. I (Political History, 1707-1761). Calcutta: Saraswat Library.

Sarkar, Sumit. 1983. *Modern India, 1885-1947.* Madras: Macmillan.

Satow, Michael, and Desmond, Ray. 1980. *Railways of the Raj.* New York: New York University Press.

Satyanarayana, K. 1975. *A Study of the History and Culture of the Andhras.* New Delhi: People's Publishing House.

Sedlar, Jean W. 1980. *India and the Greek World: A Study in the Transmission of Culture.* Totowa, N.J.: Rowman and Littlefield.

Sen, S. P. 1971. *The French in India.* New Delhi: Munshiram Manoharlal.

Sen, Sunil. 1982. *Peasant Movements in India.* Calcutta: K. P. Bagchi.

Sen, Surendra Nath. 1957. *Eighteen Fifty-Seven.* Delhi: Government of India, Ministry of Information and Broadcasting.

Seth, K. N. 1978. *Growth of the Paramara Power in Malwa.* Bhopal: Progress.

Shaha, Rishikesh. 1975. *Nepali Politics: Retrospect and Prospect.* Delhi: Oxford University Press.

Sharma, J. P. 1968. *Republics in Ancient India, c. 1500 BC-500 BC.* Leiden, Netherlands: E. J. Brill.

Sharma, Tej Ram. 1989. *A Political History of the Imperial Guptas.* New Delhi: Concept.

Sherwani, Latif Ahmed. 1986. *The Partition of India and Mountbatten.* Karachi: Center for Pakistan Studies.

Shrava, Satya. 1981. *The Sakas in India.* New Delhi: Pranava Prakashan.

Siddiqui, Iqtidar Husain. 1983. *Mughal Relations with the Indian Ruling Elite.* New Delhi: Munshiram Manoharlal.

Singh, Anita Inder. 1987. *The Origins of the Partition of India, 1936-1947.* Delhi: Oxford University Press.

Singh, Bhagat. 1990. *Maharaja Ranjit Singh and His Times.* New Delhi: Sehgal.

Singh, Fauja. 1982. *Some Aspects of State and Society under Ranjit Singh.* New Delhi: Master.

Singh, Jagdev. 1988. *Dismemberment of Pakistan: 1971 Indo-Pak War.* New Delhi: Lancer International.

Singh, K. S. 1982. *Tribal Movements in India.* New Delhi: Manohar.

Singh, Khushwant. 1963-66. *A History of the Sikhs.* 2 vols. Princeton: Princeton University Press.

Singh, Kulbir. 1980. "Trade and Industry under Maharaja Ranjit Singh." In Grewal and Banga, eds., *Maharaja Ranjit Singh and His Times,* 138-57.

Singh, Nagendra. 1972. *Bhutan: A Kingdom in the Himalayas.* New Delhi: Thomson Press.

Singh, Rajendra Pal. 1979. *Education in an Imperial Colony.* New Delhi: National.

Singh, Satya Narayan. 1992. *Political Ideas and Institutions under the Mauryas.* Patna: Janaki Prakashan.

Singh, Sukhwant. 1980. "Agricultural Production in the Punjab under Maharaja Ranjit Singh." In Grewal and Banga, eds., *Maharaja Ranjit Singh and His Times,* 253-57.

Sinha, Binod Chandra. 1977. *History of the Sunga Dynasty.* Varanasi: Bharatiya Publishing House.

Sisson, Richard, and Rose, Leo E. 1990. *War and Secession: Pakistan, India, and the Creation of Bangladesh.* Berkeley: University of California Press.

Smith, Vincent A. 1924. *Early History of Ancient India.* 4th ed. London: Oxford University Press.

Smith, Vincent. 1957. *The Early History of India.* 4th ed. Oxford: University Press.

Spate, O. H. K. 1957. *India and Pakistan.* 2nd ed. New York: E. P. Dutton.

Spencer, George W. 1983. *The Politics of Expansion: The Chola Conquest of Sri Lanka and Sri Vijaya.* Madras: New Era.

Srivastava, Ashirbadi Lal. 1966. *The Sultanate of Delhi.* Agra: Shiva Lal Agarwala.

Stein, Burton. 1980. *Peasant State and Society in Medieval South India.* Delhi: Oxford University Press.

Stein, Burton. 1989. *Vijayanagara.* Vol. 2 of Part I of The New Cambridge History of India. Cambridge: Cambridge University Press.

Stewart, A. T. Q. 1972. *The Pagoda War.* London: Faber and Faber.

Stokes, Eric. 1986. *The Peasant Armed: The Indian Revolt of 1857.* (Edited by C. A. Bayly.) Oxford: Clarendon Press.

Subbarayalu, Y. 1973. *Political Geography of the Chola Country.* Madras: Government of Tamilnadu, State Dept. of Archaeology.

Tarn, W. W. 1951. *The Greeks in Bactria and India.* Cambridge: Cambridge University Press.

Thapar, Romila. 1973. *Asoka and the Decline of the Mauryas.* Oxford: Oxford University Press.

Thapar, Romila. 1978. *Ancient Indian Social History: Some Interpretations.* New Delhi: Orient Longman.

Thapar, Romila. 1984. *From Lineage to State: Social Formations in the Mid-First Millennium B.C. in the Ganga Valley.* Bombay: Oxford University Press.

Thapar, Romila. 1987. *The Mauryas Revisited.* Calcutta: K. P. Bagchi.

Tickoo, Champa. 1980. *Indian Universities*. Bombay: Orient Longman.

Tinker, Hugh. 1974. *A New System of Slavery: The Export of Indian Labour Overseas, 1830-1920*. London: Oxford University Press.

Tinker, Hugh. 1976. *Separate and Unequal: India and the Indians in the British Commonwealth, 1920-1950*. Vancouver, Canada: University of British Columbia Press.

Trench, Charles Chenevix. 1988. *The Indian Army and the King's Enemies, 1900-1947*. London: Thames and Hudson.

Tripathi, Ram Prasad. 1981. *Studies in Political and Socio-Economic History of Early India*. Allahabad: Neeraj Prakashan.

Tripathi, Rama Shankar. 1967. *History of Ancient India*. 3rd ed. Delhi: Motilal Banarsidass.

van Leur, Jacob C. 1955. *Indonesian Trade and Society*. The Hague: W. van Hoeve.

Weller, Jac. 1993. *Wellington in India*. 2nd ed. London: Longman.

Wilson, A. Jeyaratnam. 1988. *The Break-Up of Sri Lanka*. London: C. Hurst.

Wolpert, Stanley. 1982. *Roots of Confrontation in South Asia*. New York: Oxford University Press.

Woodcock, George. 1966. *The Greeks in India*. London: Faber and Faber.

Yapp, Malcolm E. 1980. *Strategies of British India*. London: Oxford University Press.

Yazdani, G. 1960. *The Early History of the Deccan*. 2 vols. London: Oxford University Press.

Ziring, Lawrence, ed. 1982. *The Subcontinent in World Politics*. Rev. ed. New York: Praeger.

Zograph, G. A. 1982. *Languages of South Asia*. London: Routledge and Kegan Paul.

INDEX

(All numbers refer to book page numbers; numbers in **bold** type refer to pages containing maps.)